GCSE

te Revision and Practice

Contents

Section One — General Stuff

Section Two — Weather, Travel and Holidays

Section Three — Town and Local Area

Section Four — School and Work

Section Five — Free Time and Hobbies

Section Six — Shopping, Food and Drink

Contents

Section Seven — Myself, Family, Friends and Life at Home

Section Eight — Letters and Communication

Section Nine — The Wider World

Section Ten — Grammar

Published by Coordination Group Publications Ltd.

Editor: Jennifer Underwood

Contributors:
Encarna Aparicio-Domínguez, Martin Chester, Simon Cook, Taissa Csáky, Richard Fleetham, Gemma Hallam, Catriona Macrae, Pippa Mayfield, Deborah McNee, Kate Redmond, Katherine Reed, Edward Robinson, Emma Singleton, Katherine Stewart, Gillian Wallis, James Paul Wallis, Graham Whittaker.

With thanks to Tanya Anderson, Patricia Bolatti, Rachel Garlick, Latefa Mansarit and Gillian Wallis for the proofreading.

Audio CD recorded, edited and mastered at Bright Blue Studios by Charley Darbishire, featuring the voices of Nagore Calvo, Abel Díaz Avendaño, Bettina Hermoso-Gómez, Maria-Angeles Solera García and Julia Tortosa Corbí.

AQA material is reproduced by kind permission of the Assessment and Qualifications Alliance.
Edexcel examination questions are reproduced by permission of Edexcel Ltd.
OCR examination questions are reproduced by kind permission of OCR.

ISBN-10: 1 84146 388 4
ISBN-13: 978 1 84146 388 9

Website: www.cgpbooks.co.uk
Printed by Elanders Hindson Ltd, Newcastle upon Tyne.
Clipart from CorelDRAW®

Numbers and Amounts

Welcome to page one. Ease yourself in gently with a few numbers.

Uno, dos, tres — One, two, three...

0	cero
1	uno (un), una
2	dos
3	tres
4	cuatro
5	cinco
6	seis
7	siete
8	ocho
9	nueve
10	diez

11	once
12	doce
13	trece
14	catorce
15	quince
16	dieciséis
17	diecisiete
18	dieciocho
19	diecinueve

(1) 11 to 15 all end in 'ce'. But 16, 17, 18 and 19 are 'ten and six' etc.

If a Spanish word has an accent, you stress it on that syllable when you say it, e.g. 'veintiDÓS'.

(2) All twenty-something numbers are rolled into one — "veintiuno" etc.

21	veintiuno
22	veintidós
23	veintitrés
31	treinta y uno

After 30, numbers are joined by "y" (and), but written separately — "treinta y uno" etc.

(3) Most 'ten-type' numbers end in 'nta' (except 'veinte').

20	veinte	60	sesenta
30	treinta	70	setenta
40	cuarenta	80	ochenta
50	cincuenta	90	noventa

Ciento becomes "cien" unless it's followed by a number.

(4) When you get to hundreds and thousands, just put ciento, doscientos, mil (etc) before the number.

100	ciento (cien)
101	ciento uno
200	doscientos
500	quinientos
923	novecientos veintitrés
1000	mil
1 000 000	un millón

A date is written like an ordinary number:

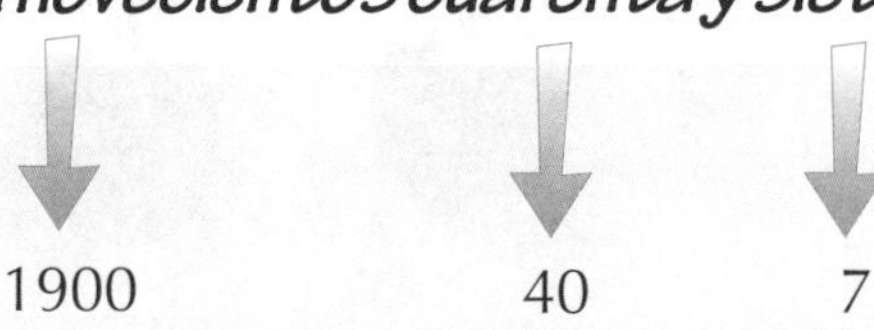

You can count on this coming up in the exam

You should know a bit about numbers already. That means you shouldn't find this page too much like hard work. It's probably a good idea to go over this stuff again though, just to make sure you know it.

Numbers and Amounts

It's not just numbers you need to know — here's more number-related stuff.

First, second, third — they're a bit different...

These always end in "o" for masculine things or "a" for feminine things.

1st	primero, primera	6th	sexto/a
2nd	segundo/a	7th	séptimo/a
3rd	tercero/a	8th	octavo/a
4th	cuarto/a	9th	noveno/a
5th	quinto/a	10th	décimo/a

When "primero" or "tercero" appear in front of a masculine word, they always drop the "o" — "el primer baile" = the first dance.

Tome la segunda calle a la izquierda. = Take the second street on the left.

1st is written $1^{\underline{o}}$, or $1^{\underline{era}}$. 2nd is written $2^{\underline{o}}$ or $2^{\underline{a}}$, etc.

¿Cuánto? — How much?

These words for how many or how much are important. There are a fair few to learn there, but write each one out in different sentences — make sure you don't cheat and skip any.

Tengo todas las manzanas. = I have all the apples.

all the (masc. plural): todos los
other: otros/as
some: unos/as
several: varios/as
many: muchos/as
few: pocos/as

Cada manzana es verde. = Every / each apple is green.

all the (singular): todo el / toda la

This is basic stuff, but it's absolutely vital

You really do need to learn how to say where things are, and use words about quantities of things. This is just the sort of thing that examiners love, so be prepared, and learn it now.

Times and Dates

Time — it's one of the most important things — especially if you want to do well in your Spanish.

¿Qué hora es? — What time is it?

There are loads of ways of saying the time in English, and there are in Spanish too.

¿Qué hora es? = What time is it?

1) Something o'clock:

It's 1 o'clock: Es la una
It's two o'clock: Son las dos
It's 8pm: Son las veinte horas / son las ocho

2) Quarter to and past, half past:

(It's) quarter past two: (Son) las dos y cuarto
(It's) half past two: (Son) las dos y media
(It's) quarter to three: (Son) las tres menos cuarto

3) '... past' and '... to':

(It's) twenty past seven: (Son) las siete y veinte
(It's) twelve minutes past eight: (Son) las ocho y doce minutos
(It's) ten to two: (Son) las dos menos diez

4) The 24-hour clock:

03.14: (Son) las tres horas catorce minutos
20.32: (Son) las veinte horas treinta y dos minutos
19.55: (Son) las diecinueve horas cincuenta y cinco minutos

If you can't tell the time, don't count on a top grade

It's no joke if you can't understand times in Spanish. It's pretty likely that there'll be some Spanish bloke telling you what time the train leaves in your listening exam, so be prepared for it by learning this page.

Times and Dates

Be ready for questions about dates in the exam — and learn how to say when your birthday is.

You use 'el' for all the days of the week

Without these words you won't be able to understand when anything's happening.

Days of the week:

Monday: lunes
Tuesday: martes
Wednesday: miércoles
Thursday: jueves
Friday: viernes
Saturday: sábado
Sunday: domingo

Days of the week are all masculine.

Don't put capital letters on them.

lunes	martes	miércoles	jueves	viernes	sábado	domingo
					1	2
3	4	5	6	7	8	9
10	11	12	13	14	15	16
17	18	19	20	21	22	23
24	25	26	27	28	29	30

Hago las compras ***los martes****.* = I go shopping on Tuesdays (every Tuesday).

Voy ***el martes****.* = I'm going on Tuesday.

Some useful words about the week:

today: hoy
tomorrow: mañana
yesterday: ayer
the day after tomorrow: pasado mañana
the day before yesterday: anteayer
week: la semana
weekend: el fin de semana
on Monday: el lunes
on Mondays: los lunes

Months: enero, febrero, marzo, abril...

Spanish month names bear a striking resemblance to the English ones.
— make sure you learn what's different.

January: enero
February: febrero
March: marzo
April: abril
May: mayo
June: junio
July: julio
August: agosto
September: se(p)tiembre
October: octubre
November: noviembre
December: diciembre

Se va ***en julio****.* = He's leaving in July.

Months are all masculine.

Don't put capital letters on them.

You need to say when you do things

As far as I can tell, most of your exam is made up of saying or understanding that you have maths on Wednesday and you went on holiday in June. Learn it now and get ahead. It'll be worth it, I promise.

Times and Dates

There's more of this date and time stuff for you to learn here — keep going.

You say "the 3 of May" instead of "the 3rd of May"

Here's how you say the date. This is bound to come up in your speaking exam — and the examiners won't be impressed if you can't tell them what the date is.

1) In Spanish, they don't say "the third of May" — they say "the three of May".

Llego el tres de octubre. = I am coming / I arrive on the 3rd of October.

Look at page 1 for help with the numbers.

2) And this is how you write the date in a letter:

Londres, 5 de marzo de 2005. = London, 5th March 2005.

See pages 114-116 for letters.

3) And here are some other useful bits:

in the year 2000: en el año dos mil
in 2006: en el dos mil seis

NOT 'dos mil y seis'

Mañana — Tomorrow... Ayer — Yesterday

Use these with the stuff on page 67 — great for sorting out your social life.

Voy a esquiar a menudo. = I often go skiing.

always: siempre
often: a menudo
seldom: pocas veces
sometimes: a veces

See page 180 for how to say you never do something.

¿Qué haces esta noche? = What are you doing tonight?

tomorrow: mañana
yesterday: ayer
this morning: esta mañana
this afternoon / evening: esta tarde
tonight: esta noche
tomorrow morning: mañana por la mañana

this week: esta semana
next week: la semana próxima
last week: la semana pasada
every fortnight: cada quince días
every day: todos los días
at the weekend: el fin de semana

Now you can ask someone out in Spanish

It's pretty useful to be able to say '¿Qué haces esta noche?' to a stunning Spanish lad or lass, but even more important, this stuff is crucial if you want more marks in your GCSE. Fantastic.

Quick Questions

These Quick Questions should just ease you gently in and make sure that you've learnt the first half of this section. If you've forgotten anything, have another look at it. The answers are in the back of the book, so you can see how you've done.

Quick Questions

1) Write down in words the Spanish for the numbers from 11 to 20.
2) Now write down in Spanish the odd numbers in the 20s.
3) What is the Spanish for: 26, 31, 45, 54, 66, 78, 87, 99, 101, 2005?
4) Write the Spanish for: 21 apples, 31 CDs, 101 dogs, 100 euros.
5) Your friend tells you that she was born in mil novecientos ochenta y nueve. What year is that?
6) Write down the Spanish for tomorrow, yesterday, tonight, every day, tomorrow morning.
7) "Mi habitación está en el tercer piso". Which floor does your friend say her room is on? How would you tell her that your room is on the first floor?
8) You are told: "Tome la segunda a la derecha y es la cuarta casa a la izquierda." Which street should you take and which is the house?
9) How would you say in Spanish: "all the bottles" and "all the cars"?
10) Write a short note to a friend saying that on Tuesdays you go to the cinema, on Wednesdays you do your Spanish homework and at the weekends you go shopping.
11) Your friend says to you: "Ayer fui a la piscina, hoy voy a la discoteca y mañana voy a salir con mis amigos". Write down in English what he said.
12) Write down in Spanish the birthdays of each member of your family: e.g. el cumpleaños de mi padre es el veintidós de abril.
13) You receive a note from your friend which says: "Llego el jueves, doce de agosto a las once y veinte de la mañana y tomo el vuelo de regreso el veintiocho a mediodía". Write down the arrangements in English.
14) Write a note in Spanish to your friend telling her that you will be arriving on Saturday, 25th July at 3 pm and that you will catch the return flight on the 10th of August.
15) Translate the following conversation into Spanish:

A: What are you doing this evening?
B: I'm going to the swimming pool.
A: Do you go often?
B: Yes, every week.
A: Every Wednesday evening?
B: Not always. Would you like to come?
A: I can't this week because I'm going to a party tonight. What are you doing tomorrow morning?
B: We sometimes go shopping on Thursdays.
A: Well, one day next week?
B: OK. But not next weekend because all the family is going to visit my uncle and aunt. Next Friday morning?
A: Great.

Being Polite

You'll lose marks (and sound rude) if you don't sound polite in the exam — it's really important.

¿Qué tal? — How are you?

Learn these phrases — they're crucial.

How are you?: ¿Qué tal?
How are you? (to a friend): ¿Cómo estás?
How are you? (formal): ¿Cómo está usted?

Say this when you're introduced to someone:

Pleased to meet you: Encantado/a
or: Mucho gusto

Change the 'o' to an 'a' if you're female.

This one doesn't change.

Por favor — Please... Gracias — Thank you

Easy stuff — maybe the first Spanish words you ever learnt. Don't ever forget them.

por favor = please **gracias** = thank you

It was nothing / you're welcome: De nada

Quisiera — I would like

It's more polite to say 'quisiera' (I would like) than 'quiero' (I want).

Here's how to say you would like a thing:

Quisiera un zumo de naranja. = I would like an orange juice.

Here's how to say you would like to do something:

Quisiera hablar. = I would like to talk.

See page 8 for other ways to ask questions.

Lo siento — I'm sorry

I'm sorry / Sorry!: Lo siento

Excuse me! (e.g. wanting to ask the way, or attract attention): Por favor / Perdone señor(a)
(e.g. wanting to get past someone): Con permiso

Learn these and learn how to use them

These little phrases are just what you need to help your social life in Spain. They'll also help loads when it comes to your exams. They're absolutely vital, so start learning them now while you've got time.

Asking Questions

You'll have to ask questions to score good marks. Learn how to do it and practise it as much as you can.

1) Make it a question with ¿ ? or tone of voice

To turn a statement into a question, just add question marks to the beginning and the end. When you're speaking, raise your voice at the end to show it's a question.

¿Tus plátanos son amarillos? = Are your bananas yellow? (Literally: Your bananas are yellow?)

See the grammar section for more on endings.

¿Tienes un coche? = Do you have a car? (Literally: You have a car?)

2) 'What' questions — stick **Qué** at the start

If your question starts with "What…", use "¿Qué…".

¿Qué comes por la mañana? = What do you eat in the morning?

¿Qué quieres hacer? = What do you want to do?

3) **Cuándo** – When... **Por qué** – Why... **Dónde** – Where

There are lots of other question words you can slot into a sentence at the start instead of 'Qué'. Look at these question words — then cover them up and learn them.

¿Cuándo vuelves a casa? = When are you coming home?

When?:	¿Cuándo?
Why?:	¿Por qué?
Where?:	¿Dónde?
How?:	¿Cómo?
How much?:	¿Cuánto?
How many?:	¿Cuántos/as?
At what time...?	¿A qué hora?

¿Quién rompió la ventana? = Who broke the window?

What?:	¿Qué?
Is...?:	¿Es...?

Who / whom?:	¿Quién?
Which...?:	¿Cuál?

You have to be able to ask basic questions properly

This page is full of question words — start by learning them all. Shut the book and write down all the question words. Look back for the ones you missed and try again till you get them all.

Opinions

It pays to have an opinion, in more ways than one. Learn how to say what you think.

¿Qué piensas de...? — What do you think of...?

All these phrases mean the same thing — 'What do you think of ...?'. Look out for them.
If you can use them all your Spanish will be more interesting — which means more marks.

Finding out someone's opinion:

What do you think?:	¿Qué piensas?
What do you think of...?:	¿Qué piensas de...? / ¿Qué te parece...?
What's your opinion of...?:	¿Cuál es tu opinión de...?
Do you find him/her nice?:	¿Le encuentras simpático/a?
	¿Te parece simpático/a?

¿Qué piensas de mi novio? = What do you think of my boyfriend?

Pienso que está loco. = I think he's mad.

Juan me parece muy simpático. = I think Juan's very nice.

I think...

I think that ... :	Pienso que ...
	Creo que ...
I think ... is ... :	... me parece ...

Say what you think — it'll impress the examiner

Being able to say you like or dislike something is a good start, but make the effort to learn something a bit more expressive too.

Liking things

I like... :	Me gusta (singular)...
	Me gustan (plural)...
I like... a lot:	Me gusta(n) mucho...
I love:	Me encanta(n)...
I'm interested in... :	Me interesa(n)...
I find... great:	Encuentro ... fantástico

When you like more than one thing, remember to add the "n".

Me gusta el fútbol, pero no me gusta el tenis de mesa.

= I like football, but I don't like table tennis.

Disliking things

I don't like... :	No me gusta...(singular)/
	No me gustan...(plural)
I don't like at all... :	No me gusta nada...(singular)/
	No me gustan nada...(plural)
...doesn't interest me:	...no me interesa
I find ... awful:	Encuentro ... horrible/muy mal
I can't stand...:	No aguanto...
I hate...:	Odio...

Other useful phrases

It's all right:	Vale
I prefer... :	Prefiero...
It's fine:	Está bien
I don't mind / care:	Me da igual

The examiner wants to know you have your own opinions

It might seem hard to believe, but they really do want you to say what you think. Make sure you learn one way to say 'I like' and 'I don't like' first, then add all the fancy bits afterwards.

Opinions

Don't just say you like or hate something — make sure you can say why too.

Use words like 'bueno' (good) to describe things

Here are a bunch of words to describe things you like or don't like.
They're rather easy to use, so it really is worth learning them.

good:	bueno/a	*fun, amusing:*	divertido/a	*nice (person):*	simpático/a
great:	estupendo/a	*excellent:*	excelente	*nice / kind:*	agradable
great:	fenomenal	*fantastic:*	fantástico/a	*marvellous:*	maravilloso/a
beautiful:	precioso/a		magnífico/a	*bad:*	malo/a
friendly:	amable	*fabulous:*	fabuloso/a	*awful:*	horrible
		interesting:	interesante	*boring:*	aburrido/a

Owen es estupendo.

= Owen is great.

Los niños son horribles.

= The children are awful.

See p.144 for help with plural adjective endings.

To say 'because' say 'porque'

Congratulations, you have an opinion, so you're officially undull.
But to reach the coveted rating of 'interesting',
you need to know how to back it up with 'porque'.

'porque' is ultra-important — forget it at your peril.

Me gusta esta película porque los actores son muy buenos.

= I like this film, because the actors are very good.

Pienso que este libro es horrible porque la historia es aburrida.

= I think this book is awful, because the story is boring.

Don't mix up 'por qué', and 'porque'

Be careful not to mix up "why" and "because".
They're almost the same — but not quite:

WHY = POR QUÉ

BECAUSE = PORQUE

Learn all this, especially 'porque'

It's no good only knowing how to ask someone else's opinion, or how to say 'I think', without being able to say what and why you think. All these phrases are easy — learn them now.

Quick Questions

These questions are designed as a warm-up, just to check that you've got the hang of all the stuff in this section. The answers are in the back, so you can check how you're doing. You shouldn't find them too stressful, but if you get some wrong, go back and look at that page again. By the time you try the exam questions on pages 12-15, you should be pretty comfortable with the basics, and you'll find things a lot easier that way.

Quick Questions

1) Write down the Spanish for:
   please; thank you; you're welcome; I'm sorry; pleased to meet you.
2) What does "¿Qué tal?" mean in English?
3) How would you say in Spanish: "How are you?" to the following people?
   a) a friend b) the old lady next door
   c) a colleague of your penfriend's father d) someone your own age
4) You are in a bar in Spain. Attract the waiter's attention in Spanish.
5) Someone is blocking the doorway and you want to get past him/her. What would you say in Spanish?
6) Your friend's mother asks you: "¿Qué quieres hacer?" What is she asking you?
   Tell her that you would like to telephone your parents.
7) Give three different ways of asking your friend Elena what she thinks of Madonna.
8) Ask your friend: "Who is going to the party?"
   The answer is: "Todo el mundo, pero Elena no." What does your friend say? You want more information, so you ask: "When is the party?" "Which day is it?" "What time does it start?" "How are we getting there?" "Why isn't Elena going?"
9) How would you ask your friend: "How many rooms are there in the house?" and "How many CDs do you have?" in Spanish?
10) Write a short note in Spanish to say that you're interested in languages, that you find computers great but that you're not interested in table tennis (el tenis de mesa) and you think that football is awful.
11) Your friend says to you: "Me gusta mucho tu camiseta pero me parecen horribles tus zapatos". What is she saying about your clothes?
12) Your friend says: "¿Prefieres (un) té o (un) café?" What is he saying? You answer in Spanish that you don't mind.
13) How would you say that you love table tennis but you hate bananas?
14) How would you say that you like Spanish (el español) but you hate biology (la biología)?
15) Write down the Spanish words for the following:
    friendly; kind; awful; good; bad; marvellous.
16) Say you don't like this film because the actors are awful.
17) Say that Sally is beautiful, Emma is nice and Carlos is bad.
18) Write down the Spanish word for 'why'.
19) Now write down the Spanish word for 'because'.
20) Translate this sentence: "Pienso que Elena es fenomenal pero creo que su amigo Raúl es aburrido porque no le gusta el fútbol."

Listening Questions

Track 1

1 ¿Qué hora es? Pon el número adecuado en cada casilla.

1 

2 

3 

4 

5 

a) ☐ b) 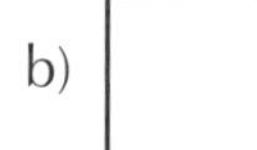 c) 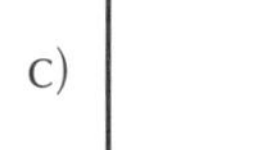

Track 2

2 ¿Cuándo es el cumpleaños de...? Completa la tabla **en español**.

Ejemplo	**a)**	**b)**	**c)**	**d)**
Berta	Julián	Marisa	Víctor	Sergio
15 de julio				

Track 3

3 Rosaura habla de su rutina. Escribe si las siguientes frases son **Verdaderas** o **Falsas** **(V/F)**.

a) Rosaura practica el tenis dos veces por semana. ☐

b) Rosaura y su familia van a misa los sábados. ☐

c) Rosaura fue al cine la semana pasada. ☐

d) Rosaura y su familia van de vacaciones todos los años en el mes de julio. ☐

Speaking Question

Try this role play for some speaking practice. This is a fairly simple one to get you started.

Candidate's Role

You're talking to your Spanish correspondent.

- Saluda, tu nombre
- Qué piensas de España
- Lo que más te gusta y por qué.

!

At higher level, you'll often get an unpredictable question that you can't prepare in advance.

Your teacher will play the part of your correspondent and will speak first.

Get a friend or parent to read the teacher's part for you.

Teacher's Role

Hablas con tu corresponsal. Yo soy tu corresponsal.

1 Hola, soy Antonio. ¿Cómo te llamas?

2 ¿Qué piensas de España?

3 ¿Qué es lo que más te gusta de España y por qué?

4 Y ¿qué opinas de los españoles? — *Here's that unpredictable question.*

Here's an example of what you could say. It's only an example to give you some ideas, so don't learn it off by heart or anything like that, (especially if your name isn't John).

Sample Conversation

1 Hola, soy Antonio. ¿Cómo te llamas?

¿Qué tal, Antonio? Yo me llamo John. Encantado de conocerte.

This is a polite way of saying you're pleased to meet them.

2 ¿Qué piensas de España?

Pienso que es un país fantástico.

3 ¿Qué es lo que más te gusta de España y por qué?

Lo que más me gusta es el clima porque en invierno no hace tanto frío como en Inglaterra.

You can't just say what you like — you need to give a reason here to get the marks.

4 Y, ¿qué opinas de los españoles?

Me parece que son muy simpáticos y amables.

Reading Question

1 Lee estos anuncios.

Anuncios

Se vende chalet con piscina, 15 km de Valencia, 4 habitaciones, 3 baños, cocina y garaje, 150 m², 150.000 €. Más información 963 47 65 89. Inmobiliaria El Mar, Avenida San Joaquín 17, 3°, A, 46003 Valencia.

Julio Fuentes (13-5-1985), quisiera intercambiar amistad con chicos y chicas de 18 a 25 años, en español o inglés, mandar foto, Pza. Conde de Monforte 75, bajo, 47045 Valladolid.

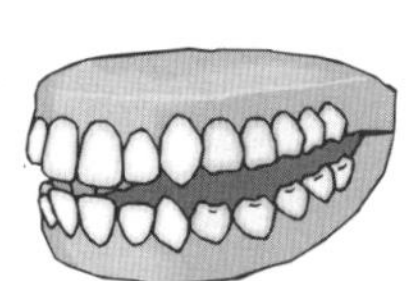

Clínica Dental. Dr J. Gómez. 15 años de experiencia profesional. Ortodoncia. Prótesis. Cirugía Dental. Horario: de 9 a 20. Cerrado en agosto por vacaciones. Teléfono. 824 00 73. Fax. 824 00 76. Urgencias 034 83 87 66 66.

Responde **en español** a las siguientes preguntas:

a) ¿Cuánto cuesta el chalet?

....

b) ¿Cuál es el teléfono de la inmobiliaria?

....

c) ¿Cuándo nació Julio Fuentes?

....

d) ¿En qué ciudad vive Julio Fuentes?

....

e) ¿Cuándo toma vacaciones el Dr J. Gómez?

....

Writing Question

1 Tu corresponsal te ha enviado una carta.

¡Hola!

Me llamo Vicente Martínez y soy estudiante en el colegio Guadalaviar de Madrid. Llegaré a Inglaterra el sábado siete de marzo; tengo ganas de conocerte para practicar mi inglés. En mi colegio tenemos seis clases cada día. No estudio demasiado porque casi todas las asignaturas son aburridas y difíciles; pero mi asignatura favorita es el inglés porque es interesante y fácil de aprender. No me gusta nada la comida de mi colegio; prefiero la comida que prepara mi madre en casa. Me encanta practicar deportes, pues pienso que el ejercicio es bueno para la salud.

Escribe pronto. Un abrazo.

Responde a la carta de tu amigo Vicente Martínez.

Responde a estas preguntas:

Make sure you include all these points in the answer, or you won't get full marks.

- ¿En qué colegio estudias? ¿Cuántas clases tienes al día?
- ¿Qué horario tienes? ¿Qué es lo que más te gusta de tu colegio y por qué?
- ¿Qué es lo que menos te gusta de tu colegio? ¿Por qué?
- ¿Qué cosas buenas tiene tu colegio? ¿Y qué cosas son malas? ¿Por qué?
- ¿Qué te gusta hacer cuando no estás en el colegio?

Revision Summary

This section is all the absolute basics. You need to know all this backwards by the time you get into the exams. All the bits on your opinions, and on times (including today, tomorrow, every week, on Mondays etc.) can make a huge difference to your marks. The best way to check you know it all is to do all these questions — if you get stuck or get it wrong, go back over the section and have another try at the questions until you get them right every time.

1) How do you say these numbers in Spanish?
a) 22 b) 35 c) 58 d) 71 e) 112 f) 2101

2) What are these in Spanish? a) 1st b) 2nd c) 5th d) 10th e) 25th f) 52nd

3) What do these words mean? a) cada b) unos

4) Ask 'What time is it?' in Spanish.
Look at your watch, and say what time it is, out loud and in Spanish.

5) How would you say these times in Spanish? a) 5.00 b) 10.30 c) 13.22 d) 16.45

6) Say all the days of the week in Spanish, from Monday to Sunday.

7) How do you say these in Spanish? a) yesterday b) today c) tomorrow

8) How do you say the date of your birthday in Spanish?

9) '¿Qué haces esta noche?' means 'What are you doing tonight?'
How would say 'What are you doing —
a) this morning?' b) this afternoon?' c) next week?'

10) 'Practico pocas veces deportes' means 'I seldom do sport.'
How would you say:
a) 'I do sport every day.' b) 'I often do sport.' c) 'I sometimes do sport.'

11) How would you say: a) 'I would like some coffee.' b) 'May I have a coffee?'
c) 'I'm sorry' (give two ways).

12) How do you say these in Spanish? a) Please b) Thank you c) How are you?

13) 'Cantas' means 'You sing' or 'You are singing'. What do these questions mean?
a) ¿Por qué cantas? b) ¿Dónde cantas? c) ¿Qué cantas?
d) ¿Cantas bien? e) ¿Cuándo cantas? f) ¿Cantas?

14) How would you say these things in Spanish?
Give at least one way to say each of them.
a) I like Elvis Presley. b) I don't like Elvis Presley.
c) I find Elvis Presley interesting. d) I love Elvis Presley.
e) I find Elvis Presley awful. f) I think that Elvis Presley is fantastic.

The Weather

You may be asked about the weather in the speaking exam. Or you might have to listen to a weather forecast in your listening exam — or you may be in Spain planning a picnic...

¿Qué tiempo hace? — What's the weather like?

These short sentences are the ones you definitely can't do without — and they're easy.

Está lloviendo. = It's raining.

It's snowing: Está nevando
The sky's clear: Está despejado
It's cloudy: Está nublado
It's foggy: Hay niebla
It's stormy: Hay tormenta

Of course, it doesn't always rain, so here are a few others you could use:

Hace frío. = It's cold.

You can use any of these words after 'Hace...'.

warm: calor
windy: viento
sunny: sol
hot: mucho calor
nice: buen tiempo
bad: mal tiempo

¿Qué tiempo hará mañana? — What will the weather be like tomorrow?

This is quite easy, and it sounds impressive:

See pages 4-5 for more on times and dates, and page 171 for the future tense.

Mañana lloverá / va a llover. = It will rain tomorrow.

next week: la semana próxima
on Tuesday: el martes

It'll snow: nevará / va a nevar
It'll rain: lloverá / va a llover
It'll thunder: habrán truenos
It'll be hot: hará calor / va a hacer calor
It'll be cold: hará frío / va a hacer frío
It'll be windy: hará viento / va a hacer viento
It'll be cloudy: estará nublado / va a estar nublado

El pronóstico del tiempo — The weather forecast

Tricky Stuff

OK, here's a real weather forecast. You won't know all the words, but you don't need to. Look at the words you do know and have a guess.

Work through this one, and see if you can figure out which bit means what. Any words you don't know are in the dictionary at the back of the book.

El tiempo de hoy
Hoy hará calor en España.
Mañana hará viento en el sur
y estará nublado en el norte.
Lloverá en la costa.

today: hoy
in the south: en el sur
in the north: en el norte

When you've figured it out as best you can, check it here to see if you got it all right.

Today's Weather Forecast
Today it will be warm in Spain. Tomorrow it will be windy in the south and cloudy in the north. It will rain on the coast.

You have to talk about the weather

This stuff on weather and forecasts nearly always comes up in the exams — so you've got to do it. Still, all you need to do is learn the main sentences and the bits of vocabulary on this page.

Countries

You're a foreigner in Spain so you need to be able to say what country you're from and what your nationality is. You need to learn some others too as they may well come up in your exams.

¿De dónde eres? — Where do you come from?

A useful pair of phrases — and they're easy to learn. If the country you're from isn't somewhere here, look it up in a dictionary.

Soy de Inglaterra. Soy inglés/inglesa. = I come from England. I am English.

Wales: (del país) de Gales
Northern Ireland: de Irlanda del Norte
England: de Inglaterra
Scotland: de Escocia

Welsh: galés/galesa
Northern Irish: norirlandés/norirlandesa
English: inglés/inglesa
Scottish: escocés/escocesa

¿Dónde vives? = Where do you live?

Vivo en Inglaterra. = I live in England.

IMPORTANT BIT:
You must add 'a' on the end and drop the accent for women and girls (see page 138).
Soy inglesa.

Learn these foreign countries

Names of countries come in handy all the time — for talking about holidays, future plans, current events, football... you get the picture.

France: Francia (fem.)
Germany: Alemania (fem.)
Italy: Italia (fem.)
Spain: España (fem.)
Austria: Austria (fem.)
Holland: Holanda (fem.)
America: América (fem.)
USA: los Estados Unidos (masc. pl.)

French: francés/francesa
German: alemán/alemana
Italian: italiano/a
Spanish: español/a
Austrian: austríaco/a
Dutch: holandés/holandesa
American: americano/a
North American: norteamericano/a

IMPORTANT: Don't use a capital letter for inglés, francés etc.

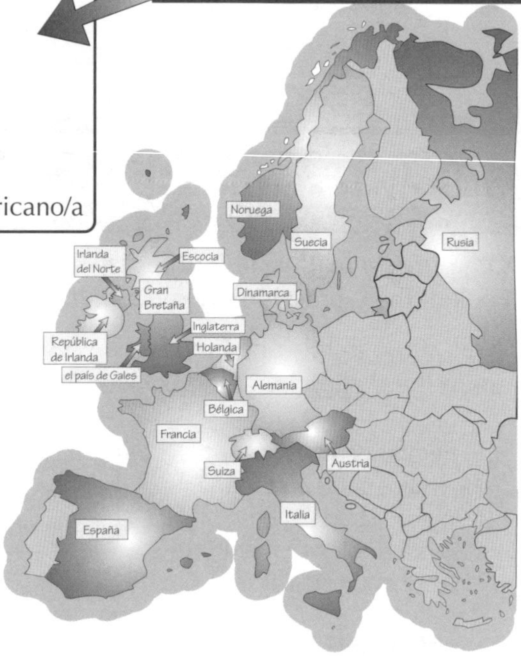

For extra marks, learn these places as well:

Belgium: Bélgica (fem.)
Denmark: Dinamarca (fem.)
Norway: Noruega (fem.)
Switzerland: Suiza (fem.)
Great Britain: Gran Bretaña (fem.)
The United Kingdom: el Reino Unido
Sweden: Suecia (fem.)
Russia: Rusia (fem.)
Europe: Europa (fem.)
Africa: África (fem.)

This is the geography part of Spanish GCSE

Find an atlas and see how many of the countries you know in Spanish. With the ones where the Spanish word is a bit like the English, check you've got the spelling right — like Holanda.

Hotels and Hostels Vocabulary

Holidays are another exam favourite. This page has all the words you need to know about hotels, hostels and camping. Still, at least camping in Spain isn't usually as soggy as it is in the UK...

Las vacaciones — Holidays

Booking the right kind of room in the right kind of hotel is really important to examiners.

Things you might want to ask for

room: una habitación
double room: una habitación doble
single room: una habitación individual

General

holiday: las vacaciones
abroad: el extranjero
person: la persona
night: la noche

Verbs used in hotels

to reserve: reservar
to stay: alojarse/quedarse
to cost: costar
to leave: irse

Here's the vocabulary for the kind of accommodation you want:

guest house: la pensión

hotel: el hotel

full board: la pensión completa
half board: la media pensión

campsite: el camping

youth hostel: el albergue juvenil

More holiday vocab to learn

You may need to ask about your room, where things are in the hotel, and paying the bill.

Parts of a hotel.

restaurant: el restaurante
dining room: el comedor
lift: el ascensor
stairs: la escalera
car park: el aparcamiento
lounge: el salón

Extra words for camping.

tent: la tienda
sleeping bag: el saco de dormir
to camp: acampar
pitch (noun): la plaza, el terreno
drinking water: el agua potable

Things about your room.

key: la llave
balcony: el balcón
bath: el baño
shower: la ducha
washbasin: el lavabo

Paying for your stay.

bill: la cuenta
price: el precio

There's vocab, vocab everywhere

OK, I admit this is just a load of vocabulary. If you want to really learn how to use and understand these words you need to write out at least one sentence for each one. It's the only way to learn it.

Booking a Room / Campsite

You'll often have to ask about booking rooms in the exam. Learn how to ask about camping too.

¿Tiene habitaciones libres?

Do you have any rooms free?

Quisiera una habitación individual . = I'd like a single room.

If you want to talk about different kinds of bookings, use the vocab you've just learnt on page 19.

double room: doble
room with a bath: con baño
room with a balcony: con balcón

Quisiera quedarme aquí dos noches . = I'd like to stay here for two nights.

Put the number of nights you want here. See page 1 for more numbers.

IMPORTANT BIT:
If you're staying for one night, use "una noche".

¿Cuánto es por noche para una persona ? = How much is it per night for one person?

If there's more than one person, use dos personas, tres personas etc.

La tomo. = I'll take it. ***No la tomo.*** = I won't take it.

¿Se puede acampar aquí? — Can I camp here?

Even if you're not into the outdoor life these phrases will be useful in your exams.

Quisiera una plaza para una noche . = I'd like a pitch for one night.

Put how long you want to stay in here.

pitch (place for a tent): la plaza

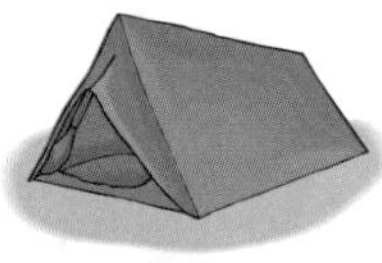

tent: la tienda

You might need these phrases too:

Is there drinking water here? ¿Hay agua potable aquí?
Can I light a fire here? ¿Puedo hacer un fuego aquí?
Where can I find...? ¿Dónde hay...?

caravan: la caravana

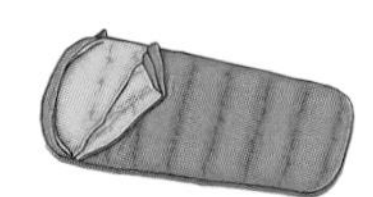

sleeping bag: el saco de dormir

You may have to book ahead. See page 115 for information on how to write a formal letter.

There's no time for camping — you've got Spanish to learn

Even if you're never going to go on holiday to Spain, learn this page. Make sure you know all the example sentences, and practise writing out variations using all the extra vocab until you're sure.

Quick Questions

If you don't have a quick, thorough warm-up you might strain a brain cell or two when you do the exam questions. So take the time to run through these simple questions and get the basic facts straight before you leap into the real exam questions. Go on — you know it makes sense.

Quick Questions

1) Write down the Spanish for: it's cold; it's sunny; it's hot; it's stormy.
2) How would you say to your Spanish friend: "It's nice weather here. What's the weather like in Spain?"
3) The weather forecast says:
   "Mañana hará generalmente buen tiempo por todo el país. En el sur el cielo estará despejado y hará sol y mucho calor. En el norte estará un poco nublado y lloverá en la costa." What is the forecast?
4) Translate this forecast into Spanish:
   In the north of England tomorrow it will rain and it will be very cloudy. In the south, it will be stormy. In Wales it will be very windy and it will snow in the Scottish mountains.
5) How would you tell your Spanish friend: "Next week it will be very cold and it will snow on Tuesday"?
6) How would you ask someone in Spanish: "Where do you come from?"
7) How would an American girl tell a Spanish person that she comes from the USA and that she is not English?
8) Write down the Spanish for:
   a) a French girl b) a German boy c) two Dutch boys
   d) two Italian girls e) a Scottish boy f) three Welsh girls
9) Translate the following dialogue into English:
   A: ¿Adónde vas de vacaciones? ¿Al extranjero?
   B: Sí, este año volveremos a España.
   A: ¿Por qué?
   B: Porque se puede garantizar el sol.
   A: ¿Había un problema el año pasado?
   B: Sí, el verano pasado mis padres decidieron acampar y nos quedamos en un camping en Bélgica. Llovió todo el tiempo. La plaza estaba bajo los árboles, la tienda y los sacos de dormir se mojaron, no había agua potable y no se podía hacer fuego.
   A: ¡Qué desastre!
   B: Y tú, ¿adónde vas?
   A: Vamos a un camping en Bélgica. ¡Nos vamos mañana por la mañana!
10) Give the Spanish for:
   a) holiday b) a guest house
   c) a youth hostel d) a caravan
11) Give the Spanish words for: a single room; a car park; the dining room.
12) How would you politely ask for the bill in Spanish at the end of your stay?

Asking Where Things Are

In the exam, they won't just get you to book a room — they can get you to do a whole load more. Here's how to ask people where things are.

Ask where things are — use '¿Dónde está...?'

Knowing how to ask where things are is very important — learn these useful phrases.

¿Dónde está el comedor, por favor? = Where is the dining room, please?

car park: el aparcamiento
games room: la sala de juegos
telephone: el teléfono

See page 19 for more things you might need to ask about.

¿Dónde están los servicios? = Where are the toilets? (plural)

Understand how to find things

Está en el tercer piso. = It's on the third floor.

fourth floor: cuarto piso
second floor: segundo piso
first floor: primer piso
ground floor: la planta baja

For higher floor numbers, see page 2.

These are other words you might need when you describe where something is.

outside: fuera
on the left / right: a la izquierda / derecha
straight on: todo recto / derecho
upstairs: arriba
downstairs: abajo
at the end of the corridor: al final del pasillo

You'll get questions like this in the listening exam

The best way to check you know this stuff is to cover up the page and try to scribble the words down. Once you know the vocab, get on with writing down full sentences using it.

Asking for Information

Here's some more stuff you might need to ask while you're on your holidays in Spain.

¿Cuándo... ? — When is... ?

¿Cuándo se sirve el desayuno, por favor? = When is breakfast served, please?

lunch: el almuerzo / la comida
evening meal: la cena

Se sirve a las ocho. = It's served at eight o'clock.

For more times, see page 3.

Find out what there is to do

Here's how you find out what a town's got to offer.

¿Puede darme información sobre el parque zoológico, por favor?

= Can you give me information about the zoo, please?

For more things you could ask about, see pages 34 and 62.

the sights of Madrid: los monumentos de Madrid
the museum: el museo

You can find out what there is to do by going to the *tourist information office:* la oficina de turismo.

¿Cuándo abre el museo? = When does the museum open?

close: cierra

the exhibition: la exposición
the gallery: la galería

Learn all this stuff for your speaking exam

Examiners love those "pretend you're on holiday in Spain" questions — that's where this stuff is handy. Even if you've never been to the tourist information centre in your life, learn about it now.

Excursions

You need to be able to ask about little trips that you can go on when you're on holiday.

Ask about 'las excursiones'

¿Tiene unos folletos sobre excursiones por Sevilla ?
= Do you have any leaflets about excursions around Seville?

the museums in Toledo: los museos de Toledo

¿Qué clase de excursión quiere hacer? = What kind of excursion do you want to go on?

Quisiera visitar Aranjuez . = I'd like to visit Aranjuez.

go to a museum: visitar un museo
see the castle: ver el castillo

¿Cuánto es? = How much is it?

Son treinta euros por persona. = It costs 30 euros per person.

Understand how to get there

the train: el tren

Este autocar va a Aranjuez. El autocar sale del ayuntamiento a la una y media . = This coach goes to Aranjuez. The coach leaves from the town hall at half past one.

from the church: de la iglesia
from the market: del mercado

at 2 o'clock: a las dos
at 3.15: a las tres y cuarto
at midday: a mediodía

Learn this page to really impress the examiner

The examiners want you to be able to organise lots of little trips to see the local attractions. They don't seem to realise that you'd probably rather stay by the hotel pool and work on your tan. That's life, sadly.

Talking about your Holiday

Everyone wants to bore people by telling them all about their holidays. By the time you've finished this page you'll be able to bore people in Spanish... and get good marks.

¿Adónde fuiste? — Where did you go?

Fui a los Estados Unidos hace dos semanas. = I went to the USA two weeks ago.

Spain: a España
France: a Francia
Ireland: a Irlanda

a week ago: hace una semana
a month ago: hace un mes
in July: en julio
in the summer: en el verano

Other dates and times: pages 4-5.
Points of the compass: page 36.
A bigger list of countries: page 18.

¿Con quién fuiste de vacaciones?

Who did you go on holiday with?

Fui de vacaciones con mi familia por un mes. = I went on holiday with my family for a month.

my brother: mi hermano
my friends: mis amigos/as

a fortnight: quince días
two weeks: dos semanas

For past tenses, see pages 172 to 177.

For friends and family, see page 96.

¿Qué hiciste? — What did you do?

You need to be able to say what you did on holiday — learn it well.

Fui a la playa. = I went to the beach.

to the disco: a la discoteca
to a museum: a un museo

Me relajé. = I relaxed.

This is a reflexive verb — see page 179.

I enjoyed myself: Lo pasé muy bien
I played tennis: Jugué al tenis
I had a great time: Lo pasé bomba

For other sports and activities, see page 62.

For other places, see pages 33- 34.

¿Cómo fuiste allí? = How did you get there?

Remember the little word 'allí', which means 'there' — it's a useful one (see page 153 for more on this).

Fuimos allí en coche. = We went there by car.

bike: en bici (bicicleta)

For 'I went', 'she went' etc, see page 174.

For more types of transport, see pages 38-39.

Make something up if you need to, as long as it sounds good

You need to understand other people talking about their holidays and talk about your own holidays. Cover the page up, write down the phrases, then check your answers. Do it again until you're sure.

Talking about your Holiday

Details — the examiners love them. So plough on and learn this stuff as well.

¿Qué tiempo hacía? — What was the weather like?

No description of your holiday would be complete without giving a rundown of the weather.

Hacía sol y hacía calor. = It was sunny and it was warm.

it was raining: llovía
it was snowing: nevaba

it was cold: hacía frío
it was windy: hacía viento

See page 17 for more ways of talking about the weather.

¿Cómo fueron tus vacaciones? — How was your holiday?

You can never have too many opinions as far as Spanish GCSE is concerned. You need to say that you liked or didn't like your holiday, and also give a reason why.

¿Cómo fue el viaje? = How was the journey?

Me gustaron porque la gente era muy simpática. = I liked it, because the people were very nice.

No me gustaron. = I didn't like it.

Así así. = So-so.

¿Adónde irás? — Where will you go?

For more on the future tense, see the grammar section — page 171.

You've got to be able to talk about the future — things that you will be doing...

Where will you go?
¿Adónde irás?

I'm going to go to the USA in two weeks.
Voy a ir a los Estados Unidos dentro de dos semanas.

How will you get there?
¿Cómo irás?

I'm going to go by plane.
Voy a ir en avión.

What will you do?
¿Qué harás?

I'm going to go to the beach.
Voy a ir a la playa.

Who will you go on holiday with?
¿Con quién irás de vacaciones?

I'm going to go on holiday for a month with my family.
Voy a ir de vacaciones con mi familia por un mes.

Tricky Stuff Tricky Stuff

Tricky Stuff Tricky Stuff

Exotic holidays — and all they talk about is the weather

More details = more marks. Simple. You can always make up a holiday you didn't have, or invent things you did, as long as you know the Spanish words for it. Just be prepared.

Quick Questions

You should know the routine by now — the Quick Questions run over the basic facts, and then the practice Exam Questions test you the way you'll be tested in the real exam. Don't panic, just take a deep breath and get started.

Quick Questions

1) What is the Spanish for: upstairs; downstairs; outside?
2) Write down the Spanish for: on the left; on the right; straight on.
3) In a Spanish bar how would you ask where the toilets are?
4) You receive the reply:
   "Están por allí al final del pasillo, en el patio, la tercera puerta a la izquierda." Where are they exactly?
5) At the hotel, ask if they have a car park and a telephone.
6) The receptionist replies: "El aparcamiento está a la derecha del hotel y hay un teléfono en cada habitación, pero el teléfono público está aquí en Recepción". Give the relevant information to your friend.
7) Ask at what time the evening meal is served.
8) The reply is: "Se sirve en el comedor del primer piso entre las nueve y las once y media." Tell your friend what this means.
9) In the Tourist Office, how would you ask in Spanish if they could give you information about the sights of the town?
10) The reply is: "Pues, aquí tiene un folleto sobre los monumentos, los museos y la galería que hay en la ciudad". Tell your friend in English what you have been given.
11) Ask what time the museum opens.
12) You hear this announcement: "El autocar que va a Granada sale de delante del hotel a las diez menos quince. Vuelve a las dieciocho quince." What are you being told?
13) Give the Spanish for the following expressions of time:
    a fortnight ago; last summer; this year; in two weeks' time.
14) Translate the following dialogue into English:
    A: ¡Hola! ¿Vuelves de vacaciones, no?
    B: Sí, sí. Volví hace dos días solamente.
    A: ¿Adónde fuiste?
    B: Pasé una semana en Miami y luego quince días en Francia.
    A: ¿Con quién fuiste?
    B: Fui a los Estados Unidos con mi familia pero viajé a Francia con unos amigos.
15) Translate the following dialogue into Spanish:
    A: I went to Italy with some friends.
    B: What was the weather like?
    A: It was sunny but it wasn't hot.
    B: What did you do there?
    A: We went to the beach, I played tennis and I went to the market to do some shopping … I relaxed.

Listening Questions

Track 4

Juan está hablando de sus vacaciones. Su amiga le pregunta:
¿Qué hiciste? ¿Con quién? Escribe la letra correcta en cada casilla.

	¿Qué hiciste?	¿Con quién?
Ejemplo	Fui a la playa	B
1	Jugué al tenis	
2	Fui de compras	
3	Visité un museo	

	¿Con quién?
A	Mi madre
B	Mi hermano
C	Mi padre
D	Mi tía
E	Mis primos
F	Mi hermana
G	Mi tío

Track 5

4 Raquel habla de sus próximas vacaciones. Contesta las siguientes preguntas **en español**.

a) ¿Cuándo va a pasar sus vacaciones en Francia?

....

b) ¿Cómo irá?

....

c) ¿Qué le interesa hacer durante su estancia en París?

....

Track 6

5 Carlos está hablando con la recepcionista del Hotel Alhambra.
Termina las siguientes frases **en español**.

a) Carlos quiere reservar una habitación ....

b) Todas las habitaciones dobles disponen de .... y ....

c) Carlos quiere quedarse para .... noches.

d) En total cuesta .... euros.

Speaking Question

Remember to get someone else to read the teacher's part for you.
Think about what you're going to say before you start the role play.

Candidate's Role

You are talking to your Spanish friend:

- Tus vacaciones preferidas
- Tus dos razones
- !
- Tus vacaciones ideales (dos detalles)

Your teacher will play the part of your friend and will speak first.

Teacher's Role

Estás hablando con tu amigo/a español/a. Yo soy tu amigo/a.

1 ¿Adónde prefieres ir de vacaciones?

2 ¿Por qué?

3 ¿Adónde irás de vacaciones el año próximo?

4 ¿Cuáles serían tus vacaciones ideales?

Remember, you don't have to tell the truth. Just say something that's easy.

Sample Conversation

1 ¿Adónde prefieres ir de vacaciones?

Prefiero ir a la costa.

2 ¿Por qué?

Porque me encanta tomar el sol en la playa y me gusta nadar en el mar.

Try not to use 'me gusta' twice in one sentence — it's more interesting to use something like 'me encanta'.

3 ¿Adónde irás de vacaciones el año próximo?

Voy a pasar dos semanas en Italia con mis padres.

4 ¿Cuáles serían tus vacaciones ideales?

Me gustaría ir a los Estados Unidos porque mis tíos viven en Florida, y me encantaría ir a los parques temáticos de 'Disneyland'.

Try and give a few reasons here — remember you need to give at least two details to get the marks.

Reading Question

1 Your Spanish friend Roberto has sent you a postcard telling you about his holiday.

¡Hola! En el mes de mayo pasé una semana en Edimburgo, Escocia, con mis padres y mis abuelos. Viajamos a Escocia en avión y alquilamos un coche en el aeropuerto. Nos quedamos en un hotel de cuatro estrellas en el centro de la ciudad.

Vi muchos sitios interesantes, por ejemplo, el castillo, la catedral, las calles estrechas y muchos monumentos. Por las tardes íbamos de excursión en coche. El viernes fuimos al lago muy grande 'Loch Ness', ¡pero no vimos el monstruo!

Por las noches cenamos en el restaurante del hotel pero no me gustaba nada la comida. Antes de acostarme jugaba a las cartas con mis abuelos o escuchaba música. La verdad es que me aburría bastante por la noche. Sin embargo me gustaron mis vacaciones. Escocia es un país muy bonito y la gente es muy simpática. Desafortunadamente hacía frío y viento todos los días, pero no llovía. ¿Y tú, dónde pasaste tus vacaciones y con quién?

Answer the questions below **in English**.

a) Who did Roberto go on holiday with?

....

b) What day did they visit Loch Ness?

....

c) What did Roberto do after dinner? Give **two** details.

i) ....

ii) ....

d) What does Roberto think of Scottish people?

....

e) What was the weather like in Scotland? Give **two** details.

....

Writing Question

1 Tu amigo/a español/a te ha mandado un e-mail:

Acabo de hablar con mis padres sobre el tema de las próximas vacaciones y han decidido que vamos a hacer camping en Francia. ¡Qué aburrimiento! No me gusta ni la naturaleza ni la tranquilidad y ¡no hablo francés! Lo peor es que quieren pasar un mes allí.

Además, todos mis amigos van a pasar sus vacaciones en la costa en España. Van a pasar todos los días en la playa y todas las noches en las discotecas. ¡Qué rabia! Mis padres no me dejan ir de vacaciones con mis amigos porque piensan que soy demasiado joven. ¡No es justo! ¿Qué piensas?

Escribe una respuesta a tu amigo/a. Responde a estas preguntas:

- ¿Adónde vas de vacaciones normalmente, y con quién?
- ¿Te gusta hacer camping? ¿Por qué?
- ¿Qué tipo de vacaciones prefieres y por qué?
- ¿Has ido de vacaciones con tus amigos alguna vez? ¿Qué hiciste?
- ¿Qué planes tienes para tus próximas vacaciones?
- ¿Qué consejo darías a tu amigo/a?

If you want full marks you need to answer all these questions. If you haven't been on holiday with your friends, you need to make something up here.

The last question is often the part where you have to give your own opinion.

Revision Summary

These questions are here to make sure you know your stuff. Work through them all and check which ones you couldn't do. Look back through the section to find out the answers, then have another go at the ones you got stuck on. Then look up any you still can't do. Keep going till you can do all of them — so you know you've really learnt it.

1) Your Spanish friend Juan Antonio wants to know what the weather is like where you are. Say that it is cloudy and raining, and cold.

2) You've just listened to the forecast. Say that tomorrow it will be hot.

3) Write down the four countries in the UK and five other countries, in Spanish.

4) Write down the nationality to go with each of the places — eg 'German', 'Welsh' or whatever (but in Spanish).

5) What are these in Spanish?
a) hotel b) youth hostel c) campsite d) guest house

6) You get to a hotel in Spain. Ask them if they have any free rooms.

7) Say you want one double room and two single rooms. Say you want to stay five nights. Say you'll take the rooms.

8) Ask when breakfast is served, out loud and in Spanish.

9) You arrive at a campsite. Ask if there are any places. Ask if there is drinking water.

10) You arrive in Granada with your family and go to the tourist information office. How do you ask for information about the sights?

11) There's an excursion to a nearby museum. Ask for a leaflet about the excursion.

12) Ask what time the bus leaves from the town hall.

13) You've just been on holiday to Italy. You went for two weeks with your sister. You went there by plane. You relaxed and enjoyed yourself. Say all that in Spanish.

14) Teresa went on holiday two months ago, and Javier went a year ago. How would they tell you that, in Spanish?

15) How would you ask someone how their holiday was? What would they reply if they'd liked it?

16) Say that next year you want to go to Gran Canaria, because the weather is hot there.

Names of Buildings

If you're going to talk about your town, you need to know the names for buildings.

Learn all these **edificios** — buildings

These are the basic, 'learn-them-or-else' buildings. (Building = el edificio.)
Don't go any further until you know all of them.

the bank: el banco

the butcher's: la carnicería

the church: la iglesia

the theatre: el teatro

the railway station: la estación (de ferrocarril)

the post office: Correos (masc.)

the baker's: la panadería

the cinema: el cine

the supermarket: el supermercado

the market: el mercado

the castle: el castillo

the library: la biblioteca

Any of these words could come up in the exam

These are the most basic buildings that are likely to turn up in your exam. This is the bare minimum you need to learn. Cover up the page and try to write all the words down.

Other Buildings

Actually there are absolutely loads of buildings you need to know. Like these:

Here are some more shops you need to know

See page 78 for more shops.

the shop:
la tienda

the cake shop:
la pastelería

the newsagent, sweet shop:
el kiosco / quiosco

the chemist's:
la farmacia

the department store:
los grandes almacenes

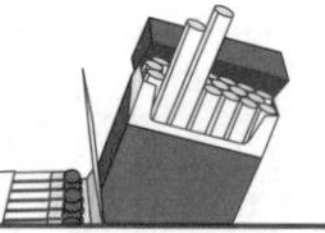

tobacconist's:
el estanco

(You can buy stamps here.)

Here are some touristy bits you should learn

the hotel:
el hotel

the youth hostel:
el albergue juvenil

the tourist information office:
la oficina de turismo

the restaurant:
el restaurante

the zoo:
el zoo

the museum:
el museo

the airport:
el aeropuerto

And finally, a few more important places

the town hall:
el ayuntamiento

the cathedral:
la catedral

the park:
el parque

the shopping centre:
el centro comercial

the university:
la universidad

the swimming pool:
la piscina

the sports ground:
el campo deportivo

the bull ring:
la plaza de toros

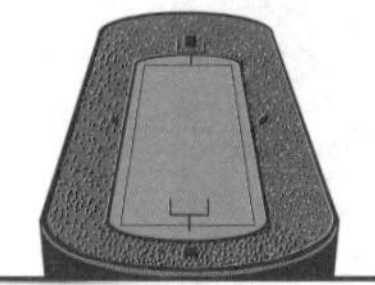

the leisure centre:
el polideportivo

the stadium:
el estadio

the school: el instituto,
el colegio, la escuela

the hospital:
el hospital

Take a bit of time to learn the names of these buildings

Learning vocab is really dull, but it will come up in the exam. Cover the page and try to write all these words down. Then look back and have another go at the ones you got wrong. Repeat as necessary.

Asking Directions

You're probably going to get at least one question about asking directions.

¿Dónde está... ? — Where is... ?

It's really easy to ask where a place is — say '¿Dónde está...?' and stick the place on the end.

¿Dónde está la estación, por favor? = Where is the station, please?

¿Hay una biblioteca por aquí? = Is there a library near here?

¿Está lejos de aquí? — Is it far from here?

If the place you're looking for is miles away, you don't just want to set off walking there.

¿Está el cine lejos de aquí? = Is the cinema far from here?

the tourist office: la oficina de turismo
the park: el parque
the museum: el museo

Está a dos kilómetros. = It's two kilometres away.

a hundred metres: a cien metros
near: cerca *far:* lejos

Tricky Stuff Tricky Stuff Tricky Stuff

Use 'para ir a...?' to ask the way

You may need to ask directions in one of the role plays that come up in the speaking exam.

¿Por favor, señor, para ir al banco? = Excuse me please, how do I get to the bank?

(to a woman): señora

to the station: a la estación *to the castle:* al castillo
to the library: a la biblioteca

IMPORTANT BIT
Replace this with any place, using "al" for "el" words and "a la" for "la" words. See page 138.

You'll need all this vocab for directions:

go straight on: siga todo recto / derecho
go right: gire a la derecha
go left: gire a la izquierda
on the corner: en la esquina

just round the corner: justo a la vuelta de la esquina
(i.e. really near)
go right at the traffic lights: gire a la derecha en el cruce de los semáforos
straight on, past the church: todo recto, pasando por delante de la iglesia
take the first road on the left: tome / coja la primera a la izquierda

Look at page 2 for more stuff on 1st, 2nd, etc.

Tricky Stuff Tricky Stuff Tricky Stuff

You need to be confident about asking for directions

Cover up, scribble it down, check what you got wrong, and try it again. That's the way to learn this stuff. Keep at it until you know it all — then you'll be really ready for the exam. There's a lot to learn.

What You Think of Where You Live

Examiners don't just want to know where you live, but what it's like there too.

¿Dónde vives? — Where do you live?

See page 18 for more countries.

Vivo en Barrow. = I live in Barrow.

Barrow está en el noroeste de Inglaterra. = Barrow's in the north-west of England.

north: el norte *south:* el sur *south-east:* el sureste
east: el este *west:* el oeste *in the north of Scotland:* en el norte de Escocia

You have to talk about life '**en tu ciudad**' — 'in your town'

¿Qué hay en tu ciudad? = What is there in your town?

Hay un mercado. = There's a market.

See pages 33-34 for more buildings and places.

¿Te gusta vivir en Barrow? = Do you like living in Barrow?

Me gusta vivir en Barrow. = I like living in Barrow.

I don't like: No me gusta

¿Cómo es Barrow? — What is **Barrow** like?

If you want a really good mark, make sure you're ready to give more details.

If you live in a village or small town it's 'el pueblo', so any adjectives you use with it will need to end in an 'o' not an 'a'.

La ciudad es muy interesante. = The town is very interesting.

boring: aburrida
great: estupenda
dirty: sucia
clean: limpia
quiet / peaceful: tranquila

Hay mucho que hacer. = There's lots to do.

There's not much: No hay mucho
There's always something: Siempre hay algo

There's nothing to do: No hay nada que hacer

Put them all together and make longer sentences — you'll get extra marks if you get it right.

Me gusta vivir en Barrow, porque siempre hay algo que hacer. = I like living in Barrow, because there's always something to do.

See pages 9-10 for more on opinions.

No me gusta vivir en Bogville, porque no hay nada que hacer. = I don't like living in Bogville, because there's nothing to do.

Tricky Stuff Tricky Stuff Tricky Stuff

Tricky Stuff Tricky Stuff Tricky Stuff

There's always something to say, if you know how to say it

If you do come from a really dreary place which has nothing going for it, you can make things up (within reason) — but chances are there'll be something to say about a place near you.

Quick Questions

These Quick Questions will test you on everything in the first part of this section.
Make sure you can answer all of these questions before you move on to the next part.

Quick Questions

1) What is the Spanish for:
   the leisure centre; the town hall; the library?
2) Which shop would you go to in order to buy stamps in Spain?
3) In a Spanish street how would you politely stop a lady passer-by and ask if there is a bank round here?
4) You receive the reply:
   "Sí, hay dos o tres, pero el más cerca está justo a la vuelta de la esquina."
   What is she telling you exactly?
5) How would you ask, in Spanish: "Where is the cathedral?"
6) You are told:
   "Está cerca del castillo en la Plaza Mayor en el centro de la ciudad."
   Where is the cathedral exactly?
7) Ask the person if it's far.
8) The reply is: "No, no. Está a doscientos metros ... a diez minutos a pie.".
   Relay the information to your friend.
9) How would you ask someone in the street: "How do I get to the town hall?"
10) How would you say in Spanish that you live in a town in the north-west of England?
11) Translate the following dialogue into English:
    A: Por favor, señora, ¿para ir al museo?
    B: Pues, siga todo recto hasta los semáforos. Gire a la izquierda, tome la primera calle a la derecha y está a mano derecha.
    A: ¿Hay mucho que ver?
    B: Sí, mucho. Hay muchas cosas interesantes y siempre hay algo que hacer.
12) Translate the following dialogue into Spanish:
    A: What's the town where you live like?
    B: Well, it's a small town and it's very quiet.
    A: Do you like living there?
    B: Not much. It's boring.
    A: What is there in your town?
    B: There's no cinema, there's one swimming pool and a market on Tuesdays. There's nothing to do at the weekend.
    A: You would like the town where I live because there's lots to do. There are lots of shops, a stadium, a zoo and a big park.

Catching the Train

Vehicle vocabulary is really useful for the speaking exam. Learn how to talk about trains — not like a parrot, but so you can actually use the vocabulary.

Quisiera tomar el tren — I'd like to take the train

Here's how to buy a ticket.

¿Hay un tren para Madrid? = Is there a train to Madrid?

to Toledo: para Toledo *to Malaga:* para Málaga

Un billete sencillo para Madrid, de primera clase. = One single to Madrid, first class.

two: dos
three: tres

single(s): billete(s) sencillo(s) / billete(s) de ida
return(s): billete(s) de ida y vuelta

first class: de primera clase
second class: de segunda clase

Un billete de ida y vuelta para Madrid, por favor. = One return ticket to Madrid, please.

¿Cuándo va a viajar? — When are you travelling?

This is more complicated, but important. You won't get far (in Spain or your exam) without it.

Quisiera ir a Santander el sábado. = I would like to go to Santander on Saturday.

today: hoy *next Monday:* el lunes próximo *on the tenth of June:* el diez de junio

¿Cuándo sale el tren para Santander? = When does the train leave for Santander?

¿Cuándo llega el tren a Santander? = When does the train arrive in Santander?

¿De qué andén sale el tren? = Which platform does the train leave from?

More vocab... Yes, it's dull, but it's also vital to know as much as you can:

to depart: salir
departure: la salida
to arrive: llegar
arrival: la llegada
to get on: subir a
to get off: bajar de

ticket: el billete
timetable: el horario
Spanish rail network: RENFE
the railway: el ferrocarril
delay: el retraso
left luggage: la consigna

to change (trains): hacer transbordo, cambiar
platform / line: el andén / la vía
the waiting room: la sala de espera
ticket window: la taquilla
smoking: fumadores
non-smoking: no fumadores

Learn this and you'll always be on time in Spain

You'd better make sure you can answer all the questions on travelling that could be thrown at you in an exam. It's boring, but when it comes to the exam, you'll wish you'd bothered.

All Kinds of Transport

Here's what you need to know about other forms of transport. This is another of those topics that you'll need to know really well — and you need to know loads of vocabulary for it too.

¿Cómo vas? — How do you get there?

Voy a pie. = I go on foot.

Normalmente voy a la ciudad en autobús.

= I normally go into town by bus.

Voy en tren.

= I go by train.

by bus: en autobús
on the underground: en el metro
by bike: en bici (bicicleta)
by car: en coche
by motorbike: en moto (motocicleta)
by coach: en autocar
by boat: en barco
by plane: en avión

La salida y la llegada — Departure and arrival

You really do need these kind of questions when you're travelling.

¿Hay un autobús para Córdoba? = Is there a bus to Córdoba?

a plane: un avión   *a coach:* un autocar   *a boat:* un barco

¿A qué hora sale el próximo autobús para Almería? = When does the next bus to Almería leave?

the (next) coach: el (próximo) autocar   *the (next) boat:* el (próximo) barco

¿Cuándo llega el avión a Barcelona? = When does the plane arrive in Barcelona?

¿Qué autobús...? — Which bus...?

No doubt about it — you need to be able to ask which bus or train goes where.

¿ Qué autobús va al centro, por favor? = Which bus goes to the town centre, please?

Which train... : ¿Qué tren...

to the airport: al aeropuerto
to the harbour / port: al puerto

You need to know how to get around on public transport

A doddle. Well, it will be if you bother to learn it now. This stuff's straightforward, really. All of the words and phrases behave themselves — "I go..." is "Voy..." and that's that. Simple.

Changing Money and Lost Property

You hope everything's going to go smoothly when you're on holiday, but just in case, prepare yourself for the worst. Losing something in Spain is a popular topic in exams. Learn this for peace of mind.

El cambio — The bureau de change

Look at pages 78 & 1 for more on money and numbers.

This comes up all the time in the speaking exam.

Quisiera cambiar dinero, por favor. = I would like to change some money, please.

some English money: dinero inglés   *£50:* cincuenta libras esterlinas

Quisiera cambiar este cheque de viaje, por favor. = I would like to cash this traveller's cheque, please.

these traveller's cheques: estos cheques de viaje

La comisaría — The police station

Tricky Stuff Tricky Stuff Tricky Stuff

Here's another situation likely to come up in the speaking test — but it's a bit trickier.

He perdido mi bolso. = I've lost my bag.

¿Dónde perdió su bolso? = Where did you lose your bag?

Perdí mi bolso en la estación. = I lost my bag at the station.

For more buildings & places, see pages 33-34

my bag: mi bolso   *my passport:* mi pasaporte   *my purse:* mi monedero
my money: mi dinero   *my key:* mi llave   *my camera:* mi cámara

Alguien me ha robado el bolso. = Someone has stolen my bag.

Me robaron el bolso hace una hora. = My bag was stolen an hour ago.

Tricky Stuff Tricky Stuff Tricky Stuff

¿Cómo es? — What is it like?

See pages 79 & 144 for more on colours and descriptions.

This little describing phrase is really handy — and not just for lost property either.

Mi monedero es pequeño y negro. = My purse is small and black.

blue: azul   *big:* grande   *old:* viejo/a   *made of leather:* de cuero

It's best to learn this stuff before you need to use it

This is pretty useful stuff. You never know when you might need to report something lost or stolen to the police. You know what to do — cover up the page and check you know it. It'll come in useful.

Quick Questions

There's only one sure way to do well in the exam — learn the basics then practise lots of exam questions to see what it'll be like on the day. We've made it as easy as we can for you, so get on with it and do it. The only other way is to kidnap a Spanish person and get them to sit the exam for you, and that's far more complicated (and illegal).

Quick Questions

1) Write down the Spanish for:
   a second class return ticket; non-smoking; departures; waiting room.
2) How would you say: "I'd like to take the boat to Palma"?
3) How would you ask: "Which bus goes to the airport?"
4) You are told: "El número treinta y tres. ¡Ahí viene uno!" What information are you given?
5) How would you tell your Spanish friend that you would like to go to Barcelona on Friday?
6) Put into Spanish: "Normally I walk to school but yesterday I went by bike."
7) Write a sentence to explain that last year you went to Spain by boat but that this summer your family and you are going by plane.
8) How would you tell a Spanish policeman that someone had stolen your purse?
9) In a bank, tell the cashier that you'd like to change some money.
10) She replies: "Sí. ¿Cuánto quiere cambiar?" What does she want to know?
11) Tell her that you want to change £30 sterling in traveller's cheques.
12) Translate the following dialogue into English:
    A: Por favor, señor ¿cuándo hay un tren para Barcelona?
    B: Sale uno cada media hora.
    A: ¿A qué hora sale el próximo?
    B: A las nueve cincuenta, pero el tren lleva un retraso de unos doce minutos.
    A: Y ¿cuándo va a llegar a Barcelona?
    B: Pues, normalmente a las diez treinta y cinco.
    A: Quisiera dos billetes de ida y vuelta de primera clase.
    B: ¡Aquí tiene!
    A: ¿De qué andén sale?
    B: Vía dos.
    A: Gracias.
    B: ¡Buen viaje!
13) Translate the following dialogue into Spanish:
    A: Excuse me. I've lost my bag.
    B: Where did you lose it?
    A: I lost it in the park behind the town hall.
    B: What is it like?
    A: It's quite big, very old, and made of black leather.
    B: What is there inside?
    A: All my money, my passport and the keys to the apartment.
    B: OK. I will telephone the town hall.

Listening Questions

Read through the questions thoroughly before you start listening to the CD tracks. Don't forget, you can listen to each track twice, so you don't have to get everything the first time round.

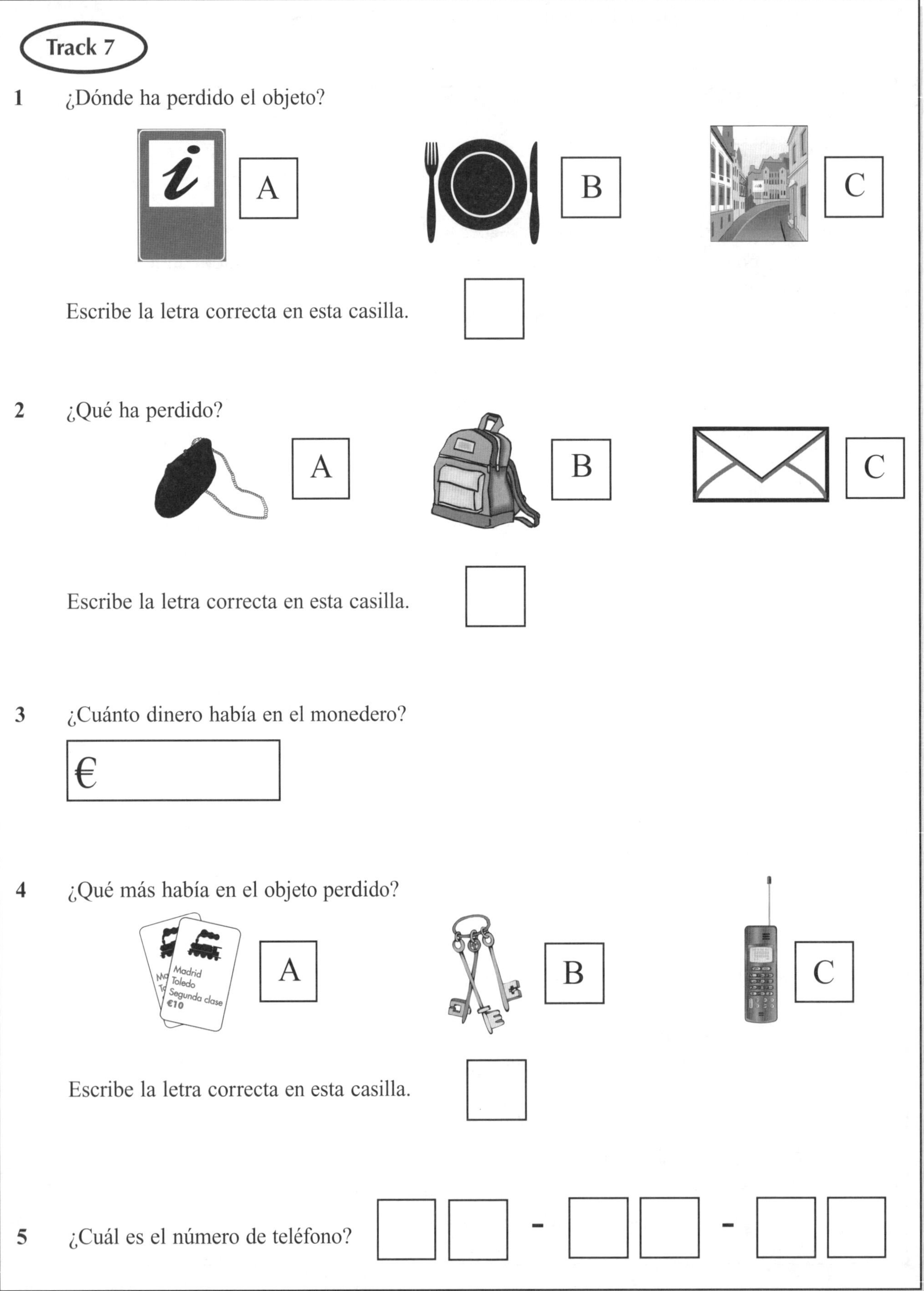

Track 7

1 ¿Dónde ha perdido el objeto?

A B C

Escribe la letra correcta en esta casilla.

2 ¿Qué ha perdido?

A B C

Escribe la letra correcta en esta casilla.

3 ¿Cuánto dinero había en el monedero?

€

4 ¿Qué más había en el objeto perdido?

A B C

Escribe la letra correcta en esta casilla.

5 ¿Cuál es el número de teléfono? ☐☐ - ☐☐ - ☐☐

Speaking Question

Have a go at this role play.

Candidate's Role

You need to travel to Granada on the train, but your train isn't there. You need to reach Granada **today**. You speak to an employee at the train station.

- Tu problema
- !
- ¿Salidas?
- ¿Dónde?

Your teacher will play the part of the station employee and will speak first.

Teacher's Role

Hablas con un empleado en la estación de trenes. Yo soy el empleado.

1 ¿En qué puedo ayudarle?

2 Lo siento pero el tren para Granada ha salido hace una hora.
El próximo tren sale mañana a las nueve. ¿Por qué no puede viajar mañana?

3 ¿Por qué no coge el autobús? Es más rápido.

4 No sé exactamente. Tiene que ir a la estación de autobuses.

5 Está justo a la vuelta de la esquina.

Here's an example of what you could say.

Sample Conversation

1 ¿En qué puedo ayudarle?
Quiero viajar a Granada, pero el tren no ha llegado.

2 Lo siento pero el tren para Granada ha salido hace una hora. El próximo tren sale mañana a las nueve. ¿Por qué no puede viajar mañana?
Necesito viajar a Granada hoy, porque mañana tengo que empezar un curso en la universidad.

This is a handy way of saying that you have to do something.

3 ¿Por qué no coge el autobús? Es más rápido.
Buena idea. ¿Cuándo sale el autobus?

You didn't know that the teacher was going to suggest the bus when you were preparing this.

4 No sé exactamente. Tiene que ir a la estación de autobuses.
¿Dónde está la estación de autobuses?

5 Está justo a la vuelta de la esquina.

Reading Question

1 Read this passage written by a Spanish teenager, and answer the questions below.

> Me gusta vivir en Granada porque no está muy lejos de la costa ni de la montaña. Mi familia va a menudo a pasar el fin de semana en Nerja, un pueblo en la costa. Otras veces, preferimos ir a la montaña para hacer alpinismo en Sierra Nevada.
>
> Para mí también es muy importante salir con mis amigos. Hay mucho que hacer aquí para los jóvenes. Las tiendas y los grandes almacenes son buenos y en verano vamos al parque para practicar deportes y charlar. Hay una piscina al aire libre y un polideportivo. Cuando hay carnavales y fiestas, por ejemplo en Semana Santa, salimos a la calle para ver las procesiones religiosas.
>
> Hay muchos turistas, claro, porque hay un montón de monumentos conocidos. Las calles están llenas de tráfico y hay que esperar mucho tiempo antes de entrar en algunos sitios.

Answer the following questions in English:

a) Why is Granada a nice place to live? Mention **three** things.

....

....

....

b) What activities can you do there in the summer? Mention **two** things.

....

....

c) What is one disadvantage of living in Granada?

....

Writing Question

1 Tu corresponsal español/a te ha mandado una carta.

> ¡Hola!
>
> ¿Qué tal? Yo no estoy muy bien. Acabo de saber que mi padre tiene un nuevo trabajo. Nos mudamos de casa y nos marchamos de Valencia en agosto de este año. Tenemos que ir al norte de España. Estoy muy nerviosa porque tendré que cambiar de instituto y estar lejos de mis amigos.
>
> Vamos a vivir en un pequeño pueblo a diez kilómetros del centro de la ciudad de Oviedo. Tengo miedo y estoy triste porque ya han decidido mis padres y no puedo hacer nada para cambiar la situación.
>
> ¡Escríbeme pronto!

Escribe una respuesta a tu corresponsal.

Responde a estas preguntas:

- ¿Cómo son tus experiencias de vivir en el campo y en la ciudad?
- ¿Cuáles son las ventajas y las desventajas de los pueblos y de las ciudades?
- ¿Tienes amigos que viven lejos? ¿Estás en contacto con ellos?
- ¿Te gusta dónde vives?
- ¿Te llevas bien con tus padres?
- ¿Tienes consejos para tu corresponsal?

Revision Summary

To do well in GCSE Spanish, you mainly just need to learn the key vocab and phrases, and be able to adapt them to different questions. Do that, and you're onto a winner. But if you don't know the phrases, you've got a problem. These questions will check that you know everything you need from this section. Keep trying them until you can do them all.

1) You've arrived in Seville and are writing to your penfriend María Eugenia about the sights. How do you say that there's a castle, a swimming pool, a university, a zoo, a museum and a theatre?

2) Write down five shops and five other buildings you might find in a town (apart from the ones above).

3) You need to go to the chemist's. How do you ask where it is, and how far away it is?

4) What do these directions mean: "La farmacia está a un kilómetro de aquí. Gire a la derecha, tome la primera calle a la izquierda, siga todo recto hasta la iglesia. La farmacia está a la derecha."

5) A Spanish tourist has come to see your home town and is looking for the youth hostel. Tell him to go straight on, turn left at the traffic lights and the youth hostel is on the right.

6) Say that you like living in your town, there's loads to do and it's quite clean. Say there's a sports centre and a cinema.

7) Julio doesn't like living in a town because it's very big and dirty. What would he say in Spanish?

8) Pilar doesn't like living in the country because it's boring and too quiet. What would she say in Spanish?

9) You're at a Spanish train station. Say that you'd like to travel to Bilbao on Sunday.

10) How do you say these in Spanish?
    a) the platform   b) the waiting room
    c) the timetable   d) non-smoking
    e) the departure

11) Ask for three return tickets to Pontevedra, second class. Ask what platform the train leaves from and where the waiting room is. Ask if you have to change trains.

12) You've missed the bus to Vigo. Ask when the next bus leaves and when it arrives in Vigo.

13) You've lost your purse — tell the police, and say that you lost it in the bakery, an hour ago.

School Subjects

There's no way to avoid school and jobs, however much they stress you out.
Great news though — learn all this really well for your exams and you'll have less to worry about.

¿Qué asignaturas estudias? — What subjects do you do?

Write out your timetable in Spanish and learn it all.

You don't need to use 'el/la or los/las after 'Estudio...'.

Estudio español. = I do Spanish.

Physical Education
PE: la educación física

Arts and Crafts
art: el arte
drawing: el dibujo
music: la música

Languages
French: el francés
German: el alemán
Spanish: el español
Italian: el italiano
English: el inglés

Humanities
history: la historia
geography: la geografía
philosophy: la filosofía
religious studies: la religión

Sciences
science: las ciencias
physics: la física
chemistry: la química
biology: la biología

Numbers and Stuff
maths: las matemáticas
ICT: la informática
business studies: las ciencias empresariales

¿Cuál es tu asignatura favorita? — What's your favourite subject?

Or your least unfavourite subject if that's how you feel about it all...

¿Cuál es tu asignatura favorita / preferida? = What is your favourite subject?

Mi asignatura preferida es el español. = Spanish is my favourite subject.

Prefiero la biología. = I prefer biology.

There's more on how to say what you like and don't like on pages 9–10.

Me gustan las matemáticas. = I like maths.

Odio el deporte. = I hate sport.

You need to learn this school vocabulary

Play around with this page until you've got it firmly lodged in your brain. Make sure you can say all the subjects you do, and at least understand the ones you don't do when you hear them.

The School Routine

Not the most exciting of pages ever, but it's worth all the effort when you get tricky questions on school routine. Go for short snappy sentences — that way they're easier to remember.

¿Cómo vas al instituto? — How do you get to school?

Practise saying the sentence you're going to use in the speaking exam. Don't stop there though — any of the other variations could come up in the other exams, so learn the lot of them.

Voy al instituto en coche. = I go to school by car.

on foot: a pie
by bus: en autobús
by bike: en bicicleta

Use "en" with the form of transport, but "a" for "pie" (on foot).

Una clase — A lesson

Write out all these sentences and practise slotting in the right times and numbers for your school.

Las clases comienzan a las nueve. = School begins at 9.00.

Las clases terminan a las tres y cuarto. = School ends at 3.15.

Tenemos ocho clases por día. = We have 8 lessons per day.

Cada clase dura cuarenta minutos. = Each lesson lasts forty minutes.

El recreo es a las once. = Break is at 11.00.

lunch break: la hora de comer

For more on times, see page 3 in 'General Stuff'.

Hacemos una hora de deberes por día. = We do one hour of homework every day.

This could come up in any of the exams, so be prepared

Don't forget the phrases for your exciting school routine, and the sentences for saying how you go to school. Remember the handy phrase 'por día' — you can stick it in loads of sentences.

School Rules and Activities

School is still about 99% of your life so it makes sense that you're expected to talk about it in Spanish. Reading this page out loud is a great way of practising for your speaking exam.

¿Qué haces en tus ratos libres?

What do you do in your free time?

For more on hobbies, see page 63.

Hago deporte. = I do sport.

I play in a band: Toco en un grupo.
I collect stamps: Colecciono sellos.
I play on the computer: Juego en ordenador.

¿Cuánto tiempo hace que...? — How long...?

This isn't here because I like it. It's here because it could be in your exam. So learn it.

¿Cuánto tiempo hace que aprendes español? = How long have you been learning Spanish?

Be careful to use the present tense — you don't say 'I have been' as in English. See pages 165-166.

Aprendo español desde hace tres años. = I've been learning Spanish for three years.

El horario etc. — The timetable etc.

This is all a bit more tricky and also fairly random, but if you want a top mark, you need to learn it.

Tenemos seis semanas de vacaciones en el verano. = We have six weeks' holiday in the summer.

8 weeks: ocho semanas *5 days:* cinco días

at Christmas: en Navidad *at Easter:* en Semana Santa

Hay tres trimestres. = There are three terms.

Las reglas son estrictas. = The rules are strict.

Llevamos uniforme en el instituto. = We wear a uniform at school.

See page 79 for more on colours and page 81 for more clothes.

Nuestro uniforme es un jersey rojo, pantalones grises, una camisa blanca y una corbata verde. = Our uniform is a red jumper, grey trousers, a white shirt and a green tie.

Tricky Stuff Tricky Stuff Tricky Stuff

You need to be able to drone on about your school life

Spanish numbers are vital for this section, so make sure you know them. Close the book and see how much of it all you can remember — the more you can reel off about your school, the better.

Classroom Language

We all have our 'off' days, so it's really useful to be able to ask someone to repeat something, or spell out a word you're not sure about. The stuff at the top of the page is useful, too.

¡Siéntese! — Sit down!

Learn these three short phases to avoid the wrath of a scary teacher.

¡Levántate! = Stand up!   ***¡Siéntate!*** = Sit down!   ***¡Silencio!*** = Be quiet!

¿Habla usted español? — Do you speak Spanish?

We all make mistakes and misunderstand things sometimes, but if you can ask for help, you might not make the same mistake twice.

¿Entiendes? = Do you understand?   ***¿Cómo se escribe?*** = How do you spell that?

(No) entiendo/comprendo. = I (don't) understand.

¿Cómo se pronuncia? = How do you pronounce that?

¿Cómo se dice en español? = How do you say that in Spanish?

If you don't understand say "No entiendo"

These phrases can be vital in your speaking exam. Even if the worst happens, it's far better to say 'I don't understand' in Spanish than to shrug, give a cheesy smile and mumble something in English.

¿Me puedes explicar esta palabra? = Can you (informal) explain this word?

Can you (formal): puede

¿Qué quiere decir eso? = What does that mean?

¿No es correcto? = Is that wrong?   ***No lo sé.*** = I don't know that.

No es correcto. = That's wrong.   ***Eso es.*** = That's right.

¿Puede repetir eso, por favor? = Can you repeat that, please?

This stuff could come up in any of your exams

You can save yourself from an embarrassing silence and get credit for asking the examiner to repeat something at the same time — don't be afraid to use these phrases in your speaking exam if you need to.

Quick Questions

By the time exam day comes you'll need to know the facts in all these Quick Questions and all the exam questions. It's not easy, and there is a lot to learn, but it's the only way to get good marks, so it's well worth the effort.

Quick Questions

1) Give the Spanish (with el/la/los/las) for:
PE; ICT; science; the third term; subjects; the rules.
2) What is your friend asking you: "¿A qué hora empiezan las clases?"
3) Say that your classes start at 9.00 a.m.
4) Ask: "What time do your lessons end?" in Spanish.
5) How would you say in Spanish: "I like maths and I like chemistry but I hate physics"?
6) "¿Cuál es tu asignatura preferida?" What does your friend want to know?
7) Say what your favourite subject is, and give at least one reason.
8) Translate the following dialogue into English:

   A: ¿Cuánto tiempo hace que vas a este instituto?

   B: Vengo aquí desde hace dos semanas solamente.

   A: ¿Te gustan las clases?

   B: No entiendo todo y las clases duran una hora ... es muy largo tiempo.

   A: Sí, pero hay el recreo y la hora de comer y tenemos dos meses y medio de vacaciones en el verano.

   B: ¡Qué suerte!

   A: ¿Cuántas vacaciones tienes tú en tu país?
9) Tell your friend how much holiday you have and when.
10) "Aquí no llevamos uniforme", says your friend. What are you being told?
11) Write a short paragraph to describe your school uniform.
12) Translate the following into Spanish:
Usually I walk to school with my friends but sometimes we go by car. On Monday morning my first lesson is Spanish. I've been learning Spanish for two years. After Spanish I do music. I like music because I play in a group in my free time. After break I do business studies but I don't like the teacher and I don't understand business studies.
13) Ask your friend what he/she does in his/her free time.
14) "¿Cómo se escribe tu apellido?" What are you being asked?
15) "¿Habla usted inglés?" What are you being asked?
16) In your Spanish speaking exam you don't quite catch what your teacher said. How would you tell your teacher that you do not understand and that you would like the phrase repeated?
17) What are you being told to do:
a) ¡Silencio! b) ¡Levántate! c) ¡Siéntate!
18) What does "Eso es" mean?

Jobs and Gender

There are lots of jobs on these two pages — and you need to recognise all of them because any of them could pop up in your listening or reading exams.

Female versions of jobs can be tricky

There are hard and fast rules to how the female version of a job is formed, but there are also exceptions to every rule. The only way to be sure you get the female version right is to learn it.

This table shows how most names for female jobs are formed.
It's a good guide, but won't work for every job.

	**Masculine**		**Feminine**	
	el ingeniero		la ingeniera	*(an "o" ending becomes "a")*
	el doctor		la doctora	*("or" becomes "ora")*
	el contable		la contable	*("e" just stays the same)*

The **gender** of a job depends on who's doing it

The gender of the job is always masculine for a man and feminine for a woman, although sometimes the only thing that changes is the article — "el dentista" or "la dentista".

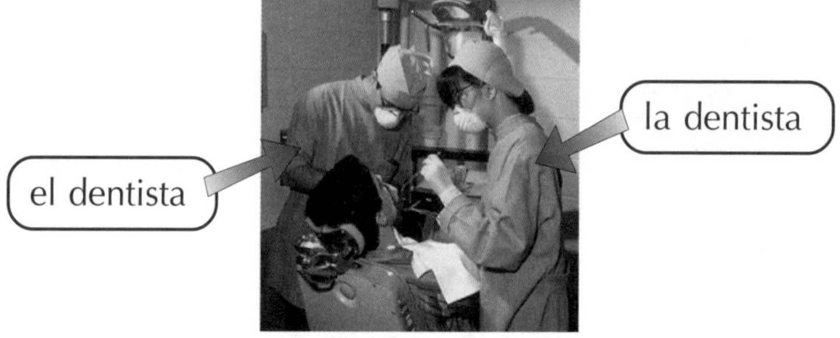

It's very important to get the gender right

It's hard to remember to change the word ending for each gender, but it's not that complicated really. Just remember, o for male, and a for female, except for a few trickier exceptions.

Types of Job

There are more jobs here than you can shake a stick at — and any of them could pop up in your Spanish exams. The jobs you and your family do are extra important.

You need to know lots of **different** jobs

Get-your-hands-dirty jobs
mechanic: el/la mecánico/a
electrician: el/la electricista
plumber: el/la fontanero/a
chef: el/la cocinero/a
baker: el/la panadero/a
butcher: el/la carnicero/a

Medical jobs
dentist: el/la dentista
chemist: el/la farmacéutico/a
nurse: el/la enfermero/a
doctor: el doctor, la doctora / el/la médico/a

Arty jobs
actor/actress: el actor, la actriz
musician: el/la músico/a

More jobs
shop assistant: el/la dependiente/a
journalist: el/la periodista
teacher: el profesor, la profesora
hairdresser: el/la peluquero/a
policeman/woman: el policía, la mujer policía
postman/woman: el cartero, la mujer cartero
estate agent: el/la agente inmobiliario/a

Grey-suit-type jobs
accountant: el/la contable
secretary: el/la secretario/a
engineer: el/la ingeniero/a

Being a student or having a part-time job
student: el/la estudiante
part-time worker: trabajador a tiempo parcial / trabajadora a tiempo parcial

Mi padre — My father, **Mi madre** — My mother

Pick easy-to-say jobs to put in these sentences for your whole family — then learn them.

For more stuff about families, see page 96. For more about numbers, see page 1.

Mi padre es vendedor. = My father is a shop assistant.

My brother: Mi hermano
My sister: Mi hermana

chef: cocinero
doctor: médico

Remember: don't put 'un' or 'una' before the job description. Just put 'es' and the job.

Mi madre trabaja treinta y cinco horas por semana. = My mother works 35 hours a week.

five days: cinco días

You need to learn more than just the jobs your family do

Start with the jobs you find easiest to remember, then try and learn the rest. Remember, the jobs that your family do are the most important, but you need to understand the others too.

Jobs You Do

You'll need to talk about your <u>own job</u> as well, assuming you've got a Saturday job or something. If not, you could be asked about what sort of job you'd <u>like</u>. Be prepared for these types of question.

Tengo trabajo a tiempo parcial — I have a part-time job

Make these easier by choosing <u>easy</u> jobs and <u>simple</u> values — if only the rest of life was like that.

Tengo trabajo a tiempo parcial. = I've got a part-time job.

Soy carnicero/a. = I am a butcher.

You can find more jobs to put into this box on page 53

Gano cinco libras por hora. = I earn £5 per hour.

£3.00 per hour: tres libras por hora
£15 per week: quince libras por semana

Say **what job** you'd like to do and why

Tell those examiners the job you'd like to do with a short and simple <u>reason</u> why — easy.

Quisiera ser médico, ... = I would like to become a doctor, ...

Use "ser" (to be) to say what kind of job you'd like to do.

... porque el trabajo sería interesante. = ... because the job would be interesting.

difficult: difícil *fun:* divertido *easy:* fácil

For more words to say what you think of something, see pages 9–10.

Learn your answer to this question in advance

It's pretty likely that they're going to ask you what job you'd like to do. You need to have the answer to this question on the tip of your tongue — if you don't know, make something up.

Plans for the Future

If your idea of future plans is what you're doing next weekend, then you'll need to come up with some ideas about what you plan to do when you've left school pretty quick. Make it up if necessary.

¿Qué te gustaría hacer después del instituto? — What would you like to do after school?

Quisiera estudiar para el bachillerato. = I would like to do A-levels.

'El bachillerato' is the Spanish equivalent of A-levels; except that they do more subjects.

Quisiera tomar un año sabático. = I would like to take a year out.

Quisiera estudiar geografía. = I would like to study geography.

Quisiera ir a la universidad. = I would like to go to university.

Give **short, sharp reasons** for your answers

Tricky Stuff

Work out an explanation for the answer you've given above. Keep your explanations short, clear and simple. For example 'I want to take a year out so that I can travel' — nice and concise.

Quisiera estudiar música, porque quiero ser músico/a. = I would like to study music, because I want to be a musician.

ICT: informática
maths: matemáticas

accountant: contable
teacher: profesor / profesora

For all the different school subjects see page 47.

Quisiera prepararme para el bachillerato, porque después quiero estudiar biología. = I would like to do A-levels, because I want to study biology afterwards.

Never mind 'after school', you need to revise first

Sometimes the exam seems like a big looming mystery, but things like the stuff on this page come up year after year in the exams. Learn it all and you'll be laughing. Honestly. It's worth the effort.

Quick Questions

Give these Quick Questions a try, and once you've got them right, you should be ready to move on to the exam questions. If you're still not sure about some of the answers, go back and check out the bits you got wrong. Don't move on to the next section until you're sure.

Quick Questions

1) Give the Spanish for a part-time job.
2) Write down the feminine form of the following professions:
   el doctor — el contable — el dependiente
   el policía — el actor
3) Write down the masculine form of the following professions:
   la ingeniera — la dentista — la mecánica
   la actriz — la trabajadora
4) Who works in these places?
   la carnicería — la panadería — la peluquería
   la farmacia — el hospital — la cocina
5) What is your friend telling you: "Mi padre es fontanero y trabaja treinta y nueve horas por semana y mi hermana es secretaria y trabaja a tiempo parcial"?
6) Choose two people you know (family or friends) and write a sentence in Spanish for each of them describing what they do for a living.
7) "¿Cuánto ganas?" What is your friend asking you?
8) Say in Spanish that you earn £5 an hour.
9) Translate the following dialogue into English:
   A: Tengo un trabajo a tiempo parcial en una tienda. Trabajo los sábados por la mañana desde las siete hasta mediodía y gano ocho euros cincuenta por hora.
   B: ¿Te gustaría trabajar en una tienda después del instituto?
   A: ¡Qué va! Todavía no he decidido lo que quiero hacer en el futuro pero sé que no quiero ser dependiente. ¿Y tú?
   B: Yo quiero prepararme para el bachillerato porque después quiero estudiar informática en la universidad.
   A: Tendrías que estudiar mucho porque sería difícil ¿no?
   B: Sí, pero sería muy interesante y ¡ganaría mucho dinero!
   A: Pues, ¡buena suerte!
10) Write a sentence in Spanish to say what job you would like to do in the future and give at least one reason for your choice.
11) Write another sentence in Spanish saying which job you would definitely not want to do in the future and give at least one reason for your choice.
12) Translate the following into Spanish:
   A: What would you like to do after your exams?
   B: I'd like to be an accountant because they earn a lot of money.

Listening Questions

Get your teeth into these practice exam questions, and see how much you really know.

Track 8

1 ¿Qué clases tiene Ana cada día? Rellena el horario **en español**.

	lunes	**martes**	**miércoles**	**jueves**	**viernes**
8.30	inglés		inglés	arte	inglés
9.20				arte	
10.10	**recreo**	**recreo**	**recreo**	**recreo**	**recreo**
10.40		ciencias			
11.30	informática	ciencias			
12.20	**recreo**	**recreo**	**recreo**	**recreo**	**recreo**
12.40	música			ed. fisica	
1.30				ed. fisica	

Track 9

2 Raquel habla de su familia. Escribe el número correcto en cada casilla.

1	Carlos (padre)	**2**	Nuria (madre)	**3**	Sara (hermana)	**4**	Raquel

a) Hace un trabajo muy duro. ☐

b) Trabaja tres días por semana. ☐

c) Quiere ser diseñadora. ☐

d) Ahora no tiene que trabajar los fines de semana. ☐

Speaking Question

This is the kind of role play you might be given to do in an exam.
Have a go at this one for practice.

Candidate's Role

You're talking to your Spanish friend about school.

- Tu asignatura favorita
- Razón
- Ratos libres
- Di qué quieres hacer cuando termines el instituto.
- Trabajo en el futuro (**dos** detalles)

Your teacher will play the part of the friend and will speak first.

Here's what your teacher would say, followed by an example of what you could say.

Teacher's Role

Estás hablando con un/una amigo/a español/a. Yo soy tu amigo/a.

1 ¿Cuál es tu asignatura favorita?

2 ¿Por qué?

3 ¿Qué haces en tus ratos libres después de las clases?

4 ¿Qué trabajo te gustaría hacer en el futuro y por qué?

Sample Conversation

1 ¿Cuál es tu asignatura favorita?

Mi asignatura preferida es la geografía.

These reasons might sound a bit ropy, but at least they show you can speak Spanish.

2 ¿Por qué?

Me interesa aprender cómo vive la gente en los países extranjeros, y cómo evitar los problemas del medio ambiente, por ejemplo.

3 ¿Qué haces en tus ratos libres después de las clases?

Juego al fútbol con mis amigos y toco la guitarra.

This is good because there's lots of detail here.

4 ¿Qué trabajo te gustaría hacer en el futuro y por qué?

Quisiera tomar un año sabático para viajar por todo el mundo. Después, me gustaría ser periodista porque es un trabajo interesante y conoces a mucha gente nueva.

Reading Question

1 Don Pelayo, director del instituto 'El Cid Campeador', habla del horario de clases.

> Las clases en el instituto 'El Cid Campeador' empiezan a las nueve de la mañana y terminan a las cinco de la tarde. Los alumnos que viven lejos vienen al instituto en autobús. Tenemos seis clases cada día, que duran una hora: dos clases por la mañana, antes del recreo, y dos clases después del recreo. El recreo es a las once y dura media hora y la comida es a la una y media. Algunos alumnos van a casa a comer y otros comen en el instituto. Por la tarde, los alumnos estudian asignaturas como informática, música, taller de teatro y religión.
>
> Todos los alumnos estudian dos idiomas extranjeros: inglés y alemán. Tenemos dos programas de intercambio: uno con un instituto en Colonia, Alemania y el otro con un instituto en Manchester. Hay tres trimestres cada año y las vacaciones de verano duran dos meses.
>
> Las reglas del instituto son estrictas y todos los alumnos deben llevar uniforme: pantalones negros, camisa blanca, corbata azul y zapatos negros. Las chicas llevan una falda negra y no llevan corbata. Los pantalones vaqueros están prohibidos.

Responde **en español** a las siguientes preguntas:

a) ¿A qué hora terminan las clases?

....

b) ¿Cuántas clases hay antes del recreo?

....

c) ¿Qué idiomas estudian los alumnos de este instituto?

....

d) ¿Cuánto tiempo duran las vacaciones de verano?

....

e) ¿Qué tipo de ropa no se puede llevar en el instituto?

....

Writing Question

1 Lee estos dos anuncios publicados en el periódico 'La Gaviota' el día 24 de junio.

Consultorio médico busca recepcionista. Horario laboral: de lunes a viernes (9.00 a 17.00). Buena presencia. Sueldo: 200 € por semana. Mandar CV con fotografía a la atención de la Sra. Pérez. Plaza Covadonga 17, B, 080067 Barcelona.

Se necesita camarero/a para Hotel 'El Cisne Blanco'. Dominio de inglés y español. Jóvenes entre 18 y 25 años. Experiencia previa esencial. Interesados enviar CV y dos referencias al Sr. González. Carretera de Granada s/n. 12356 Málaga.

Escribe una carta solicitando **uno** de los trabajos.

Incluye la siguiente información:

- Periódico y fecha en que viste publicado el anuncio
- Trabajo que quieres solicitar.
- Tus datos personales
- Tus estudios académicos
- Otras cualificaciones/habilidades
- Experiencia profesional
- Razón(es) por la(s) que quieres el trabajo
- Intereses personales

If you get stuck with letter writing, look at page 115 for some hints.

Revision Summary

Go through these questions — if you can answer them all without looking anything up, bravo. If there are some you can't do, look them up. Then try again, until you can do them all with no problems. It might take a while, but let's face it, you can't expect to learn it all in one day.

1) Say what all your GCSE subjects are in Spanish (or as many as possible). I guess one of them will be 'el español'...

2) What is your favourite subject? What subject(s) don't you like? Answer in Spanish.

3) María goes to school by bike, but Carlos goes by car. How would each of them say how they get to school?

4) How would you say that your lunch break begins at 12:45pm and that you have one hour?

5) How do you say that you have six lessons every day, each lesson lasts fifty minutes and you have to do homework?

6) John is describing his school to his Spanish penfriend Miguel. How would he say that there are three terms, that he wears a school uniform and that the rules are very strict?

7) How do you say that you've been learning Spanish for five years and German for four years?

8) Your teacher has just said a long sentence in Spanish and you don't understand. How would you ask him or her to repeat it?

9) You still don't understand. What could you say now? How do you ask how to spell the word that is confusing you?

10) How do you say these jobs in Spanish? (Give both the male and female versions if they're different.) a) engineer b) actor c) policeman d) hairdresser e) accountant f) doctor

11) Say what jobs your parents do.

12) You have a part-time job as a salesperson in a shop. You work for three hours on Saturday and you earn £4.50 an hour. Write down how you'd tell your Spanish penfriend José all about it.

13) Susana wants to study physics. How does she say that she wants to do the 'bachillerato' so that she can go to university? How does she say her favourite subjects are maths, physics and chemistry?

14) Pablo wants to take a year out after school and study later. How does he say this?

15) Write down the Spanish names of four jobs that you might possibly do in the future and four that you wouldn't be caught dead doing. For the one you like best and the one you like least, give reasons.

Sports

I was never much good at sport — I could never remember the vocabulary. OK, maybe you don't need to know it perfectly, but you've got to be able to recognise these words if they turn up.

¿Practicas algún deporte? — Do you do any sport?

Here are some of the sports you could see mentioned in an exam:

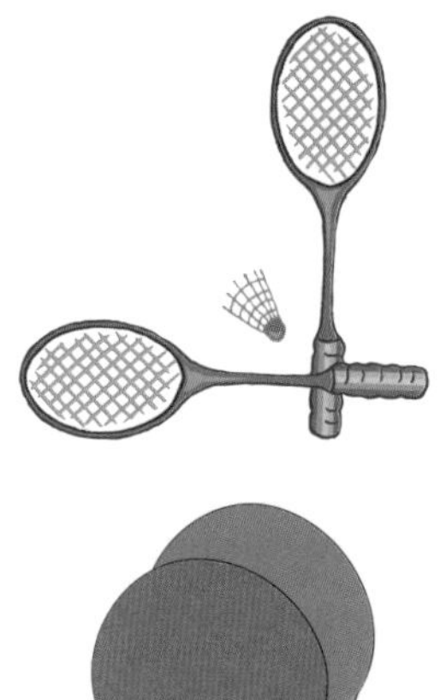

Names of sports

badminton: el bádminton
football: el fútbol
match: el partido
game: el juego
tennis: el tenis
table tennis: el tenis de mesa, el ping pong
squash: el squash
hockey: el hockey

And here are some outdoor sports that you might also see:

Verbs for outdoor sports

to go fishing: ir de pesca
to go out: salir
to run: correr
to cycle: hacer ciclismo
to swim: nadar
to ski: esquiar, hacer esquí
to go for a walk: dar un paseo
to play: jugar
to walk, hike: hacer senderismo
to jog: hacer footing/futing

You also need to be able to recognise the words for where you go to do sport:

Places you can do sports

sports centre, leisure centre: el polideportivo, el centro de deportes
swimming pool: la piscina
sports field: el campo de deportes
gymnasium: el gimnasio
park: el parque
ice rink: la pista de hielo

You need to know your sports

It sounds odd, but even if you don't like sport, make something up if they ask you that in the exam. You also need to know how to recognise all the other sports, too. There's a lot of vocabulary to learn here.

Hobbies

More lists. This time it's hobbies. Same thing applies — you won't need them all, but any one of them could turn up. But first learn the ones that apply to hobbies you do.

¿Tienes un pasatiempo? — Do you have a hobby?

General but vital

hobby: el pasatiempo
interest: el interés
club: un club (de...)
member: el/la miembro

Other important nouns

chess: el ajedrez
film: la película
performance: la sesión
play (in a theatre): la obra de teatro

Verbs for indoor activities

to dance: bailar
to collect: coleccionar
to sing: cantar
to read: leer

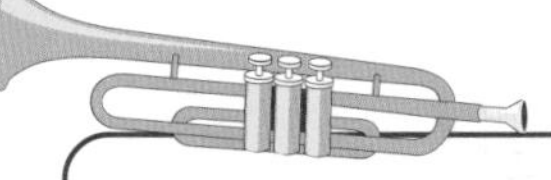

Musical instruments

violin: el violín
flute: la flauta
drum kit: la batería
clarinet: el clarinete
guitar: la guitarra
trumpet: la trompeta
piano: el piano
cello: el violoncelo

Musical words

band, group: el grupo
CD: el CD, el disco compacto
DVD: el DVD
video: el vídeo
instrument: el instrumento
cassette: el casete, la cinta
concert: el concierto
record: el disco
hi-fi: el equipo de música

To see how to use verbs with different people, see pages 164-177.

You'd better think of some hobbies to talk about

Sport and hobbies are common enough topics — you need a good spread of vocabulary, especially for anything you're involved with. If you aren't into any of this stuff, pretend you are.

Sports and Hobbies

What you do in your free time comes up in the exams every year. You have to be able to say what you get up to, and give opinions on other hobbies. It's must-learn stuff.

¿Qué haces en tus ratos libres?

That means, "What do you do in your free time?"
Practise writing some of your own sentences about your free time.

Los fines de semana juego al fútbol. = I play football at weekends.

Every day: Todos los días
Every week: Todas las semanas
Twice a month: Dos veces al mes

badminton: al bádminton
tennis: al tenis

You can find more sports on page 62.

Toco el piano. = I play the piano.

IMPORTANT
If you're talking about games, use 'jugar a', but with instruments, it's 'tocar'.

Soy miembro de un club de tenis. = I'm a member of a tennis club.

chess club: club de ajedrez
squash club: club de squash

Handy hint: if you need to talk about any sport club just put 'club de' and the name of the sport.

¿Te gusta el fútbol? — Do you like football?

Here's how to say what you think of different hobbies — good phrases to know even if you don't really care.

Sí, me encanta el fútbol. = Yes, I love football.

Creo que el fútbol es aburrido. = I think football's boring.

the cinema: el cine
hiking: el senderismo

exciting: emocionante
interesting: interesante

¿Por qué piensas eso? = Why do you think that?

For agreeing and disagreeing you can use these phrases:

I think that too / I agree: Estoy de acuerdo
I don't think that / I disagree: No estoy de acuerdo
That's true: Es verdad
That's not true: No es verdad

No me gusta correr porque es difícil. = I don't like running because it's difficult.

music: la música

boring: aburrido/a

Think up some answers to this sort of question

It's easy to get bogged down in all the vocab here — but there's no need. Practise using it in sentences — the sort of thing you'd stick in a letter or say in a speaking exam.

Quick Questions

Time to see if you've really been learning all those lists, or just looking at the pictures. Try these Quick Questions, and if there are any you can't remember, go back and find the answer. That way, by the time you come to do the exam you should know them all.

Quick Questions

1) How would you say in Spanish: "My parents go hiking every weekend"?
2) Write down in Spanish: "In winter we go skiing".
3) Your friend tells you: "Mis padres salen a hacer footing todas las tardes." What are you being told?
4) Ask your friend if she does any sport.
5) The reply is: "Sí claro, soy miembro de un club de tenis de mesa. Tenemos partidos dos veces al mes." What are you being told?
6) Tell your friend in Spanish that you like going to the sports centre to play badminton every Sunday from six till eight.
7) Write a sentence in Spanish to tell your friend that your brother is a member of a tennis club and that your sister plays the drums in a band.
8) Give the Spanish for:
   an ice rink; a cassette; a flute; I go fishing.
9) Tell your friend in Spanish that you went to the gym.
10) Your friend asks: "¿Cómo era?" What is he/she trying to find out?
11) Translate the following dialogue into English:
    A: ¿Tienes un pasatiempo?
    B: Sí, aprendo a tocar la guitarra porque me encanta la música. ¿Y tú?
    A: Escucho los discos compactos en mi equipo de música.
    B: ¿Tienes muchos CDs?
    A: Sí, muchos. Mi padre colecciona viejos discos de los años setenta pero no me gusta esa música porque creo que es aburrida ¿no estás de acuerdo?
    B: ¿Por qué piensas eso?
    A: Pues, no es interesante.
    B: No estoy de acuerdo. Esa música es emocionante porque tiene mucho ritmo.
    A: Eso no es verdad.
12) Translate the following dialogue into Spanish:
    A: How was the concert last night?
    B: Great! The band was fantastic. I sang and danced all night.
    A: I couldn't go.
    B: Why not?
    A: Because there was a match. I swim for the school team. I love swimming.
    B: I don't like swimming because I think it's dangerous.
    A: Why?
    B: Because I can't swim!

Going Out

Heading out? — then buying tickets, opening times and finding where things are are essential.

¿Cuánto cuesta? — How much does it cost?

¿Cuánto cuesta una sesión de natación? = How much does it cost to go swimming?

tennis: de tenis *cycling:* de ciclismo

Cuesta un euro. = It costs 1 euro.

Cuesta un euro la hora. = It costs 1 euro per hour.

¿Cuándo está abierta la piscina? — When is the swimming pool open?

¿Cuándo está abierta la piscina? = When is the swimming pool open?

closed: cerrado/a
open: abierto/a

sports centre: el polideportivo
ice rink: la pista de hielo

Abre a las nueve y media y cierra a las cinco. = It opens at half past nine and closes at five o'clock.

Quisiera una entrada, por favor. = I'd like one entrance ticket, please.

two entrance tickets: dos entradas

...por aquí? — ...near here?

¿Hay un teatro por aquí? = Is there a theatre near here?

a sports field: un campo deportivo
a bowling alley: una bolera

play tennis: jugar al tenis
go for walks: pasear

¿Se puede nadar por aquí? = Can people swim near here?

For hobbies & more places, see pages 33-34 & 62.

You need to learn these key phrases

Nothing too problematic here — provided you learn your stuff that is... A lot of this vocabulary will turn up in different situations — going out, asking for directions, buying tickets. It's worth learning.

Inviting People Out

You have to organise your own social life, too. Learn how to invite people out in Spanish.

¡Salimos! — Let's go out

Here's one way to suggest a trip out: ***Vamos a la piscina.*** = Let's go to the swimming pool.

to the theatre: al teatro *to the park:* al parque

Your mate might answer:

Sí, me encantaría. = Yes, I'd love to. ...OR... ***No, gracias.*** = No, thank you.

Good idea: Buena idea.
Great!: ¡Estupendo!

It's always good to give a reason if you say no:

I'm sorry: Lo siento.
Unfortunately I can't: Desafortunadamente no puedo.
I don't have enough money: No tengo bastante dinero.

You'll pick up extra marks if you use '**preferiría**' to say what you'd prefer to do:

Preferiría jugar al fútbol.

= I'd prefer to play football.

¿Dónde nos encontramos? — Where shall we meet?

You might decide to meet in front of the town hall:

Nos vemos delante del ayuntamiento. = Let's meet in front of the town hall.

at your house: en tu casa
beside the church: al lado de la iglesia

For other places, see pages 33, 34 and 78.

Your friend might ask what time:

¿A qué hora nos encontramos? = What time shall we meet?

You'd reply:

Nos encontramos a las diez. = We'll meet at 10 o'clock.

two thirty: las dos y media
twenty to five: las cinco menos veinte

This kind of stuff will impress the examiners

Arranging a meeting looks like a tricky topic. There's quite a bit of vocabulary to get to grips with. Then it's practising sentences, I'm afraid. Remember to give reasons and say what you'd prefer.

Cinema and Concerts

There's lots of vocabulary here about going to the cinema or to a play or concert. Some of it's a bit dull, I'm afraid, but that's the price you have to pay if you want to do well in your exam.

¡Vamos al cine! — Let's go to the cinema!

It's a good move to check the price first:

¿Cuánto cuesta una entrada? = How much does one ticket cost?

You should get a reply something like this:

Una entrada cuesta cinco euros.

= One ticket costs 5 euros.

How much do two tickets cost?:
¿Cuánto cuestan dos entradas?

Watch out — you need plural endings for more than one ticket.

Here's your bog-standard 'give us a ticket' phrase:

Quisiera dos entradas, por favor. = I'd like two tickets, please.

el espectáculo = show, performance
el concierto = concert
la película = film
la obra de teatro = play
la sesión = performance
empezar = start/begin
comenzar = start/begin
terminar = finish

Finding out when things start and end is a good plan too:

¿A qué hora empieza la sesión?

¿A qué hora termina la película?

Comienza a las ocho y termina a las diez y media. = It starts at 8 o'clock and finishes at half past ten.

¿Era buena la película? — Was the film good?

Yep, opinions again — you've got to be able to give your thoughts.

¿Qué piensas de la película? = What do you think of the film?

Era bastante buena. = It was quite good.

very good: muy buena
bad: mala
boring: aburrida

If you're talking about 'el concierto' or 'el espectáculo' you'll need 'bueno'/ 'malo'/ 'aburrido' etc.

Meeting times and ticket prices often turn up in the listening exam

Concerts, plays, cinemas — they all use the same vocabulary for buying tickets and asking what time the show starts. The only way to do this is to learn it. It may be dull, but it'll get you a good grade.

TV and Radio

OK, you can have too much of a host family — you may just prefer to watch the box instead. That's where this page comes into its own — it's got a lot of useful conversational phrases.

Ask politely: ¿Puedo...? — May I...?

Sometimes you may just want mindless entertainment:

¿Puedo ver la televisión, por favor? = May I watch TV, please?

listen to the radio: escuchar la radio
use the telephone: hacer una llamada telefónica

At other times there may be a particular show you want to catch:

¿A qué hora empieza el programa? = What time does the programme start?

El programa empieza a las ocho y termina a las nueve y media. = The programme starts at eight and finishes at half nine.

Watch out — it's el programa **not** la... don't get it wrong.

Here's a common question about what you like to watch:

¿Qué programas te gusta ver? = What programmes do you like to watch?

And here's how to answer it:

Me gusta ver Westenders. = I like to watch Westenders.

¿Qué has hecho recientemente? — What have you done recently?

Half the fun of seeing a film or hearing a new song is telling your mates about it:

Hace poco vi 'Gladiator'. = I saw 'Gladiator' recently.

Last week: La semana pasada
Two weeks ago: Hace dos semanas
A month ago: Hace un mes

heard: escuché
read: leí

the new song by Stairs:
la nueva canción de Stairs
the new novel by Martin Amis
la nueva novela de Martin Amis

You'll need to learn all the stuff on this page

Hmmm — it may look like a random selection of media-type sentences but that's what your exam could be like. They could ask you any of this stuff — not just the easy bits, so make sure you've learnt it.

What Do You Think Of...?

Giving opinions is one of those things the examiners are especially looking out for. It's popped up in a few places with specific topics, but it's worth getting this general vocab learnt too.

Use 'creo que...' or 'pienso que...' to give your opinion

Creo que este grupo es bueno. = I think this band is good.

this team: este equipo
this magazine: esta revista
this music: esta música

bad: malo/a
excellent: excelente
boring: aburrido/a
quite good: bastante bueno/a
fantastic: fantástico/a

Opinion words

¿Te gusta...? — Do you like...?

Sometimes you may also have to ask about somebody else's opinions.

¿Te gusta este grupo? = Do you like this band?

this film: esta película
this newspaper: este periódico
this book: este libro

Here's an answer:

No me gusta este grupo. Creo que es malo.

These are linked. If the first bit is masculine, then the second bit must be masculine too.

You may want to check the other person agrees with what you've just said:

¿Estás de acuerdo? = Do you agree?

...or... *Creo que este periódico es aburrido. ¿Y tú?*

= I think this newspaper is boring. And you?

And in reply:

Estoy de acuerdo. = OK / I agree.

It doesn't matter what your opinion is, so long as you can say it

Giving your opinion about things gets you big marks in the exam. It's all a matter of having the vocab at your fingertips, ready to use. And the best way to have that is, you've guessed it, lots of practice.

Quick Questions

Try these Quick Questions and test how much you've learnt in this section.

Quick Questions

1) Give the Spanish for: a show, a play, a performance, a song.
2) Write down in Spanish: "How much does it cost to play tennis?"
3) The attendant tells you: "Cuesta cinco euros cincuenta la hora". How much does it cost?
4) Ask the attendant when the ice-rink is open. The reply is: "Por la mañana abre a las siete y media y cierra a la una del mediodía." Between what times is it open?
5) Ask your friend, in Spanish, if one can swim in the river.
6) Ask your friend, in Spanish, whether there is a ten-pin bowling alley nearby.
7) How would you ask, in Spanish, for two tickets for the ten-pin bowling?
8) Write the Spanish for: unfortunately; I would prefer; I'm sorry.
9) Your friend says: "¡Vamos al teatro!" What are they saying?
10) In Spanish, how would you say that you are sorry but unfortunately you can't because you don't have enough money?
11) Suggest to your Spanish friend that you go for a walk.
12) Your friend says: "La película empieza a las siete y veinticinco y termina a las diez menos diez". What are the times of the film?
13) Your friend says: "Hace poco escuché una canción estupenda en la radio pero no sé el nombre de la cantante". What is she telling you about the song?
14) Write down in Spanish: "Last week I read the new novel by Terry Pratchett."
15) Suggest to your friend, in Spanish, that you go to the cinema.
16) How would you say, in Spanish: "Good idea. I'd love to"?
17) Ask your friend, in Spanish: "When shall we meet?"
18) "Nos vemos en la esquina de tu calle cerca de la parada del autobús número treinta. ¿Entiendes?" Where are you meeting?
19) Write down the Spanish for:
    a) this programme b) this magazine c) this team d) this film
20) How would you ask, in Spanish: "May I use the phone?"
21) Explain to your Spanish friend what programmes you like to watch on the television and give at least one reason why you like them. Then ask her what programmes she likes.
22) Translate the following dialogue into English:
    A: ¿Qué has hecho recientemente?
    B: Pues, hace poco fui al cine.
    A: ¿Era buena la película?
    B: ¡Fenomenal! Fue una película de horror. Me encanta este tipo de película. ¿Y tú?
    A: No, creo que estas películas son aburridas. Preferiría ver una película romántica porque es más interesante, ¿no estás de acuerdo?
    B: ¡Qué va! No estoy de acuerdo en absoluto.
    A: Pues, ¡no vamos a salir juntos al cine!
    B: Pues, vamos a la bolera.
    A: Desafortunadamente no tengo bastante dinero, lo siento.
    B: No importa, voy a pagar yo.
    A: ¡Estupendo! Gracias.

Listening Questions

Track 10

1 Unos amigos españoles están hablando de sus pasatiempos.
Escribe el número correcto en cada casilla.

1	Sandra	2	Pilar	3	Carmen	4	Roberto

a) ¿A quién no le gusta ver la televisión? ☐

b) ¿Quién es una persona deportista? ☐

c) ¿A quién le gusta salir de casa? ☐

d) ¿Quién es una persona musical? ☐

Track 11

2 Termina las siguientes frases **en español**.

a) Eva y Luisa se encuentran a las ....

b) Una sesión de patinaje cuesta .... euros.

c) Se ven delante de ....

Track 12

3 Beatriz and Lucía are talking about films. Answer the questions below **in English**.

a) What does Beatriz think of the character 'Bridget Jones'?

....

b) What does Lucía think of Tom Cruise?

....

c) What do they decide to do instead of going to the cinema?

....

Speaking Question

Now try this speaking role play.

Candidate's Role

You are talking about what you'd like to do today with your Spanish friend.

- Lo que quieres hacer y por qué.
- ¿Cúando?
- ¿Cómo ir?
- !

Your teacher will play the part of the friend and will speak first.

Get a friend or parent to read this part with you.

Teacher's Role

Estás hablando con tu amigo/a español/a sobre lo que vais a hacer hoy. Yo soy tu amigo/a.

1 ¿Salimos entonces?

2 Sí, muy buena idea.

3 A las once.

4 Vamos a ir en coche, con mis padres. Dime, ¿qué haces normalmente los fines de semana en tu país?

Here's an example of some of the things that you could say.

Sample Conversation

1 ¿Salimos entonces?

Sí, vamos a la piscina. Me encanta nadar.

2 Sí, muy buena idea.

¿Cuándo quieres ir?

You've been told the teacher is your friend — remember to address him or her as "tú" throughout.

3 A las once.

Bien. ¿Cómo vamos a ir?

4 Vamos a ir en coche, con mis padres. Dime, ¿qué haces normalmente los fines de semana en tu país?

Pues, normalmente los sábados jugamos al fútbol, y por la tarde vamos al cine, o a una fiesta. Me gusta mucho bailar con mis amigos.

Reading Question

1 Opiniones sobre los deportes.

Miguel
Paso todo mi tiempo libre practicando deporte. Me divierto mucho con mis amigos y es importante para mí estar en el aire libre. Además, hay que hacer mucho deporte para mantenerse en buena salud.

Rocío
Es sano practicar deporte de vez en cuando. Sin embargo, me gusta tener una vida equilibrada con un poco de todo. Practicar deporte sin nada más no es útil. Es bueno leer y charlar con tus amigos también.

Puri
Tengo demasiado trabajo que hacer. Con los exámenes en junio, prefiero estudiar todo el tiempo. En mi opinión, el deporte es una pérdida de tiempo y estoy demasiado cansada para salir después de un día en el instituto.

Esther
El deporte está bien hasta cierto punto; una o dos veces a la semana. Por otro lado, hay gente que practica deporte todos los días y no tienen tiempo para otras cosas interesantes.

¿Qué opinión tienen estos chicos sobre los deportes?
Escribe **P** (Positiva); **N** (Negativa); **P+N** (Positiva y negativa).

Ejemplo	**Miguel**	**P**
a)	Rocío	
b)	Puri	
c)	Esther	

Writing Question

1 Has recibido un e-mail de tu amiga española, Beatriz.

¡Hola!

Mi madre me dice que tengo que hacer más ejercicio pero no me gusta nada la idea. Odio la educación física en el instituto, sobre todo los deportes de equipo. Fuera del instituto, no tengo tiempo. Tengo muchos deberes en este momento y prefiero descansarme delante de la televisión. No tengo ganas de ir al polideportivo ni al gimnasio. ¡Que aburrimiento!

Un abrazo

Beatriz

Escribe una carta a Beatriz **en español**. Menciona todos los detalles.

Menciona:

- Los deportes que practicas
- Qué hiciste como deporte la semana pasada
- Qué piensas de los deportes
- Cómo organizas tu tiempo libre
- Las facilidades deportivas que hay en tu región

Pregunta:

- Algo sobre las instalaciones deportivas que hay en la región de tu amiga

Revision Summary

These questions really do check what you know and don't know — which means you can spend your time learning the bits you're shaky on. But it's not a good idea to do this one day, then forget about it. Come back to these a day later and try them again. And then a week later...

1) What is the Spanish for each of these sports, and for the place where you would do them?
   a) football b) swimming c) squash d) skating
2) Escribe cinco pasatiempos que te gustan, y cinco que no te gustan.
3) Write down as many words as you can to do with playing or listening to music.
4) Juan Martín asks Marisol if she has a hobby. She says that she plays the guitar, goes cycling and reads books. Write down their conversation in Spanish.
5) Francisco and Anne are having an argument. Francisco says that he likes tennis because it's exciting. Anne finds tennis boring and difficult. Write down their conversation in Spanish.
6) Say you go for walks at the weekend and you're a member of a table tennis club.
7) You want to play squash. Ask when the sports centre is open and how much it costs to play squash. Ask for two tickets.
8) How would you ask:
   a) if there's a sports centre near here?
   b) if you can play badminton near here?
9) Say that you'd like to go to the cinema, but unfortunately you haven't got enough money. Suggest going for a walk instead.
10) Quieres ir a un concierto. El concierto empieza a las nueve y media y termina a las diez y media. Una entrada cuesta cinco euros. ¿Cómo se dice eso en inglés?
11) What questions would you have to ask to find out the information in Q.10?
12) You're at your penfriend's home. Ask if you can listen to the radio. Say that you also like watching TV.
13) Think of a film you saw recently and one you saw a month ago, and say this in Spanish. (You don't have to translate the film title into Spanish.)
14) You like the group 'The Sheep Shearers', but you think 'Desmond and the Dreamboats' are excellent. How would you tell someone that in Spanish?
15) How would you ask your penfriend if he/she agrees? (There are two ways.)

Where and When

This section gives you all the key facts you need to know about shopping and eating — at last, a section after my own heart.

¿Dónde está...? — Where is...?

A really useful question, this one. We've covered it already, but it's so important that we put it in again:

¿Dónde está el supermercado, por favor? = Where is the supermarket, please?

butcher's: la carnicería
baker's: la panadería
grocer's: la tienda de comestibles

The word order's the same in English and Spanish here.

Ask when shops open using '¿cuándo...?' — 'when...?'

All very well going shopping, but let's not forget Spain is the land of siesta — opening times may vary.

¿Cuándo está abierto el supermercado? = When is the supermarket open?

shut: cerrado/a

Or any other shop — see the next page for vocabulary.

¿Cuándo cierra el supermercado? = When does the supermarket close?

opens: abre

El supermercado cierra a las siete. = The supermarket closes at 7:00 pm.

For times, see page 3 in the General Stuff section.

Try out these sentences with the names of other places

When you've learnt these, use them with other vocabulary that you've learnt — ask when the museum opens, or where the swimming pool is. There's more vocabulary on the next page to help you.

Shops

Here's some vocabulary for you. Learn the names of these shops before your exam.

Las tiendas — shops

chemist's: la farmacia
book shop: la librería
newsagent: el quiosco
department store: los grandes almacenes
shopping centre: el centro comercial

cake shop: la pastelería
sweet shop: el quiosco/la confitería
stationer: la papelería
fishmonger's: la pescadería
market: el mercado
delicatessen: la charcutería
hypermarket: el hipermercado

La moneda española — Spanish money

Spanish money's easy. There are 100 cents in a euro, like there are 100 pence in a pound.

This is what you'd see on a Spanish price tag:

= 5 euros 50 cents

This is how you say the price: *'Cinco euros y / con cincuenta céntimos'*

Now you're ready to shop 'til you drop

Better do some revision first, though. It's best to get on and learn all these different types of shop. Some of them are bound to be in your exam, and who knows which ones it'll be, apart from the examiners.

Saying What You'd Like

Now here's a handy page — this is how to say what you want when you're shopping in Spain.

Quisiera... — I would like...

Quisiera is ultra polite — it's more formal than 'quiero' (I want), and it's more common in Spain.

Quisiera una barra de pan, por favor. = I'd like a loaf of bread, please.

Quisiera unos pantalones; mi talla es la cuarenta y seis. = I'd like a pair of trousers. I'm size 46.

Important Bit: Another good way to say 'I would like' is 'Me gustaría ...'

shoe size: el número de pie
size: la talla

Continental Sizes

dress size		*shoe size*	
10	38	5	38
12	40	6	39
14	42	7	40
16	44	8	41
18	46	9	42

You don't need to learn these sizes, but they might be handy for shopping in Spain or Latin America.

For clothes, see page 81.

They might ask what colour you want — ¿De qué color...?

Colours go after the noun, and have to agree with it (most change to end in 'a' if the noun's feminine and 's' or 'es' if it's plural).

Quisiera unos pantalones azules. = I'd like a pair of blue trousers.

Colours: los colores

black: negro/a
white: blanco/a
red: rojo/a
yellow: amarillo/a
green: verde
blue: azul
brown: marrón
orange: naranja
pink: rosa
purple: púrpura / morado/a
light blue: azul claro
dark blue: azul oscuro

Quisiera una falda roja. = I'd like a red skirt.

Quiero vs quisiera — 'I want' doesn't get

Saying what you want is an absolutely vital thing to learn. Spend some time on colours too, especially getting the right ending. Have a look at page 144 to learn all about adjective endings — it's important.

Shopping: The Basics

Ah the roar of the crowds, the push of the queues — we all have to shop sometime... often in the exams. Shopping is one of those essential topics you'd be advised to get under your belt.

¿En qué puedo servirle? — Can I help you?

First you've got to be able to ask if the shop has what you want.

¿Tiene pan, por favor? = Do you have any bread, please?

You'd expect a reply like: ***Sí, allí está.*** = Yes, there it is. ***No, no tenemos.*** = No, we don't have any.

You can say what you'd like using 'Quisiera...':

Quisiera quinientos gramos de azúcar, por favor. = I'd like 500g of sugar, please.

1kg: un kilo *2kg:* dos kilos

The shop assistant might say:

¿Algo más? = Anything else? ...or... ***¿Eso es todo?*** = Is that everything?

You could reply: ***No, gracias.*** = No, thank you.

Sí, por favor, también quisiera una patata. = Yes, I'd like a potato as well, please.

¿Lo quiere? — Do you want it?

To buy or not to buy — that is the question... and here are the answers...

Lo/La quiero. = I'll take it. (Literally = I want it)

No lo quiero. No me gusta el color. = I don't want it. I don't like the colour.

lo = masculine things, la = feminine

It's too small: Es demasiado pequeño/a.
It's too expensive: Es demasiado caro/a.

Tricky Stuff

Learn how to ask for what you want

The trick with shopping is knowing the basic vocabulary first — it's a nightmare trying to bluff your way through an exam if you don't know the words. Practising these phrases helps.

Clothes and Pocket Money

More lists of vocabulary, I'm afraid — but it's all everyday stuff that turns up frequently. Apart from clothes, there's a bit of vocabulary for pocket money and sales. There's a lot to learn here.

La ropa — Clothing

Me gusta este zapato. = I like this shoe.

No me gustan estos zapatos. = I don't like these shoes.

shirt: la camisa
skirt: la falda
jumper: el jersey, el suéter
socks: los calcetines
shoe: el zapato
shoes: los zapatos
dress: el vestido
coat: el abrigo
hat: el sombrero
T-shirt: la camiseta, el niki
suit: el traje
jacket: la chaqueta
tie: la corbata
glove: el guante
gloves: los guantes
pair of tights: las medias
shorts: los pantalones cortos
raincoat: el impermeable
a pair of socks: un par de calcetines
jeans: los vaqueros, los tejanos
tracksuit: el chandal
trousers: los pantalones

El dinero de bolsillo — Pocket money

Recibo cinco libras de dinero de bolsillo por semana. = I get £5 pocket money a week.

£3: tres libras
£10: diez libras

See page 1 for numbers.

month: mes

Gasto mi dinero de bolsillo en CDs. = I spend my pocket money on CDs.

clothing: ropa
sweets: caramelos
books: libros
computer games: juegos de ordenador

Las rebajas — The sales

Advanced shopping vocab for advanced shoppers — and for picking up extra marks for vocab.

Hay rebajas en el supermercado. = There's a sale on in the supermarket.

I like shopping: Me gusta ir de tiendas / ir de compras
I particularly like shopping for books: Más que nada, me gusta comprar libros.
I often go to the bakery: Voy a menudo a la panadería.
I go shopping once a week: Voy de compras una vez por semana.

Tricky Stuff

Talking about uniforms often comes up in the exam

Never forget your clothes — it's common sense really. Some of them are dead easy — el jersey, el sombrero etc. Others need a bit more effort to learn — but they'll come in handy.

Quick Questions

There's quite a lot covered on those last pages, so here are some questions to help you check that you've taken it all in. Hopefully you know the drill by now — go through all the questions first, leaving a blank if you can't remember an answer. Then check through to make sure you got them all right. If you got one wrong or left it blank, go back through the last few pages to the relevant bit and learn it again. Repeat until you can't stand the thought of shopping, ever again.

Quick Questions

1) In which shops would these people work:
   el pastelero; el panadero; el carnicero;
   el charcutero; el librero; el farmacéutico.
2) Write down in Spanish: "Where is the nearest grocer's?"
3) Ask the shop assistant: "What time does the supermarket close?"
4) Give the Spanish for: a hypermarket; the chemist's; a stationer's; a bookshop.
5) Ask, in Spanish, if they have any bread.
6) "Sí, claro. ¿Qué desea?" replies the baker. Ask her for a loaf.
7) "¿Algo más?" she says. What does she want to know?
8) Say to her, in Spanish: "I'd like two cakes as well".
9) She says: "¡Aquí tiene!" What is she doing?
10) "¿Quiere algo más?" How would you say to her, in Spanish: "That's all, thanks"?
11) How would you say, in Spanish: "Five hundred grammes of sweets" and "Two kilos of tomatoes".
12) Your friend points to a sign which says: "GRANDES REBAJAS HOY". What is she trying to draw your attention to?
13) Write down in Spanish: computer games; clothes; sweets.
    Don't forget to say whether they're masculine or feminine.
14) How would you tell the shop assistant that you want a red skirt and that you are a size 10?
15) Your friend goes into a shop and says: "Quisiera unos zapatos negros. Tengo el número cuarenta y uno o cuarenta y dos." What does he want exactly?
16) Translate the following dialogue into English:
    A: Buenos días. ¿En qué puedo servirle?
    B: ¿Tiene camisetas como éstas pero en otros colores?
    A: ¿Qué talla lleva?
    B: ¡No sé exactamente!
    A: Pues, tenemos ésta en azul oscuro y blanco o naranja y verde. Y esta otra camiseta en blanco y negro.
    B: ¿No la tiene en blanco?
    A: Sí, pero no hay rebaja.
    B: Pues no la quiero porque no me gustan los colores y la blanca es demasiado cara. Gracias.
    A: Pues, lo siento.
17) Your Spanish friend has sent you an e-mail that includes: "¿En qué gastas tu dinero de bolsillo?" Say how much you get and what you spend it on.

Food

Any of this stuff could come up in your exam, so you need to be on your toes.

La carnicería y la tienda de comestibles — Butcher's and Grocer's

Vegetables: las verduras
potato: la patata
carrot: la zanahoria
tomato: el tomate
cucumber: el pepino
onion: la cebolla
cauliflower: la coliflor
French bean: la judía
mushroom: el champiñón
cabbage: la col
lettuce: la lechuga
pea: el guisante

Fruit: la fruta
apple: la manzana
banana: el plátano
strawberry: la fresa
lemon: el limón
orange: la naranja
raspberry: la frambuesa
peach: el melocotón
pear: la pera

Meat: la carne
beef: la carne de vaca
pork: la carne de cerdo
chicken: el pollo
lamb: el cordero
sausage: la salchicha
ham: el jamón
dry sausage: el chorizo, el salchichón
steak: el filete
fish: el pescado
seafood: los mariscos

Las bebidas y los postres — Drinks and Desserts

Mmm, my favourite vocab — this is more like it...

Drinks: las bebidas
beer: la cerveza
tea: el té
coffee: el café
milky coffee (latte style): el café con leche
wine: el vino
red/white wine: el vino tinto/blanco
orange juice: el zumo / jugo de naranja
mineral water: el agua mineral

Desserts: los postres
cake: la tarta / el pastel
biscuit: la galleta
ice cream: el helado
chocolate: el chocolate
sugar: el azúcar
cream: la nata
pancake: el crep
yogurt: el yogur
honey: la miel
jam: la mermelada

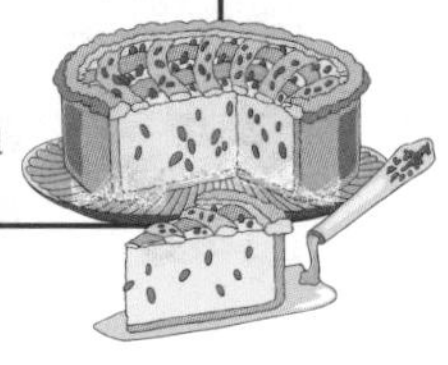

This page is making me hungry

You know what you have to do with a page stuffed with vocabulary like this one. There's no way to tell what'll come up in the exam, so if you're sensible you'll learn all of it. It shouldn't take too long.

Food

Some absolute basics here — and some Spanish specialities that could just pop up in the exam.

Otros alimentos — Other foods

Here are some more basic foods to learn:

bread: el pan
bread roll: el panecillo
egg: el huevo
milk: la leche
butter: la mantequilla
cheese: el queso
salt: la sal

pepper: la pimienta
rice: el arroz
pasta: las pastas
soup: la sopa
breakfast cereals: los cereales
chips: las patatas fritas
crisps: las patatas fritas

Las especialidades españolas — Spanish specialities

Here are some of the local specialities you might want to try while you're on holiday in Spain. Learn as many of these as you can.

olives: las aceitunas
spicy cold tomato soup: el gazpacho
small snacks eaten in cafés and bars: las tapas

rice dish with chicken, seafood and vegetables: la paella
deep-fried fritters with hot chocolate: churros con chocolate
a type of nougat made of almonds: el turrón

Knowing some Spanish specialities looks good in the exam

A lot of foods are similar to the English words — like el café, el chocolate, el limón, but a lot aren't. You'll just have to learn them — but make sure you can spell them as well.

Likes and Requests

You probably have some foods you can't stand, and others you love — well, here's how to say so.

Me gusta / Me gustan... — I like...

Use these expressions to talk about anything you like or dislike — they're not just for food.

(No) me gusta la nata. = I (don't) like cream.

coffee: el café

squid: los calamares *vegetables:* las verduras

(No) me gustan las manzanas. = I (don't) like apples.

Soy vegetariano/a. = I'm a vegetarian.

vegan: vegetariano/a estricto/a

¿Puede...? — Can you...?

Here's a useful phrase to learn. Use it properly and you'll be the essence of politeness.

¿Puede pasarme la sal, por favor? = Can you pass me the salt, please?

a napkin: una servilleta
the cream: la nata
the pepper: la pimienta
the sugar: el azúcar
the milk: la leche

¿Tienes hambre o sed? — Are you hungry or thirsty?

It won't do you any good to be able to say what you like if you can't tell people you're hungry first...

¿Tienes hambre? = Are you hungry?

thirsty: sed

Tengo hambre. = I'm hungry.

No gracias, no tengo hambre. = No thanks, I'm not hungry.

If you're a veggie, learn how to say it in Spanish

Make sure you can tell people what you like and don't like — it'll definitely come up in the exam. And if you're vegetarian or vegan, learn the words for vegetables and stuff you can eat.

Dinner

A lot of this is useful in different situations — not just in conversations at the dinner table. It almost always comes up in the exams — it's the sort of stuff you really need to know.

¿Te gusta la comida? — Do you like the meal?

La comida estaba buena. = The meal was good.

very good: muy rico/a
bad: malo/a
very bad: muy malo/a

La comida no estaba buena. = The meal wasn't good.

El desayuno estaba delicioso, gracias. = Breakfast was delicious, thanks.

'La comida' is usually the main meal in Spain, eaten at lunchtime. If you're talking about the evening meal, it's 'la cena'.

Tricky Stuff Tricky Stuff Tricky Stuff Tricky Stuff Tricky Stuff

¿Quisiera...? — Would you like...?

¿Quisiera tomar sal? = Would you like salt?

the pepper: la pimienta *the wine:* el vino
the butter: la mantequilla

¿Le puedo pasar una servilleta? = Can I pass you a napkin?

If you only want a little, ask for 'un poco'

These amount words are dead useful, and not just here...

Quisiera mucho azúcar, por favor. = I would like lots of sugar, please.

a bit: un poco de

Quisiera una porción grande de tarta. = I would like a big piece of cake.

He comido bastante, gracias. = I've eaten enough, thanks.

a lot: mucho

Tengo suficiente. = I have enough.

Tricky Stuff Tricky Stuff Tricky Stuff Tricky Stuff Tricky Stuff

Being polite at dinner makes a big difference

There's loads of really useful stuff on this page. There are a lot of situations where you'll need to say 'lots', 'not much', 'a little', etc. Scribble down those words and learn them.

Dinner

It's hungry work, talking about dinners and restaurants.

En el restaurante — At the restaurant

¡Camarero! = Waiter! *¡Señorita!* = Waitress!

These are what you'd use to call the waiter or waitress over...

...and these are the names of the jobs.

waiter: el camarero
waitress: la camarera

¿Me trae el menú, por favor? = May I have the menu, please?

¿Dónde están los servicios, por favor? = Where are the toilets, please?

is: está

the phone: el teléfono

See page 19 on 'hotels' for asking where things are.

Quisiera... — I'd like...

See page 84 for food vocab.

¿Tiene paella? = Do you have paella?

bread: pan
bananas: plátanos

the omelette: la tortilla
the dish of the day: el plato del día

salad: ensalada
rice: arroz
carrots: zanahorias

Quisiera / Para mí el filete con patatas fritas. = I'd like the steak with chips.

Quisiera probar... — I'd like to taste some...

Here's a handy sentence for when someone offers you something new, or you've forgotten what something tastes like.

¿A qué sabe el turrón? = What does 'turrón' taste like? (turrón = nougat)

rabbit: el conejo

¿Ha terminado? — Have you finished?

¿Puedo pagar? = May I pay? *La cuenta, por favor.* = The bill, please.

This is vital stuff

Another 'must-learn' page, I'm afraid. Restaurant vocab is useful in all sorts of situations. Start by writing it down, covering the page and learning the handy phrases and vocabulary.

At a Restaurant

Restaurant role plays aren't just about ordering food — this vocabulary will win you marks too...

¿Tiene una mesa libre? — Do you have a table free?

Don't forget — it's all about being polite.

Una mesa para cuatro, por favor. = A table for four, please.

Somos cuatro. = There are four of us.

two: dos *three:* tres

Quisiéramos sentarnos fuera. = We'd like to sit outside.

on the terrace: en la terraza

No estoy satisfecho/a — I'm not satisfied

If you want to complain about something... ***Quisiera quejarme.*** = I'd like to make a complaint.

... remember to say what you're complaining about:

La carne de ternera está poco hecha. = The veal is underdone.

The steak: El filete
The pork: La carne de cerdo
The coffee: El café

too hot: demasiado caliente
too cold: demasiado frío/a

El servicio — Service charge

Remember the service charge (the tip) — you'll be the waiter's friend forever.

¿Está incluido el servicio? = Is service included?

Some useful words you might see on a menu:

Servicio incluido (= Service included)
El cubierto (= The cover charge)
El precio fijo (= Fixed price)

Servicio incluido

Asking about the service charge sounds really impressive

This is all stuff that's sure to come up — make sure you know the vocabulary backwards, and how to use it. There's loads of really useful stuff on this page. Write down the words and learn them.

Quick Questions

These Quick Questions really won't take you long, so take a few minutes to check you've learnt it.

Quick Questions

1) Write down in Spanish:
   the vegetables; outside; pork; a strawberry ice-cream; a bottle of mineral water; one bread roll with a bit of butter and a cup of hot chocolate; one white coffee.
2) At table you are asked: "¿Me puedes pasar el azúcar, por favor?"
   What are you being asked to do?
3) How would you say, in Spanish: "Can I pass you the pepper?"
4) Ask your Spanish friend: "Do you like English breakfasts?"
5) She replies: "Sí, me gustan mucho. Son muy ricos."
   What does she say about them?
6) Tell your friend's mother that the meal was delicious and that the cake was very good.
7) How would you say, in Spanish: "Can you pass me the salt, please?"
8) Translate the following dialogue into English:
   A: Soy vegetariana.
   B: ¿Qué comes pues?
   A: Muchas cosas. Tengo suficiente con las verduras, los huevos, las pastas, la fruta y, claro, los postres ... me gustan mucho los postres.
   B: ¿Por qué no comes carne de vaca por ejemplo o el jamón?
   A: Pues, no me gusta la carne.
   B: ¿No tienes hambre sin carne?
   A: ¡Claro que no!
9) On the menu you see: "Menú a precio fijo". What does that mean?
10) You see a sign by a shop front that says:
   Especialidades de la casa : helados a su gusto ... melocotón, limón, manzana.
   What are they selling?
11) Translate the following conversation set in a restaurant into Spanish:
   A: Do you have a table free?
   B: For how many people?
   A: There are two of us. We'd like to sit on the terrace.
   B: Fine.
   A: What is the dish of the day?
   B: Spanish omelette or paella.
12) After the main course, the waitress comes over. Say that you would like a dessert.
13) At the end of the meal, call the waitress, ask for the bill and find out if the service charge is included.
14) Your friend would also like to know where the toilets are, so ask the waitress.

Listening Questions

Track 13

1 Haciendo la compra.

¿Qué compra cada persona? ¿Cuánto quiere? ¿Cuánto cuesta? Completa la tabla.

	¿Qué compra?	**¿Cuánto quiere?**	**¿Cuánto cuesta en total?**
Ejemplo i)	tomates	2 kilos	
Ejemplo ii)	jamón	8 lonchas	2,70 euros
a) i)	patatas		
ii)		1 barra	1,70 euros
b) i)			
ii)	agua sin gas	2 botellas	
c) i)		4 lonchas	
ii)		500g	

Track 14

2 En el restaurante.

¿Quién lo pide? Escribe la letra correcta en cada casilla.

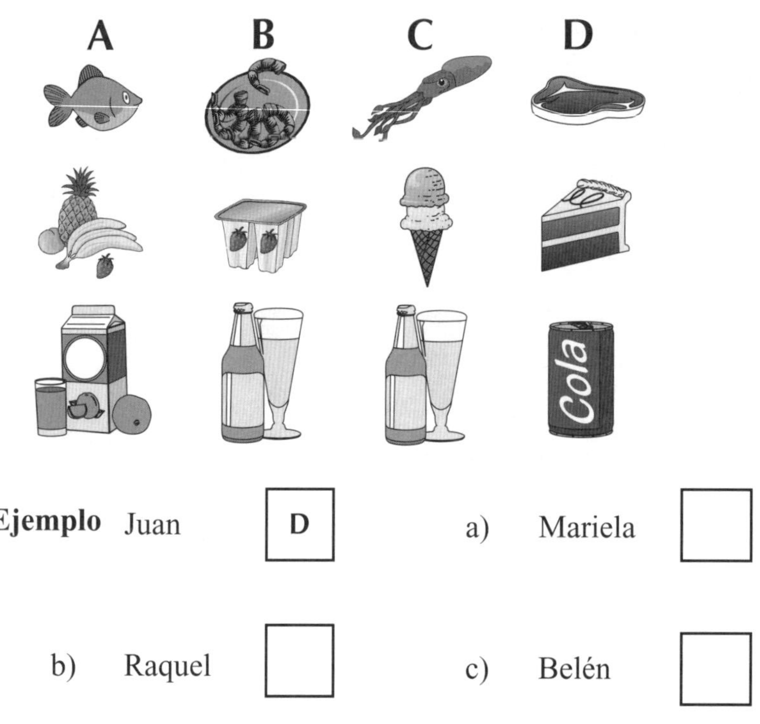

Ejemplo Juan [D]   a) Mariela [ ]

b) Raquel [ ]   c) Belén [ ]

Speaking Question

You get to complain a lot in GCSE Spanish. This time you're complaining in a restaurant.

Candidate's Role

It is the **last** night of your holiday in Spain and you are having a meal in a restaurant. You are not happy with the meal and complain to the waiter.

- Tu problema
- **Dos** detalles del problema
- Tu solución al problema
- !

Your teacher will play the part of the waiter and will speak first.

Make sure you get someone else to read the teacher's role for you.

Teacher's Role

Estás en un restaurante en España. Yo soy el/la camarero/a.

1 ¿Qué tal la comida?

2 ¿Cuál es el problema exactamente?

3 ¿Qué quiere hacer?

4 No es posible pero le invito a cenar gratis mañana. ¿Qué le parece?

5 Pues, lo siento mucho.

Sample Conversation

1 ¿Qué tal la comida?
No estoy satisfecho. Quiero quejarme.

2 ¿Cuál es el problema exactamente?
El pollo está poco hecho y mi vaso está sucio. — *Don't forget to mention 2 things here.*

3 ¿Qué quiere hacer?
Quiero un reembolso. — *This word means a refund.*

4 No es posible pero le invito a cenar gratis mañana. ¿Qué le parece?
Gracias pero no puedo porque vuelvo a Inglaterra mañana.

5 Pues, lo siento mucho.

Reading Questions

1 ¿A cuáles tiendas necesitan ir? Completa la tabla.

A	Necesito comprar una tarjeta de cumpleaños para el cumpleaños de mi madre.
B	Vamos a cenar en casa de nuestros vecinos mañana y quiero llevar una caja de bombones.
C	Mi hermana tiene dolor de garganta y tengo que encontrar un jarabe.
D	Mañana voy a merendar con mi clase y quiero comer bocadillos de chorizo y de salchichón. Ya tengo el pan.

Ejemplo	la farmacia	C
a)	la papelería	
b)	la charcutería	
c)	la confitería	

2 ¿Dónde se lleva normalmente la ropa siguiente? Completa la tabla.

Ejemplo	Se lleva una falda o un pantalón azul o negro, una camisa blanca y zapatos negros. A menudo una corbata es obligatoria.	B
a)	Se lleva los pantalones cortos, un chandal si hace frío, un par de calcetines y zapatillas de tenis.	
b)	Se lleva los vaqueros y una camiseta normalmente pero depende del tiempo. Es aconsejable llevar un impermeable y un suéter.	
c)	Las chicas llevan vestidos o faldas cortas y los chicos se ponen pantalones o vaqueros con una camisa.	

A	Una merienda en el campo
B	Al colegio
C	A la discoteca
D	Al gimnasio

Writing Question

1 Tu amiga española te ha mandado un e-mail:

¡Hola!

Estoy harta de esta situación. Mis amigos van de compras todos los fines de semana. Parece que es su pasatiempo preferido. Siempre tienen dinero para comprar música y ropa. Mis padres me dan diez euros de dinero de bolsillo por semana pero no es bastante para todo eso. ¿Qué puedo hacer?

Paula

Escribe una carta a Paula **en español**. Menciona todos los detalles.

Menciona:

- ¿Qué piensas de ir de compras como pasatiempo? ¿Te gusta?
- ¿Prefieres ir de compras con tus padres o con tus amigos?
- ¿Cuánto dinero de bolsillo recibes?
- ¿Cómo ahorras dinero?
- ¿Cómo son las tiendas en tu ciudad/ pueblo?
- Sugerencias y consejos para tu amiga

Revision Summary

This kind of thing always comes up in exam papers, so make sure you know all the vocab for shopping and meals. You know how it works — do these questions, then look up the ones you get stuck on, then go back over them and check you really can do them.

1) You're out of bread. How do you ask where the baker's is and whether it is open?

2) You have a splitting headache. Ask where the nearest chemist's is, and if it's open now. Ask what the chemist's opening hours are.

3) What are the Spanish names for
a) a stationer's b) a cake shop c) a butcher's
d) a book shop e) a sweet shop f) a supermarket?

4) You've been looking at jeans, but decided not to buy any. A shop assistant asks '¿En qué puedo ayudarle?' What do you reply?

5) You want to buy a brown jumper, size 48, and three pairs of socks. How do you say this to the shop assistant?

6) Your penfriend asks if you like their new coat. Say you don't like it, you like big red or small yellow coats. Ask how much it cost.

7) How would you ask if there's a sale on at the supermarket?

8) Ask for 1 kilo of apples. The shop assistant says: '¿Quiere algo más?' What does he mean?

9) You're telling your penfriend Claudio about your shopping habits. Say you get £5 pocket money a week, you like to buy chocolate but you don't like shopping.

10) Write down how you'd say that you like vegetables but don't like sausages. Also that you're hungry.

11) Thank your hosts for the meal, say you enjoyed it and it was delicious. Offer to pass your hostess the milk.

12) You're going out for a meal. Ask if you can have a table for two and ask where the toilet is.

13) Order steak and chips and an orange juice for you, and chicken with potatoes and carrots for your friend.

14) Attract the waitress's attention and say that you'd like the bill. Tell her that the meal was nice but the potatoes were cold. Ask if the service charge is included.

About Yourself

Talking about yourself — well, it's my favourite subject. There are all sorts of things they could ask about — it's a good idea to have a think about how to answer some of these questions now.

Háblame de ti — Tell me about yourself

¿Cómo te llamas? = What's your name? (literally, 'What are you called?')

Me llamo Ángela. = My name is Angela. (literally, 'I'm called...')

¿Cuántos años tienes? = How old are you?

Tengo quince años. = I'm 15 years old.

¿Cuándo es tu cumpleaños? = When is your birthday?

Mi cumpleaños es el doce de diciembre. = My birthday is on the 12th December.

See pages 36 and 98 for where you live, page 1 for more numbers and page 5 for more dates.

¿Dónde vives? = Where do you live?

Vivo en Lancaster. = I live in Lancaster.

¿Qué te gusta? = What do you like?

Me gusta el fútbol. = I like football.

¿Cómo se deletrea? — How do you spell that?

Here's how to pronounce the letters of the Spanish alphabet. Practise going through it out loud — yes, you'll sound daft, but you'd sound dafter getting it wrong in the exam.

A — a (like 'cat')
B — bay
C — they* (like 'think')
D — day
E — ay (like 'day')
F — efay
G — hay ('h' like 'loch')
H — achay ('ch' like catch)
I — eeh (like 'me')
J — hota ('h' like 'loch')
K — ca (like 'cat')
L — elay
M — emay
N — enay
Ñ — enyay
O — o (like 'pot')
P — pay
Q — coo
R — eray
S — essay
T — tay
U — ooh
V — oobay
W — oobay doblay
X — ekeess
Y — ee greeayga
Z — thayta*

**In southern Spain and Latin America, they say these as C — say, and Z — sayta.*

Learn how to talk about yourself — vain but necessary

Talking about yourself won't be a chore — it's a matter of practice. Don't lie too much in the speaking exam — if you say you live on Mars and your name is Norfluk you'll get caught out. Keep it simple.

About Yourself and Your Family

The examiners often want you to talk about yourself and your family. Get your answers ready now.

¿Cómo eres? — What are you like?

Soy alto/a . = I am tall.

small: pequeño/a
slim: delgado/a
fat: gordo/a
thin: flaco/a
short (in height): bajo/a
medium height: de talla mediana

Tengo los ojos marrones . = I have brown eyes.

blue: azules
green: verdes

Tengo el pelo largo . = I have long hair.

short: corto
shoulder-length: a media melena
quite long: bastante largo
dark: moreno
black: negro
light brown: castaño
blonde/fair: rubio
I'm red-haired: soy pelirrojo/a

For more colours see page 79.

Tengo una hermana — I have one sister

If you're talking about more than one person, use "se llaman", not "se llama".

Mi madre se llama Janet . = My mother is called Janet.

My father: Mi padre
My brother: Mi hermano
My sister: Mi hermana
My aunt: Mi tía
My uncle: Mi tío
My female cousin: Mi prima
My male cousin: Mi primo
My grandmother: Mi abuela
My grandfather: Mi abuelo
My friend: Mi amigo/a
My boy/girlfriend: Mi novio/a

Tengo un hermano . = I have one brother.

Try describing some of your relatives too — it's an easy way to pick up extra marks in letters to penpals.

Es baja . = She is short.

Tiene doce años. = He's 12 years old.

Tiene el pelo liso . = She has straight hair.

Tiene los ojos azules . = He has blue eyes.

Learn how to describe yourself and your family

Questions about family are a real giveaway — if you know your stuff that is. Learning this stuff will give you a big headstart — practising it will increase your chances of getting a good grade in the exam.

Pets

This stuff isn't <u>hard</u> — it's just a question of learning the vocabulary.

¿Tienes animales? — Have you any pets?

Tengo un perro. = I have a dog.

Mi perro se llama Enrique. = My dog is called Henry.

See page 79 for colours and sizes and page 96 for things like fat and thin.

Es amarillo. = He is yellow.

Practise using <u>different</u> descriptive words.

a dog:
un perro

a horse:
un caballo

a cat:
un gato

a guinea pig:
una cobaya

a rabbit:
un conejo

a mouse:
un ratón

a hamster:
un hámster

a goldfish:
un pez de colores

a bird:
un pájaro

This sort of stuff always comes up in the exam

It's simple, really. You know that they're going to ask about your home life in the exam, so all you have to do is learn it. If you don't have pets, say 'No tengo animales'. Or just make it up.

Where You Live

You need to be able to describe where you live. The more information you give, well, the more marks you're going to get for it. It stands to reason, really.

¿Dónde vives? — Where do you live?

Vivo en la calle Pitt número cuarenta y cuatro, en Lancaster.

= I live at 44 Pitt Street, in Lancaster.

Tricky Stuff Tricky Stuff

Lancaster es una ciudad con 64.000 habitantes y mucha industria.

a village/small town: un pueblo
a large town, city: una ciudad
a hamlet: una aldea

= Lancaster is a city with 64,000 inhabitants and a lot of industry.

inhabitant: el habitante

El paisaje alrededor de Lancaster es muy bonito y verde.

= The landscape around Lancaster is very beautiful and green.

Tricky Stuff Tricky Stuff

En tu casa — At your home

Vivo en una casa. = I live in a house.

a flat: un piso, un apartamento *a bungalow:* un chalet
a semi-detached house: una casa adosada

Vivo en una casa pequeña y nueva. = I live in a small, new house.

pretty: bonita *old:* vieja *modern:* moderna
big: grande *cold:* fría *green:* verde

See pages 145-146 for where to put adjectives.

Mi apartamento está cerca de un parque. = My flat is near a park.

My house: Mi casa

a shopping centre: de un centro comercial
the town centre: del centro de la ciudad
a train station: de una estación de trenes
a bus stop: de una parada de autobús
the motorway: de la autopista
the shops: de las tiendas

You must know how to say this stuff

Where you live is a great topic because you don't have to find out any new info. All you've got to do is work out how to describe your home. Write down the key phrases from this page and start learning.

Inside your Home

Saying where things are and what they're like is always good for this sort of question.

¿Cómo es tu casa? — What's your house like?

Luckily you won't need to give a full house tour in your exams —
it's just a matter of having a few things to say about your beautiful home.

¿Dónde está la cocina? = Where is the kitchen?

¿Cómo es la cocina? = What's the kitchen like?

the living room: el salón
the bathroom: el cuarto de baño
the dining room: el comedor
the bedroom: el dormitorio

¿La cocina es grande? = Is the kitchen big?

small: pequeño/a
tiny: muy pequeño/a

Remember that what you say doesn't have to be entirely true — but it does have to be in good Spanish.

¿Qué muebles hay en tu dormitorio? = What furniture is there in your bedroom?

En mi dormitorio hay una cama, dos sillas y una mesa pequeña. = In my bedroom there is a bed, two chairs and a small table.

Look at page 79 for colours.

Las paredes son púrpuras. = The walls are purple.

armchair: un sillón
sofa: un sofá
lamp: una lámpara
table: una mesa
shelf: un estante
wardrobe: un armario
cupboard: un armario
curtains: cortinas
carpet: una alfombra
fitted carpet: una moqueta
chair: una silla
mirror: un espejo
bed: una cama
double bed: una cama de matrimonio
wall: una pared

¿Tienes un jardín? — Have you got a garden?

Mi casa tiene un jardín. = My house has a garden.

My flat: Mi apartamento

Tenemos flores en nuestro jardín. = We have flowers in our garden.

a tree: un árbol
a lawn: césped

You can make this up, but the vocabulary must be right

That yellow box full of all the stuff you find in bedrooms looks a bit full, doesn't it?
So learn just a few of them properly, but make sure you can recognise them all for the exam.

Chores and Household Routines

Conversations about household routines are pretty standard exam stuff.

¿Cuándo se come...? — When do you eat...?

This vocab will come in handy for restaurants too.

¿Cuándo se cena? = When do you eat dinner?

breakfast: el desayuno
lunch: el almuerzo, la comida
dinner: la cena

eat breakfast: se desayuna
eat lunch: se almuerza, se come

Cenamos a las siete. = We eat dinner at seven o'clock.

we eat breakfast: desayunamos
we eat lunch: almorzamos, comemos

See page 3 for more times.

¿Tienes que ayudar en casa? — Do you have to help at home?

Lavo los platos en casa. = I wash up at home.

I tidy my room: Arreglo mi cuarto
I make my bed: Hago mi cama
I vacuum: Paso la aspiradora

Tengo que lavar/fregar los platos. = I have to wash up.

vacuum: pasar la aspiradora
clear the table: quitar la mesa
lay the table: poner la mesa
clean: limpiar

¿Necesitas algo? — Do you need anything?

These aren't quite household routine phrases, but they can pop up from time to time in role plays.

¿Me da un poco de pasta de dientes? = Can I have some toothpaste?

a towel: una toalla
soap: jabón

Have you (informal): ¿Tienes...

¿Tiene pasta de dientes? = Have you any toothpaste?

¿Puedo ducharme? = May I have a shower?

have a bath: bañarme

Talking about chores is better than actually doing them

OK, it might not be the most exciting way to spend your youthful years, but it's not really hard. It's about sitting down and learning the words. Then it's all down to practising. It's your choice.

Chores and Household Routines

This stuff isn't just about playing happy home life — it also works a treat for role plays. The trick is using the vocab you know in different settings — which means learning it first.

¿Le puedo ayudar? — Can I help you with that?

Here's how to offer your services when you're staying with someone.

¿Puedo fregar los platos? = Can I wash up?

vacuum: pasar la aspiradora   *clear the table:* quitar la mesa

Or for extra politeness marks:

¿Quiere que yo friegue los platos? = Would you like me to wash up?

¿Quién hace cada cosa? — Who does what?

Mi hermana Kerry pasa la aspiradora todos los días. = My sister Kerry vacuums every day.

every week: todas las semanas

Papá friega los platos. = Dad does the washing up.

washes up: friega los platos
cleans: limpia
vacuums: pasa la aspiradora
lays the table: pone la mesa

Nadie lava los platos en nuestra casa porque tenemos un lavaplatos.

= Nobody washes up in our house because we have a dishwasher.

¿Tienes tu propio dormitorio? — Do you have your own room?

Tengo mi propio dormitorio. = I have my own room.

Comparto un dormitorio con mi hermano. = I share a room with my brother.

Tricky Stuff Tricky Stuff Tricky Stuff Tricky Stuff Tricky Stuff Tricky Stuff Tricky

We can't all be as helpful as the fictional Kerry (see above)

Domestic life is so dull I can never believe they spend so much time asking about it. Still, if the marks are there to be won you might as well learn this vocab. If you think about it, it'd be pretty daft not to.

Quick Questions

Here's some Quick Questions to test you on the last seven pages.

Quick Questions

1) You are asked: "¿Cómo se deletrea su apellido, por favor?"
What are you being asked to do?
2) Your Spanish friend sends you an e-mail: "¡Háblame de ti! ¿Cómo eres?"
What are you being asked?
3) Write down your name, your age and your birthday in Spanish.
4) How would you say, in Spanish:
a) slim, b) short, c) medium height, d) shoulder-length hair?
5) Your Spanish friend writes: "Soy alta, pelirroja y tengo los ojos verdes. Mi novio también es alto; tiene el pelo negro bastante corto y los ojos marrones."
Describe your friend and her boyfriend.
6) Send your friend an e-mail describing your own basic stature, the colour and length of your hair and the colour of your eyes.
7) What do the following words mean: el hermano; el abuelo; el primo; el padre?
What are the feminine forms of them in Spanish?
8) Your friend writes: "Mi tía, que se llama Antonia, tiene treinta y nueve años. Es baja y tiene el pelo negro, liso y largo." What are you being told about his aunt?
9) Choose a person in your family and, in Spanish, say which relation he/she is, give his/her name, age and add two details about them.
10) Ask your friend if he/she has any pets.
11) Write, in Spanish: "We have a dog called Spot and a rabbit."
12) "¿Puedes describirme donde vives?" What are you being asked?
13) Tell your friend, in Spanish, that you live in a small modern house which is not far from the shops and there is a park nearby.
14) How would you tell your friend in Spanish that you live in a big industrial city of one hundred and fifty thousand inhabitants?
15) You see the following advert in an estate agent's window in Spain:
"Se vende apartamento en el tercer piso con dos dormitorios, salón, pequeño comedor y cuarto de baño moderno." Describe what's for sale.
16) Give the Spanish for: a) a garden, b) the trees, c) a lawn, d) the flowers.
17) Write a short description of your room in Spanish — the general size, the furniture in it and the basic colour scheme.
18) Ask your friend's mother what time the meals are.
19) She replies: "Bueno pues, desayunamos a las siete o las siete y media, generalmente comemos a las dos de la tarde y cenamos alrededor de las diez."
What are the arrangements?
20) How would you say in Spanish: "Every week my sister cleans our room and I vacuum"?
21) Translate the following dialogue into English:
A: ¿Tienes que ayudar en casa?
B: Sí, tengo que hacer mi cama y arreglar mi dormitorio.
A: Manuel pone la mesa y a veces friega los platos.
B: No fregamos los platos en casa porque tenemos un lavaplatos.
A: ¡Qué suerte! ¿Tu papá ayuda en casa?
B: Sí, a veces pone la mesa o pasa la aspiradora.

Parts of the Body

Knowing the names for the parts of the body is vital for those 'doctor' role plays.

El cuerpo — The body

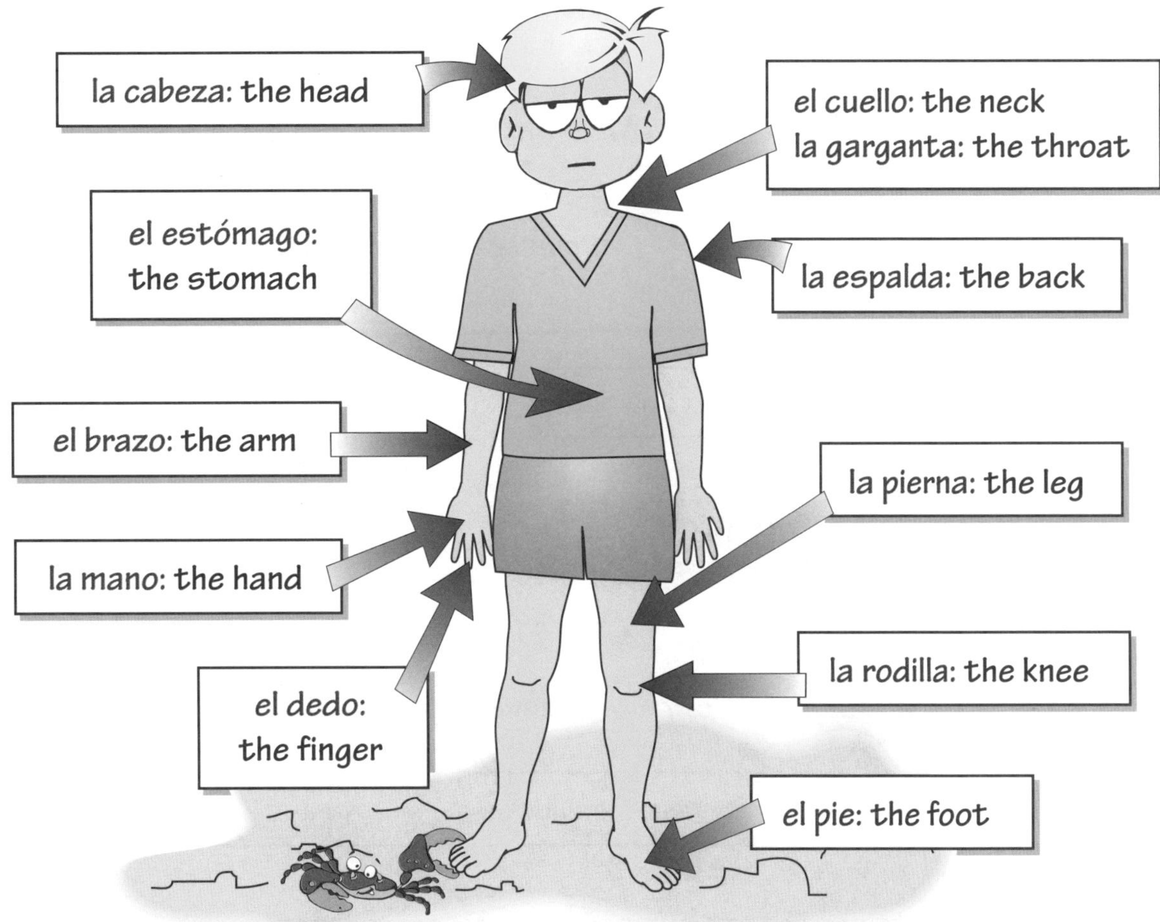

La cara — The face

Learn all the vocab on this page

Body vocab is really worth learning. There's nothing worse than a role play about a leg injury where you can't think of the word for 'leg' — it's seriously embarrassing, and you'll lose marks.

Going to the Doctor or Chemist

Body part vocab is one thing — using it is another. And don't just learn these phrases like a parrot — try using them with different vocab. Believe me, it's the only way to make sure you know them.

¿Cómo está usted? — How are you?

Saying how you feel's the most important thing — you need to be able to say what's wrong.

Estoy enfermo/a. = I am ill.

Me siento mal. = I feel ill.

tired: cansado/a

Debo ir al médico. = I need to go to see the doctor.

to the hospital: al hospital
to the chemist's: a la farmacia
to the dentist's: al dentista

Tengo calor. = I am hot.

cold: frío *thirsty:* sed *hungry:* hambre

¿Qué le duele? — What hurts?

Here's how you say which bit hurts.

Me duele el dedo. = My finger hurts.

hurt (plural): duelen

my head: la cabeza *my ears:* los oídos

Use 'dolor de...' to say where the pain is

You can use 'tengo dolor de' with any part of your body that's hurting.

Tengo dolor de estómago. = I have stomach ache.

a headache: dolor de cabeza
a sore throat: dolor de garganta
sunstroke: una insolación
a temperature: fiebre
flu: gripe

Tengo dolor de oídos. = I have earache / my ears hurt.

Practise using this phrase for pains in different parts of your body.

Estoy resfriado/a. = I have a cold.

You'll be glad you learnt this if you get sick in Spain

You know the score — practise using these phrases as much as you can. Don't panic — if you don't know how to say a particular illness in the exam, use 'dolor de' with the right part of the body instead.

Polite Conversation

Most of this is basic stuff — it'd be stupid to get it wrong, but every year people do. The thing about Spanish is if you can say stuff politely, you're bound to pick up good marks.

¡Buenos días! ¿Qué tal? — Hello! How are you?

Good day / Hello: Buenos días
Hi: Hola
Goodbye: Hasta luego / Adiós
Good evening: Buenas tardes
How are you? (informal): ¿Qué tal? / ¿Como estás?
How are you? (formal): ¿Cómo está?
Good day (to a man): Buenos días señor
Good day (to a woman): Buenos días señora/señorita

To reply to 'Buenos días', just say 'Buenos días' back. Do the same with 'Buenas tardes'.

Muy bien, gracias. = (I am) fine thanks.

Not good: No muy bien
OK: Regular
Not bad: Así así
Terrible: Fatal
Great: Maravillosamente bien

Le presento a Nuria — May I introduce Nuria?

My, life's such a social whirl. Here's how to meet and greet people:

Ésta es Maria. = This is Maria.

For a man: Éste es ...

Encantado/a.
Mucho gusto.
= Pleased to meet you.

Pasa. Siéntate. = Come in. Sit down. *(Familiar, singular)*

Pase. Siéntese. = Come in. Sit down. *(Formal, singular)*

Pasen. Siéntense. = Come in. Sit down. *(Formal, Plural)*

Muchas gracias. Es muy amable. = Thank you. That is very nice of you.

Tricky Stuff

Use 'Lo siento' to say you're sorry

Lo siento. = I'm sorry.

Lo siento mucho. = I'm really sorry.

¿Puedo sentarme? = May I sit down?

go to the toilet: ir al baño
have something to drink: beber algo

Tricky Stuff

Try and pretend you're polite, even if you're not really

It's a bit boring, I know. But grin, bear it, and most of all learn it, and you'll be fine. It'll be worth it when you turn over the exam papers, and realise you can answer all the questions.

Quick Questions

Before you get stuck into the mock exam questions on the next few pages, try answering these quick questions. They test if you've learnt the material on the last few pages properly.

Quick Questions

1) You are asked: "¿Cómo está usted?"
What does the person want to know?
2) Say that you are tired.
3) In response to "¿Qué tal?", how would you respond if:
a) you felt terrible, b) you just felt OK, c) you felt great?
4) Your Spanish friend looks at you and asks: "¿Qué tal? ¿No te sientes bien?"
What is he asking?
5) You reply that you feel ill.
6) Your friend asks: "¿Qué te duele?" What does this mean?
7) How would you say, in Spanish: "My eyes hurt"?
8) Give the Spanish for:
a) she has sunstroke b) my knee hurts c) my feet hurt
9) Your friend goes into the chemist's and asks:
"¿Tiene algo para el dolor de cabeza?" What does he/she want?
10) The chemist answers: "¿Quiere aspirina o paracetamol?"
What does this mean?
11) Give the Spanish for:
a) toothache b) stomach ache c) headache
d) earache
12) How would you say: "Come in!" to the following people:
a) two ladies who have come to take tea with your Spanish friend's mother.
b) your friend Pablo from next door.
c) a man delivering a large parcel.
13) Introduce your parents to your Spanish friend's parents by saying, in Spanish:
"This is my Dad and this is my Mum."
14) You overhear an argument:
"Son las nueve. ¿Dónde está mi desayuno? ¡Tengo hambre!"
What's the problem?
15) Translate the following three-way dialogue into English:
A: ¡Hola Rebeca! ¿Qué tal?
B: Muy bien, gracias. ¿Y tú?
A: Así así. Estoy un poco resfriado. ¡Pasa, pasa! Te presento a mi madre. Mamá, ésta es Rebeca.
B: Mucho gusto, señora.
C: ¡Encantada! ¡Siéntate, Rebeca!
B: Muchas gracias, señora.
16) Translate the following conversation in a doctor's surgery into Spanish:
A: Come in, please! Sit down! How are you?
B: My head aches, my whole body aches and I think that I have a temperature.
A: I think that you have flu. You need to go to the chemist's and you need to drink lots of water.
B: Thank you, doctor. Goodbye.

Listening Questions

It's easy to ignore the CD at the back of this book. Don't. Get it out now and do some practice.

1 ¿Cuál es el dormitorio de Susana?

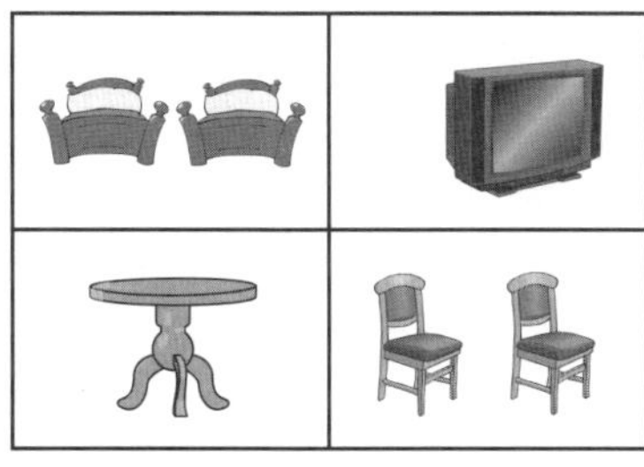

A

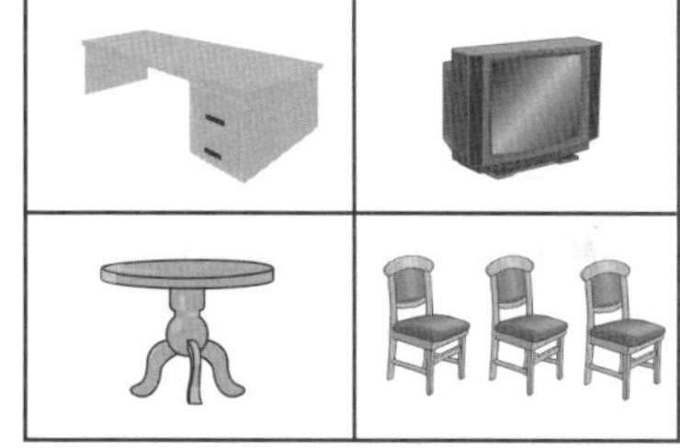

B

C

D

Escribe la letra correcta en esta casilla. 

Track 16

2 A cada persona, ¿qué le recomiendan los médicos? Completa la tabla **en español**.

	Remedio
Ejemplo	Beber agua
a)	
b)	
c)	

Speaking Question

Have a go at this role play. Get a friend or parent to read the teacher's role for you.

Candidate's Role

You are staying with your Spanish friend but realise you have forgotten some essential items. You ask your friend for some help.

- Tu problema
- **Dos** cosas que necesitas
- !
- Tu opinión de tu dormitorio

Your teacher will play the part of the friend and will speak first.

Teacher's Role

Estás en casa de tu amigo/a español/a. Yo soy tu amigo/a.

1 ¿Qué te pasa?

2 ¿Qué necesitas exactamente?

3 Todo lo que necesitas está en el cuarto de baño o te lo puedo dar. ¿Qué quieres hacer más tarde?

4 Vale, me parece muy bien. ¿Está bien el dormitorio?

Sample Conversation

1 ¿Qué te pasa?

He olvidado unas cosas que necesito para mi estancia.

2 ¿Qué necesitas exactamente?

Necesito champú y pasta de dientes.

Make sure you mention two things, or you'll lose marks.

3 Todo lo que necesitas está en el cuarto de baño o te lo puedo dar. ¿Qué quieres hacer más tarde?

Me gustaría dar un paseo por el pueblo.

4 Vale, me parece muy bien. ¿Está bien el dormitorio?

Sí, es muy grande y me encanta el color.

Reading Question

1 Has recibido una carta de tu amigo español.

> ¡Hola!
>
> Me llamo Carlos y soy tu corresponsal. Tengo quince años. Vivo en un pueblo cerca de Granada. Granada es una ciudad con mucha historia y un palacio famoso que se llama la Alhambra. La Alhambra fue construido por los árabes. Soy de talla mediana, tengo los ojos marrones y el pelo moreno. Tengo dos hermanas. Se llaman Luisa y Ana. Me encantan los animales — tengo dos gatos negros, y mis hermanas tienen dos caballos y siete conejos. Vivimos en una casa bonita, con un jardín. Tengo mi propio dormitorio. Tengo que ayudar en casa — todos los días arreglo mi cuarto, pero no hago nunca mi cama. Odio pasar la aspiradora, pero a mi hermana Luisa no le molesta así que lo hace ella. También tenemos que fregar los platos, porque no tenemos lavaplatos — ¡qué pena!

Responde **en español** a las siguientes preguntas.

a) Da **dos** detalles sobre la ciudad de Granada.

i) ....

ii) ....

b) ¿Cómo es Carlos? Da **dos** detalles.

i) ....

ii) ....

c) ¿Qué **no** hace Carlos para ayudar en casa?

....

Writing Question

1 Tu corresponsal español te ha mandado un e-mail.

> ¡Hola!
>
> Estoy cansado y muy ocupado estos días. Como mi padre trabaja en los Estados Unidos durante seis meses y mi madre trabaja muchas horas como enfermera, necesito ayudar mucho en casa. Además, ahora mi madre tiene gripe. Me levanto a las seis para salir con el perro. Por la tarde preparo la cena, y después tengo que fregar. Los fines de semana lavo el coche de mi madre. Es muy difícil, casi no tengo tiempo para salir con mis amigos. ¿Y tú, qué tal?
>
> Miguel

Escribe una carta a Miguel en español. Menciona todos los detalles.

- ¿Qué piensas de lo que dice Miguel?
- ¿Quién ayuda en tu casa?
- ¿Qué haces tú para ayudar?
- ¿Qué piensas de las tareas, en general?
- ¿Tienes bastante tiempo libre para ver a tus amigos?
- Pregunta: si Miguel tiene alguien que podría ayudarle.

Revision Summary

The idea isn't that you just do these questions and stop. To make sure you've really learnt this stuff, you need to go back through the section and look up the answers to the questions you couldn't do. Then try them all again. Your aim is eventually to be able to glide through them all with the greatest of ease.

1) An easy one to start with — give your name, age and when your birthday is to someone you've just met.

2) Describe three of your friends and say how old they are. Spell out loud their names and the names of the towns where they live.

3) Tell your penfriend what relatives you have — including how many aunts, cousins etc.

4) Your animal-loving friend has six rabbits, a bird, a guinea pig and two cats. How will she say what these are in her Spanish speaking exam?

5) Carina lives in a big house with a garden. It's near a shopping centre, a bus stop and a motorway. How would she say this in Spanish?

6) Give the names of the rooms in your home and say how many bedrooms it has. Say whether you have a garden and whether it has flowers, grass or trees.

7) Describe your bedroom in as much detail as possible.

8) You're staying with your host family and have just eaten. Ask if they would like you to help clear the table.

9) Ask if you can have a bath and if they have a towel for you.

10) Cecilia has a room to herself but Roberto shares one with his brother Xavier. How would they say this in Spanish?

11) Draw a stick man or woman and label it with as many body parts in Spanish as you can.

12) How would you say you have each of these ailments in Spanish?
a) stomach ache b) headache c) a cold d) flu

13) You're being introduced to a Spanish visitor. Say 'Good morning, how are you?' When he asks how you are, say 'I'm fine, thanks. Pleased to meet you.'

14) Ask if you may have something to drink — and say thank you.

Telephones

Answering the phone in a foreign language is a bit scary. Here's how to do it.

Una llamada telefónica — A phone call

¿Cuál es tu número de teléfono? = What is your telephone number?

If you need to be more formal, use ***su***.

Mi número de teléfono es veintiocho, diecinueve, cincuenta y seis.

= My telephone number is 281956.

Put your phone number in groups of 2, i.e. twenty-eight rather than two eight.

Answering the phone: "Soy Bob" — "It's Bob"

The trick with phone role plays is saying the things you'd actually say on the phone.

This is how you answer the phone: ***¿Dígame?*** = Hello?

These are for when you phone someone:

Hello, it's Barbara: ¡Hola! Soy Barbara
Can I speak to...?: ¿Puedo hablar con...?
Is Juana there?: ¿Está Juana?
Could Juana call me back at seven?: ¿Puede llamarme Juana a las siete?

Quisiera dejar un mensaje — I'd like to leave a message

This is a bit of a twist on the old phone role play — leaving a message. The important thing is getting all the right info across.

Have a look at this example and scribble down who called, their number and when Claudio should call back:

Hola, soy Paula. Mi número de teléfono es cincuenta y nueve, dieciocho, cuarenta y siete. ¿Puede llamarme Claudio a las siete? Gracias. Hasta luego.

La cabina de teléfono — The telephone box

¿Tiene monedas para el teléfono? = Do you have any coins for the telephone?

a phonecard: una tarjeta telefónica

Phone calls crop up in exams all the time — learn this page

Time to cover up the page and write down and learn the key bits of vocab. You've got to know how to call someone, answer the phone, and take a message. It's important.

Post Office

Post offices are great venues for role playing — perhaps because there's lots of vocab you can use. You'll be fine with a bit of practice — as long as you've learnt the words first.

¿Dónde está Correos? — Where is the Post Office?

These phrases all look a bit random, but they're the sort of thing that pop up in role plays. Start by learning the vocab then practising some phrases.

postbox: el buzón
stamps: los sellos
post office: Correos
letter: la carta

¿Dónde está el buzón, por favor? = Where is the postbox, please?

¿Hay un buzón cerca de aquí? = Is there a postbox near here?

¿Tiene sellos? = Have you got any stamps?

¿Cuánto cuestan los sellos? = How much do the stamps cost?

Señor Pablo Picasso
La Plaza Mayor
Barcelona
Spain

Quisiera mandar una carta — I'd like to send a letter

This stuff's a bit more specific — sending letters or parcels abroad or within Spain.

¿Cuánto cuesta mandar una carta a Inglaterra? = How much does it cost to send a letter to England?

a parcel: un paquete *a postcard:* una tarjeta postal

¿Cuánto cuesta mandar/enviar una carta en España? = How much does it cost to send a letter within Spain?

¿Tiene sellos para mandar una carta a Inglaterra?

= Do you have stamps for sending a letter to England?

Quisiera mandar una tarjeta postal a Inglaterra.

= I would like to send a postcard to England.

Write each phrase out — and try using it with different vocab.

Tricky Stuff Tricky Stuff

Post offices are pretty dull places, but examiners like them

Hard work's the key, I'm afraid. If you want to do well in your exam you've got to put the hours in, learning the vocab, covering up each page, and writing it out again. It'll all be over some day, honest.

Informal Letters

You're bound to have to write a letter in Spanish at some point. Just remember, the secret of writing a good letter in any language is knowing the rules.

Learn this layout for starting and finishing

Here's an incredibly short letter — it shows all the key bits you need for letter-writing.

This means Dear Juan. If you're writing to a woman, you'd put Querida instead of Querido.

You only need to put the town, not the full address.

Millom, 5 de marzo

Put where you live and the date up here. Check out page 5 for dates.

Querido Juan:

Gracias por tu carta.

This means: 'Thanks for your letter.'

Me alegró mucho recibir tus noticias.

This means: 'I was very pleased to hear from you.'

Saludos

Best wishes.

Albert

Bye for now: Hasta pronto
A hug: Un abrazo

Now you have a go — practise writing your own short letter.

You can get easy marks if you write letters properly

Think you know it? Then cover up the page and practise writing a few short letters — it's the only way to make sure. And always use plenty of nice simple phrases — say things you know how to say.

Formal Letters

Formal letters have got even more rules than informal ones. They'll come in handy for job applications or booking hotels though.

Get the **layout** and **language** right

Here's a formal letter — make sure you learn all the different parts.

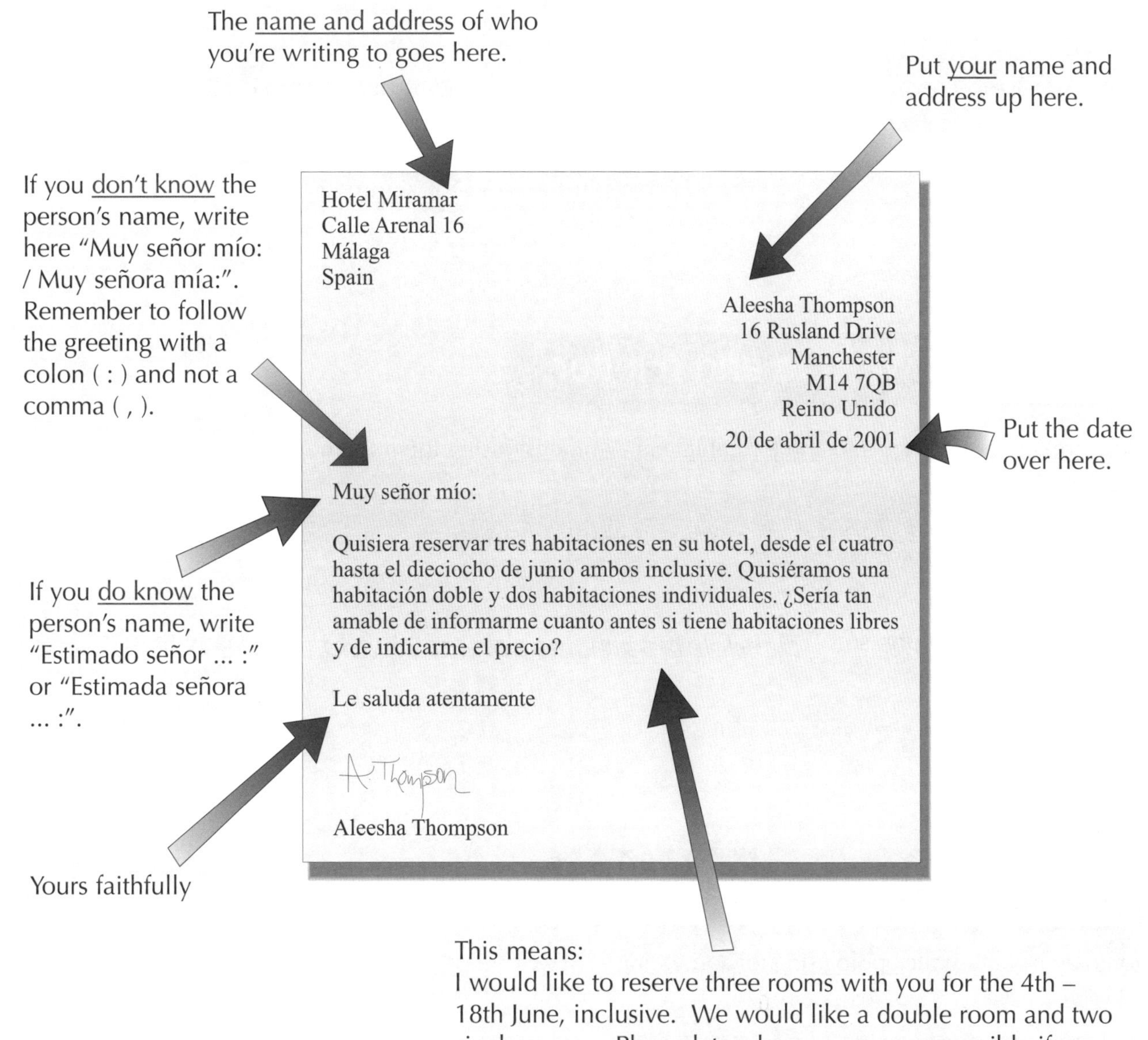

Hotel Miramar
Calle Arenal 16
Málaga
Spain

Aleesha Thompson
16 Rusland Drive
Manchester
M14 7QB
Reino Unido
20 de abril de 2001

Muy señor mío:

Quisiera reservar tres habitaciones en su hotel, desde el cuatro hasta el dieciocho de junio ambos inclusive. Quisiéramos una habitación doble y dos habitaciones individuales. ¿Sería tan amable de informarme cuanto antes si tiene habitaciones libres y de indicarme el precio?

Le saluda atentamente

A. Thompson

Aleesha Thompson

Formal letters are different — do them like this for top marks

If you know how to lay out your formal letters, and how to start and finish them properly, you're half way there. Practice is the main thing — have a go at writing your own formal letters.

Writing Letters

Learning the layout of letters is all very well, but it's only the start. Writing good letters means using lots of nice clear Spanish phrases and vocab. They don't need to be complicated — just right.

Use plenty of common phrases in your letters

¿Qué tal? = How are you?

¿Qué piensas de...? = What do you think of...?

¿Cómo va todo? = How's it all going?

Espero recibir tus noticias pronto. = I hope to hear from you soon.

This one's quite good for signing off.

Learn these ways to end a letter

Here are a couple of ways to end formal letters — practise using them till they trip off your pen.

Le saluda atentamente. = Yours faithfully / sincerely

Another useful phrase: ***Dándole las gracias por anticipado.*** = Many thanks in advance.

Use '**disculparse**' to apologise

You may have to write apologising for something — it's worth practising using sentences like this one.

Quisiera disculparme por haber dejado mi bolso en su hotel. = I would like to apologise for having left my bag in your hotel.

Learn how to finish a letter — it's really important

You need to start and finish your letters properly, if you want good marks. There are a couple of good phrases you can learn to put at the end of letters. Just go ahead and learn them.

Quick Questions

Test your knowledge of letter-writing, phoning and the Post Office with these Quick Questions.

Quick Questions

1) How would you ask Elena in Spanish for her phone number?
2) "Cuarenta y uno, veinticinco, cero siete", she replies. What number is that?
3) "Y ¿el tuyo?" she asks. Give her your phone number in Spanish.
4) Your Spanish friend says: "Hay una llamada telefónica para ti".
What are you being told?
5) The telephone rings at your Spanish friend's house and you are asked to pick it up.
What do you say first?
6) Translate the following phone conversation into English:
A: ¡Hola! Soy Ana ... ¿está Jaime?
B: Sí.
A: ¿Puedo hablar con él?
B: Es que está en la ducha.
A: ¡Ah bueno! Pues, ¿puede llamarme antes de las nueve y media?
B: Sí, le voy a dar el mensaje.
A: Gracias. Adiós y ¡hasta pronto!
B: Hasta luego.
7) You have to leave a message on an answering machine. First, give your name, then translate the following message into Spanish: "Could María Dolores call me after lunch? If I'm not in you can give a message to Jaime. The phone number is 201116. Thanks, see you later".
8) You need to phone home. Stop a passer-by and ask, in Spanish, if there's a telephone box nearby.
9) Give the Spanish for: a postcard; a parcel; Post Office.
10) You find the following note from your friend:
"Quisiera enviar una carta y cuatro postales a España. ¿Cuánto cuestan los sellos? ¿Hay un buzón cerca de tu casa o debo ir a Correos?"
What does she want to know and why?
11) How would you say, in Spanish, the following?
a) I'd like to send these two letters to England.
b) Do you have any stamps?
c) Do you have stamps for sending a letter to England?
d) How much do the stamps cost?
e) Where is the nearest postbox?
12) How would you apologise for having left the following?
a) your toothpaste in the bathroom.
b) your hat in the wardrobe.
c) your new CD in the music centre.
13) How would you write the following in Spanish?
a) Dear Sir b) Dear Madam c) Yours faithfully
d) Dear Miss Gómez e) Dear Mr. Hernández f) Yours sincerely

Listening Questions

Now you've learnt the stuff in this section, you're ready to try out some listening questions.
Get your CD player out, find somewhere quiet (or use headphones), then get started.

Track 17

1 Dejando mensajes por teléfono.

Estas personas han dejado mensajes en el contestador automático.

1 David

2 Carmen

3 Penélope

4 Señora Piqueres

¿Quién:

Ejemplo ahora puede salir? [1]

a) ahora no puede ir? [ ]

b) quiere confirmar su reservación? [ ]

c) llegará más tarde? [ ]

Escribe el número correcto en cada casilla.

Track 18

2 En Correos.

¿Qué quieren mandar? ¿A qué país? ¿Cuánto cuesta?

Completa la tabla **en español**.

	¿Qué quieren mandar?	**¿A qué país?**	**¿Cuánto cuesta?**
Ejemplo	una carta	Inglaterra	0,60 euros
a)			16,36 euros
b)	10 cartas		
c)		Australia	

Speaking Question

And now, as a special prize for finishing your listening practice, you get to have a go at this speaking role play.

Candidate's Role

You phone your Spanish friend but she is not at home.
You ask your friend's mother/father if you can leave a message.

- Tu pregunta
- Tu mensaje — *When you're preparing this, you need to think of a sensible message to leave.*
- Tus detalles (**dos** cosas)
- !

Your teacher will play the part of your friend's mother/father and will speak first.

This is the bit your teacher would read in the exam. Get a friendly helper to read it for you now.

Teacher's Role

Estás hablando por teléfono con la madre de tu amiga española. Yo soy la madre.

1 Pues, mi hija no está en casa en este momento.

2 Claro, ¿cuál es el mensaje exactamente?

3 Vale. Dame tus detalles.

4 ¡Ah! Ya sé quién eres. ¿Te gustaría visitarnos aquí en España?

This is an example of the type of thing you might want to say in the role play.

Sample Conversation

1 Pues, mi hija no está en casa en este momento.
¿Puedo dejarle un mensaje?

2 Claro, ¿cuál es el mensaje exactamente?
Quiero saber a qué hora llega el sábado.

3 Vale. Dame tus detalles.
Me llamo Joanna Brown y mi número de teléfono es cuarenta y cuatro, treinta y dos, treinta y uno.

4 ¡Ah! Ya sé quién eres. ¿Te gustaría visitarnos aquí en España?
Sí. Estaría estupendo. Gracias.

Reading Question

1 Lee el siguiente folleto de Correos:

OFICINA DE CORREOS — PRODUCTOS Y SERVICIOS

TARIFAS

	Nacionales	Internacionales
Paquetes de menos de 1.5 kg de peso	0,40 €	0,60 €
Paquetes de más de 1.5 kg de peso	1,20 €	2,00 €
Cartas y Tarjetas Postales Ordinarias	3,10 €	4,50 €
Cartas y Tarjetas Postales Certificadas	5,15 €	6,20 €
Telegramas	0,15 € por palabra	0,25 € por palabra
Fax	0,50 € por página	0,75 € por página
Servicio Urgente de Cartas	1,90 €	2,30 €
Servicio Urgente de Paquetes	7,00 €	9,60 €
Giros (envío de dinero)		
— De 5 € a 1.000 €	1,80 €	2,00 €
— Más de 1.000 €	2,05 €	2,35 €

Número de Atención al Cliente: 902 37 37 37
Reclamaciones o Quejas: 902 12 01 20

Horario de Atención Telefónica — De lunes a viernes: de 8:00 a 21:00; Sábados: de 9:00 a 13:00

Horario de Recogida — 7:00 a 20:00 (excepto domingos y festivos)

Responde **en español** a las siguientes preguntas:

a) ¿Cuánto cuesta enviar una carta certificada a Inglaterra?

....

b) ¿Cuánto tienes que pagar para enviar un fax de 2 páginas a Holanda?

....

c) ¿A qué teléfono puedes llamar si quieres hacer una reclamación?

....

d) ¿Hay servicio de recogida los domingos?

....

Writing Question

1

Cuando estabas de vacaciones en España fuiste con unos amigos a cenar en el restaurante 'Los Claveles' y perdiste tu bolso allí. Escribe una carta al director del restaurante preguntando si el bolso ha sido encontrado. Puedes incluir la siguiente información:

- Fecha en que fuiste al restaurante
- Mesa/lugar que ocupaste
- Descripción del bolso
- Objetos personales que contenía el bolso
- Tus datos personales

Revision Summary

Letters and phone calls are places you can really pick up marks if you know your stuff. The beauty is they're so structured. Once you know the vocab and the phrases it's just a matter of getting lots of practice... which is where these questions come in. Have a go at them now, then have another go if there are any you're not sure about. Then use the pages of the section to help you mark them.

1) ¿Cuál es tu número de teléfono?
(No cheating and writing it in numerals — do it in full in Spanish.)

2) What should you say when you answer the phone in Spanish?

3) Your brother's Mexican friend calls. Write down a message in Spanish for your brother, saying his friend can't go out tonight.

4) Colin phones his friend Pedro and talks to his mother. Pedro isn't in, but his mother says she will tell him Colin rang. Write down the whole phone conversation in Spanish.

5) How do you ask someone if they've got any coins for the phone?

6) Ask at the Post Office if they have stamps for sending a letter to England.

7) You have four postcards and three letters and want to send them to England.
Ask the Post Office staff how much this will cost.

8) You are in the street in Spain and want to post a letter. How would you ask someone where to find a postbox? (Try to think of two ways of saying it.)

9) Write a letter to your friend Clara. Write your address, say hello and tell her something you've done in the last week.

10) You would like to hear from her soon — how would you say that in your letter?

11) Write down one way you could end the letter.

12) You'd like to reserve 3 single rooms in a hotel in Madrid. Write a letter in Spanish to:
Hotel Glorieta, Paseo del Prado 3, Madrid.

13) How would you end a formal letter in Spanish?

14) What does this phrase mean: 'Dándole las gracias por anticipado'?
Would you use it in a formal or informal letter?

15) You have left a suitcase in a hotel room. Write a letter to the hotel staff to apologise.

Work Experience

These three pages are about work experience and going for interviews.
You might have to do a speaking role play about this topic.

¿Qué hiciste como experiencia laboral?

What did you do for work experience?

Como experiencia laboral, trabajé en la oficina de un abogado.

= For work experience I worked in a lawyer's office.

name or description of the company

Trabajé allí durante una semana y media. = I worked there for a week and a half.

¿Cómo era el trabajo? Dime qué hiciste.

How was the work? Tell me what you did.

More opinions wanted — did you or did you not like it..?

El trabajo era duro. = The work was hard.

difficult: difícil
interesting: interesante

comfortable: cómodo / cómoda
at home: en casa
isolated: aislado / aislada

Me sentía muy solo/sola. = I felt very lonely.

Mis colegas de trabajo no eran simpáticos. = My work colleagues weren't friendly.

were very friendly: eran muy simpáticos
were interesting: eran interesantes

You need to have your answers ready

If you haven't done any work experience then you can say "No hice la experiencia laboral".
I suppose you could always make something up instead, but it'd better sound convincing.

Interviews

OK, so maybe you've never applied for a job, but it's highly likely that you'll have to one day. And there just might be a job interview role play in your speaking exam.

¿Qué quieres hacer en el futuro?

What do you want to do in the future?

En mi trabajo, quiero resolver problemas. = In my job I would like to solve problems.

meet new people: conocer a personas nuevas
work with numbers: trabajar con números
help people: ayudar a la gente

See page 53 for more types of jobs, or look one up in a dictionary.

Me gustaría ser agente de viajes. = I would like to be a travel agent.

Preguntas para una entrevista — Interview Questions

Right, here are examples of the basic questions you could expect to be asked in a job interview.

¿Cómo se llama usted? = What is your name?

¿Cuántos años tiene usted? = How old are you?

¿Qué trabajo le interesa a Ud? — Which job interests you?

Quisiera trabajar como ayudante en la oficina de turismo en Madrid. = I'd like to work as an assistant in the tourist information office in Madrid.

You'll soon land that job at Real Madrid

Most of this stuff isn't new, but you need to get used to dealing with it in this context. So if you're asked to pretend you're applying for a job in a role play, it won't throw you. Revise and you'll be fine.

Interviews

A lot of the stuff in your GCSEs will be addressed to you informally, i.e. you'll be called 'tú' and not 'usted' by most exam boards. In an interview you'll always be 'usted' though.

¿Por qué quiere usted este trabajo?

— Why do you want this job?

El turismo me interesa mucho. = Tourism interests me a lot.

Quisiera mejorar mi español. = I'd like to improve my Spanish.

qualifications: los títulos (necesarios)

Tengo la experiencia necesaria, soy flexible y maduro. = I have the necessary experience, I'm flexible and mature.

responsible: responsable
hard-working: trabajador

¿Qué hizo usted en el instituto?

— What did you do at school?

Fui al instituto en Bolton. = I went to school in Bolton.

Mis asignaturas preferidas en el instituto fueron el alemán y el español. = German and Spanish were my favourite subjects at school.

¿Qué le gusta hacer?

= What do you like to do?

Me encanta la arquitectura. = I love architecture.

Me gusta viajar al extranjero. = I like travelling abroad.

Be convincing — try not to mess up your Spanish

You don't have to be a great actor, but do try and sound like you're really having a job interview if this comes up in your exam. Learn your answers to these questions while you can.

Quick Questions

You need to be able to talk about your future plans. If it doesn't come up in your speaking exam, it's bound to turn up in one of your other exams. Make sure you go through all these Quick Questions carefully.

Quick Questions

1) You are asked: "¿Hiciste una experiencia laboral?" What are you being asked?
2) Reply, in Spanish, that for your work experience you worked in the office of an accountant.
3) "Dime qué hiciste allí" says your friend. What does your friend want to know?
4) Say, in Spanish, that the work was very boring.
5) Say, in Spanish, that you spent a week there.
6) Your Spanish friend asks: "¿Qué quieres hacer en el futuro?"
   What are you being asked?
7) Say, in Spanish, that you'd like to be a lawyer and earn lots of money.
8) Your friend e-mails you: "Trabajé en un banco. Era muy aburrido porque no me interesa trabajar con los números, prefiero ayudar a la gente".
   Where did she work and what does she say about the job?
9) Translate the following conversation into English:
   A: ¿Dónde hiciste tu experiencia laboral?
   B: Trabajé durante tres semanas en un hotel de cuatro estrellas.
   A: ¿Te gustó el trabajo?
   B: Sí, bastante. Era duro, no era difícil, era interesante porque conocí a personas nuevas, pero diez horas por día es mucho, sabes.
   A: ¿Cómo eran tus colegas de trabajo?
   B: Pues, algunos eran muy simpáticos así que no me sentía sola pero otros no eran tan simpáticos.
10) Give the Spanish for:
    a) comfortable b) mature c) assistant
    d) a (school) subject e) responsible
11) How would you say in Spanish: "I would like to improve my Spanish"?
12) In English, what are the following: los títulos; las asignaturas; los problemas?
13) How would you say these sentences in Spanish?
    a) I went to school in Stroud.
    b) I love travelling.
14) You're in a job interview. Translate your role into Spanish:
    A: Buenos días. ¿Cuántos años tiene?
    B: I'm sixteen.
    A: ¿Qué trabajo le interesa?
    B: I'd like to work in a travel agency in a big town.
    A: ¿Por qué quiere trabajar allí?
    B: I like helping people and tourism interests me a lot.
    A: ¿Dónde hizo su experiencia laboral?
    B: I worked in the offices of a coach company. I worked there for two weeks.
    A: ¿Cómo fue el trabajo?
    B: The work wasn't difficult, it was interesting but the hours were very long because the coaches went abroad.
    A: ¿Qué hizo usted en el instituto?
    B: My favourite subjects were ICT and Business Studies.
    A: Pues, gracias. Le vamos a enviar una carta. Adiós.
    B: Thank you. Goodbye.

The Environment

Things get serious when the environment comes up, and you're supposed to have an opinion. It's a chance for you to maybe write or say what you think about something real and important.

El medio ambiente — ¿es importante para ti?

Is the environment important to you?

A question like this has to be answered with a yes, or a no, so remember to always listen out first for that in a listening exam, then try to figure out the reason.

No, no tengo ningún interés. = No, I'm not at all interested in it.

¡Sí! Pienso que el medio ambiente es muy importante. = Yes, I think the environment is very important.

If you're asked for your own take on a question like this, start with yes or no then explain why. Of course it'll help if you've prepared something earlier, so think about the issues now.

Give opinions and arguments

If you're really up on 'green' matters then you could get really into this, but if you're not then say so. You'll get as many marks for saying why you're not interested as you would for enthusing about it.

¡NO!

Eso no me interesa. Quiero vivir en la ciudad y no en el campo.

= It doesn't concern me. I want to live in the city not in the country.

Las flores y la naturaleza son muy aburridas. Prefiero los juegos de ordenador.

= Flowers and nature are very boring. I prefer computer games.

Me preocupa mucho el medio ambiente debido a la contaminación industrial.

= I'm really worried about the environment because of industrial pollution.

Probablemente vamos a perder la biodiversidad de nuestro planeta.

= We are probably going to lose the biodiversity of our planet.

If you don't have an opinion, make one up

There are so many different aspects of the environment you could choose to talk about — it's always better to be prepared, and have your opinions ready. Be wise and learn the basics.

The Environment and Health

You should get used to this essential environmental vocab. It could be sneaked into a reading comprehension or a listening conversation.

Essential environment vocabulary

exhaust fumes:	el humo de los coches
pollution:	la contaminación
the greenhouse effect:	el efecto invernadero
emissions:	las emisiones
to damage:	dañar
to endanger:	poner en peligro
air pollution:	la contaminación del aire
natural resources:	los recursos naturales
biodiversity:	la biodiversidad
nature:	la naturaleza

Are you taking care of yourself?

It's not just about environmental health, you know.
Your own health is another important issue you may get asked about.

La alimentación — The food you eat

This is about your normal everyday diet and how healthy it is, or isn't.

¿Comes bien? = Do you eat well?

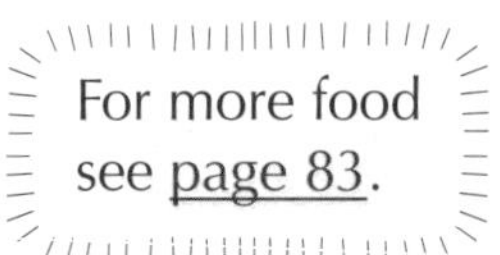
For more food see page 83.

Sí, como muchas ensaladas y frutas. = Yes, I eat lots of salads and fruit.

No, como patatas fritas casi todos los días, y bebo solamente limonada. = No, I eat chips almost every day and I only drink lemonade.

regularly: regularmente

Think about what to say to the examiner

There is loads you might want to say about these exciting things, but learning the stuff on this page is a good start. Think about what else you might want to say, look it up, then write it down and learn it.

Exercise, Smoking and Drugs

Remember, this is not a lie detector test, it's a Spanish exam. You don't have to be totally honest — you just have to learn some Spanish phrases that you think you'll be able to remember for the exam.

El ejercicio — Exercise

It doesn't matter if you don't do any exercise, just be able to say so.

¿Qué haces para mantenerte en buena salud?

= What do you do to stay healthy?

Como bien, me mantengo delgado/a y tengo mucha energía.

= I eat very healthily, stay slim and have a lot of energy.

Juego al fútbol y al tenis regularmente.

= I regularly play football and tennis.

Hago mucho deporte.

= I play a lot of sport.

Smoking, Drugs and Alcohol

¿Qué piensas de las drogas ? = What do you think of drugs?

alcohol: del alcohol

NO FUMO = I don't smoke.

Los cigarrillos me dan asco. Odio cuando la gente fuma. Los cigarrillos tienen un olor horrible. No saldría nunca con un fumador / una fumadora.

= Cigarettes disgust me. I hate it when people smoke.
Cigarettes have a terrible smell. I'd never go out with a smoker.

ME GUSTA FUMAR = I like smoking.

Sé que no es muy sano, pero me parece muy elegante fumar.

= I know it's unhealthy, but I think it's very stylish to smoke.

Whether you smoke or not, you need to have an opinion on it

You might have already discussed this stuff in PSHE, but now you need to know how to say it all in Spanish. It's tough, but it's worth learning it and practising it ready for the exam.

Celebrities

Talking about celebrities is easy. It mostly involves all the same old straightforward stuff that you need to talk about yourself and your family — start with their name, then what they do, then why you like them.

¿Admiras a las personas famosas? — Do you admire celebrities?

Pienso que Britney Spears es fantástica. = I think Britney Spears is fantastic.

Es una cantante famosa de los Estados Unidos. = She is a famous singer from the USA.

Britney es muy bonita y lleva siempre ropa de moda. = Britney looks so pretty and always wears fashionable clothes.

Canta como un ángel. = She sings like an angel.

¡Es mi heroína! = She is my heroine!

La influencia de la gente famosa — The influence of celebrities

Celebrities are often role models for young people. You may be expected to have an opinion on this and the role the media plays in the whole cult of celebrity.

¿Piensas que se puede considerar a la gente famosa como un ejemplo positivo para los jóvenes? = Do you think famous people can be seen as a positive example for young people?

¡SÍ!

¡Por supuesto! Tienen mucho éxito. = Of course. They are very successful.

Se les puede admirar. = You can admire them.

¡NO!

¡De ninguna manera! No son personas normales. = No way. They aren't normal people.

Algunas chicas piensan que deben estar tan flacas como las 'Supermodelos'. Muchas veces esto es la causa de problemas dietéticos. = Some girls think they have to be as thin as the 'supermodels'. This is often the cause of dietary problems.

USEFUL VOCAB

famous: famoso / famosa
singer: un/una cantante
anorexia: la anorexia
bulimia: la bulimia
role model: un modelo
example: un ejemplo
actor / actress: un actor / una actriz
admire: admirar
hero / heroine: un héroe / una heroína
the media: los medios (de comunicación)
influence: una influencia
responsibility: la responsabilidad
responsible: responsable
cause: causar
sportsman/woman: el/la deportista

Someone like Britney's perfect to talk about

You just need something easy to talk about. There's no point talking about some obscure actor from a low budget experimental movie in the thirties, unless you can do it in perfect Spanish.

Social Issues

Talking about social issues can seem daunting enough in your own language, let alone another one, but keep a cool head and don't start anything you can't finish.

El desempleo — unemployment

There's not really very much that needs saying here. Unemployment is bad news.

Hay muchos desempleados en la ciudad. = There are lots of unemployed people in the town.

few: pocos
some: algunos

area: la región
village: el pueblo

El desempleo en Gran Bretaña no es un problema hoy en día. = Unemployment in Britain isn't a problem nowadays.

Poca gente tiene problemas en encontrar trabajo. = Few people have a problem finding work.

La igualdad de derechos — equal rights

This is your chance for a good rant, in Spanish of course.

Pienso que la igualdad de derechos es muy importante.

unimportant: no es muy importante

= I think equal rights are very important.

Es verdad que a veces hay mucha hostilidad hacia las personas de otras razas.

discrimination: discriminación

women: las mujeres

= It's true there's sometimes a lot of hostility towards people from other races.

Me parece racista. = It seems racist to me.

sexist: sexista *unfair:* injusto

Eso me molesta. = That annoys me.

La presión ejercida por los iguales — peer pressure

Whichever country you live in, you're almost certain to fall foul of peer pressure at some point.

Me parece difícil conservar la individualidad. = I think it's difficult to stay a true individual.

Uno siempre tiene que llevar ropa de moda y es muy cara.

= You always have to wear fashionable clothes and they're really expensive.

These topics are a bit more serious

Watch your back here — it's a pretty bad idea to say that there's loads of unemployment in your area, if that's not the case. Find out some info about these topics so you don't look foolish.

Quick Questions

Here's some more Quick Questions for you to get stuck into.

Quick Questions

1) Write the Spanish (and the gender) for:
   a) air pollution b) the environment c) nature
2) What do the following mean:
   a) el humo de los coches, b) el efecto invernadero, c) los recursos naturales?
3) "¿El medio ambiente es importante para ti?" asks your friend.
   What does your friend want to know?
4) You overhear three friends discussing the environment.
   What do each of them think about it?
   a) Emilio: "Pues no, para mí el medio ambiente no me interesa porque los científicos van a resolver todos los problemas."
   b) Alicia: "Vivo en la ciudad y las emisiones de las industrias y los transportes dañan la naturaleza y contaminan el aire que respiramos."
   c) Paco: "Ah sí, me preocupa mucho porque con toda la contaminación … del aire, del mar y de la tierra … vamos a poner en peligro el planeta."
5) "Y ¿qué piensas tú?" they ask. Say, in Spanish, that you are very worried about pollution because of the greenhouse effect.
6) Give the Spanish (and the gender) for: a diet; exercise; drugs; cigarettes.
7) Your friend asks: "¿Qué comes?" What does (s)he want to know?
8) Say in Spanish: "I don't eat chips every day and I go to the gym regularly."
9) Your Spanish friends ask you: "¿Qué piensas de la gente que fuma?"
   What are they asking you?
10) How would you say, in Spanish: "I never drink alcohol and I think cigarettes are horrible"?
11) How would you say the following words in Spanish?
    a) a hero b) the media c) a singer
    d) an actress e) celebrities
12) Your Spanish friend sends you an e-mail about his opinions of famous people.
    "Muchas veces la gente famosa son modelos para los jóvenes. Se les puede admirar porque tienen mucho éxito pero no son personas normales."
    What is he saying?
13) Who is your hero/heroine? Write a short paragraph in Spanish saying why you admire him/her.
14) How would you tell your friend, in Spanish, that you wear fashionable clothes?
15) The following is part of a letter you receive from your Spanish friend:
    "Hay mucho desempleo en nuestra región sobre todo entre los jóvenes, tienen muchos problemas en encontrar trabajo. Es injusto, me parece discriminación y me molesta."
    What is your friend telling you?
16) Translate this conversation into English.
    A: ¿Qué haces para mantenerte tan delgada?
    B: Como cosas sanas. Por ejemplo como muchas ensaladas y (muchas) frutas pero no estoy flaca, sabes.
    A: Algunas chicas tienen problemas dietéticos como la anorexia porque quieren tener éxito como sus heroínas, las 'Supermodelos'.
    B: Creo que estas 'Supermodelos' tienen una mala influencia sobre los jóvenes.

Listening Questions

This is the last lot of listening questions in the book before you get to the practice exam. Scary.

Track 19

1 Unos jóvenes están hablando de sus experiencias laborales.
Termina las siguientes frases **en español**.

a) Laura trabajaba en un ....

b) Laura trabajaba desde las ocho de la mañana hasta ....

c) En el futuro Jorge quiere ser ....

d) María tenía que preparar muchas ....

e) Según María trabajar como peluquera es un trabajo mal ....

Track 20

2 Ana and Juncal are talking about the environment.
Answer the questions below **in English**.

a) What environmental problems were there in Ana's city? Write down **two** problems.

i) ....

ii) ....

b) i) Ana mentions her friend José. What is his opinion of tourists?

....

ii) Why?

....

c) Why does Ana think it's important to do something to save the planet?

....

Speaking Question

I'm sure you know by now what comes after listening — yes, it's another speaking question.

Candidate's Role

You are interested in a job you have seen advertised in Spain and phone the company for further details.

- Tu pregunta.
- **Dos** detalles del trabajo que quieres saber.
- Tu experiencia.
- !

You'll need to invent the job.

Your teacher will play the role of the secretary and will speak first.

This is the bit where you get a friend or someone to try out their acting skills and play the other part.

Teacher's Role

Estás hablando por teléfono con la secretaria de una empresa española. Yo soy la secretaria.

1 ¡Dígame!

2 ¿Qué quiere saber exactamente?

3 Vale. Estos detalles se los dará el Señor Pérez en la entrevista.
¿Qué experiencia tiene?

4 ¿Por qué le interesa este trabajo?

And just for a change... here's a sample conversation.

Sample Conversation

1 ¡Dígame!
Buenos días. Quisiera más detalles sobre el puesto de recepcionista.

Remember to be very polite in a job situation.

2 ¿Qué quiere saber exactamente?
Quiero saber cuánto paga por mes y qué son las horas de trabajo.

3 Vale. Estos detalles se los dará el Señor Pérez en la entrevista.
¿Qué experiencia tiene?
Hace seis meses trabajé en la oficina de un contable como experiencia laboral.

Remember, this is just a role play — make something up.

4 ¿Por qué le interesa este trabajo?
Me interesa este trabajo porque me gustaría mejorar mi español.

Reading Question

1 Yolanda ha escrito un artículo en una revista en el que habla de una persona muy famosa.

> Hola a todos. Soy Yolanda y os voy a hablar de la estrella del pop internacional que más me gusta. Se llama Kylie Minogue; nació el 28 de mayo de 1968 en la ciudad de Melbourne, Australia. En 1986 trabajó como actriz en una serie de la televisión australiana llamada 'Neighbours', que la hizo muy famosa. En 1987 lanzó su primer disco con la canción 'Locomotion', que se convirtió en número uno en las listas de discos de muchos países. Tengo toda la colección de sus discos. Admiro mucho a Kylie porque ha conseguido muchos éxitos como cantante y actriz. Ha aparecido en películas como 'The Delinquents' y 'Moulin Rouge'. Es muy guapa y delgada, pero es muy bajita. La ropa que lleva en sus conciertos está diseñada por Dolce & Gabbana. Siempre que puedo, me compro ropa similar a la que ella lleva. Como cantante, tiene muy buena voz. La verdad es que me da un poco de envidia porque Kylie ha tenido romances con chicos muy guapos como Michael Hutchence, el desaparecido líder del grupo INXS y, más recientemente, con el actor francés Olivier Martínez. Kylie tiene mucho talento. Ha diseñado personalmente una línea de ropa interior que ha lanzado al mercado con el nombre de 'Love Kylie'; también ha creado una muñeca que es una réplica de ella misma. Ahora se encuentra de gira por todo el mundo con su nuevo espectáculo.

Responde **en español** a las siguientes preguntas:

a) ¿Cuál es la nacionalidad de Kylie Minogue?

....

b) ¿En qué serie de televisión debutó Kylie Minogue como actriz?

....

c) ¿ En qué dos películas ha trabajado como actriz?

....

d) ¿Quién diseña la ropa que lleva Kylie?

....

e) ¿Cómo se llama la colección de ropa interior que ha lanzado al mercado?

....

Writing Question

1 Escribe un artículo para una revista en el que hables de las ventajas y las desventajas de vivir en el campo o en la ciudad.

NO A LA CONTAMINACIÓN

VIVE UNA VIDA MÁS SALUDABLE Y LIBRE DE ESTRÉS

VEN A VIVIR EN EL CAMPO

Urbanización 'Sierra del Espadán'

Situada en plena Naturaleza
Casas Adosadas o Individuales
Oficina de Venta:
Ctra A456 Puerto Blanco - Salida 2
Alicante

Puedes mencionar entre otros los siguientes temas:

- La contaminación/el aire fresco
- El tráfico/el ruido
- La salud
- La educación
- Acceso a la cultura
- La vida social

Revision Summary

By now you surely know that everything in this book is here because it's really important. This section on the wider world is all about taking your Spanish language skills and using them in other situations. You need to use your initiative and imagination maybe a touch more, and get to feel happy using what you already know to answer unexpected queries.

1) Write a full Spanish sentence explaining what you did for your work experience. If you didn't do work experience anywhere then write that down.

2) Write a Spanish sentence saying whether you liked your work experience and why, or saying whether you would have liked to do work experience and where.

3) You have two Spanish penfriends Pilar and José. Pilar wants to have a job where she works with animals and José wants to travel. How would each of them say that?

4) Write down how you'd respond to the question '¿Cómo se llama usted?'

5) How would you write a reply in Spanish to a job advert for an assistant in a bookshop? Explain why you want the job and why you think you're suitable.

6) Write down the Spanish for: a) friendly; b) responsible; c) flexible.

7) Pilar wants to know what your interests are. Tell her at least two things.

8) There's no stopping José: he's just told you he'd like to live in a remote wooden hut and be at one with nature. Tell him whether you fancy this idea and why.

9) What is the Spanish for: a) air pollution; b) emissions; c) biodiversity?

10) Write down a list of all the things you'd normally eat in a day — in Spanish, of course.

11) ¿Comes bien y regularmente?

12) ¿Por qué? / ¿Por qué no?

13) Do you play a lot of sport? Why? Why not? Answer in Spanish, of course.

14) ¿Admiras a las personas famosas? ¿A quiénes? ¿Y por qué?

15) ¿Qué piensas de la situación de las mujeres en Inglaterra hoy en día?

16) Eric thinks it's hard to stay individual nowadays. How would he say it in Spanish?

Nouns

Before you panic, this stuff is a lot less scary than it looks. It's all pretty simple stuff about words for people and objects — nouns. This is really important.

Every Spanish noun is **masculine** or **feminine**

Whether a word is masculine, feminine or plural affects a lot of things. All 'the' and 'a' words change, and as if that weren't enough, the adjectives (like big, red, shiny) change to fit the word.

EXAMPLES: *a small dog:* un perro pequeño (masculine)
a small house: una casa pequeña (feminine)

For more on this, see pages 144-146.

It's no good just knowing the Spanish words for things, you have to know whether each one's masculine or feminine too.

THE GOLDEN RULE
Each time you learn a word, remember the el or la to go with it — don't think 'dog = perro', think 'dog = el perro'

el and la

An EL in front means it's masculine.
LA in front = feminine.

Tricky Stuff

These rules help you guess what a word is

Rules of Thumb for Masculine and Feminine Nouns

Masculine nouns —
most nouns that end:
-o -l -n -r -s
-ma -pa -ta -aje
also: male people, languages, days, months, seas, rivers, oceans, and mountains.

Feminine nouns —
most nouns that end:
-a -ción -sión -tad
-tud -dad -umbre
also: female people, letters of the alphabet.

You can't tell whether a noun ending in 'e' or 'ista' is masculine or feminine, e.g.

the car: el coche
the people: la gente
the tourist (man): el turista
the tourist (woman): la turista

Learn these rules to make genders easier

The bottom line is — every time you learn a word in Spanish, you have to learn whether it's el or la. So start as you mean to go on — get into genders. They're a lot more fun that you might think.

Making Nouns Plural

Making Nouns Plural

1. Nouns in Spanish are usually made plural by adding an 's' when they end in a vowel and 'es' when they end in a consonant.

e.g. *one orange* → *two oranges*
una naranja → dos naranjas

2. Family surnames and nouns which finish in an unstressed syllable ending in 's' stay the same in the plural.

e.g. *the Jiménezs (family)*
Los Jiménez

e.g. *Tuesday* → *Tuesdays*
el martes → los martes

3. You may need to add or remove an accent when nouns become plural to keep the stress in the same place.

e.g. *one young man* → *two young men*
un joven → dos jóvenes

e.g. *one Englishman* → *two Englishmen*
un inglés → dos ingleses

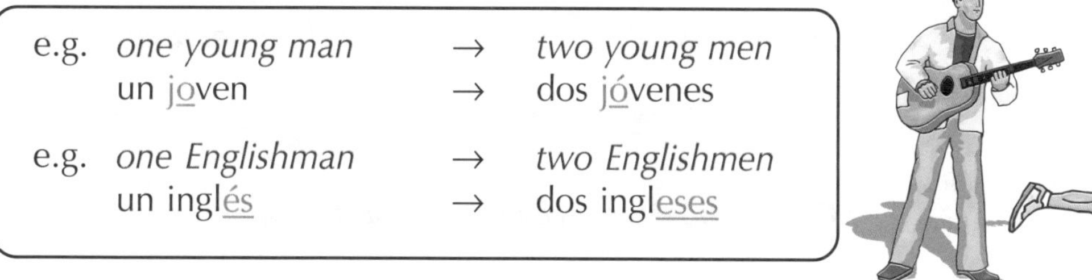

4. Nouns ending in 'z' change the 'z' to a 'c' before adding 'es'.

e.g. *one pencil* → *two pencils*
un lápiz → dos lápices

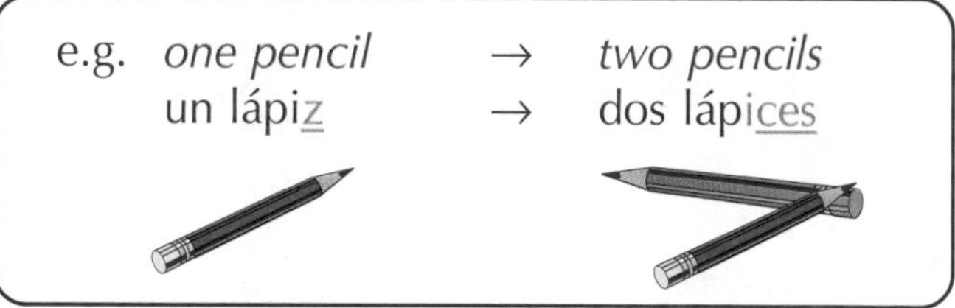

5. When you make a masculine noun plural, instead of 'el' you have to use 'los' to say 'the'. For feminine nouns 'la' becomes 'las' when it's plural — see page 141.

Top tip for PLURALS

Each time you learn a word, learn how to make it into a plural too.

Learn how to make these plural endings

There's no point pretending that grammar is fun. For most people, it's the worst part of learning a language. But it's not always hard, and once you know it, it makes life a lot simpler.

Conjunctions

Learn these joining words to help you make longer sentences, and get more marks.

Y = And

Me gusta jugar al fútbol. + ***Me gusta jugar al rugby.*** = ***Me gusta jugar al fútbol y al rugby.***

= I like playing football. = I like playing rugby. = I like playing football and rugby.

BUT if 'y' comes in front of a word beginning with 'i' or 'hi' it changes to 'e':

Hablo español e inglés. = I speak Spanish and English.

O = Or

Juega al fútbol todos los días. OR ***Juega al rugby todos los días.*** = ***Juega al fútbol o al rugby todos los días.***

= He plays football every day. = He plays rugby every day. = He plays football or rugby every day.

BUT when 'o' comes in front of a word beginning with 'o' or 'ho' it changes to 'u':

Cuesta siete u ocho libras. = It costs seven or eight pounds.

Pero = But

Me gusta jugar al fútbol. BUT ***No me gusta jugar al rugby.*** = ***Me gusta jugar al fútbol pero no me gusta jugar al rugby.***

= I like playing football. = I don't like playing rugby. = I like playing football but I don't like playing rugby.

When 'but' means 'on the contrary' it becomes 'sino':

Mi amigo no es americano sino australiano.

= My friend isn't American, but (on the contrary) he's Australian.

Porque = Because

This is a really important one you need to use to explain yourself. There's loads more about it on page 10.

Me gusta el tenis porque es divertido. = I like tennis because it's fun.

Other joining words

You don't have to use all of these, but you should understand them if you see or hear them.

well, then: pues, entonces
if: si *with:* con
as, like: como
so, therefore: por lo tanto, así (que), de manera (que)
while, during: mientras

Puedes salir si quieres. = You can go out if you want.

Tengo hambre, así que voy a comer. = I'm hungry, so I'm going to eat.

Es como su hermano. = He's like his brother.

Juega al hockey mientras llueve. = She plays hockey while it's raining.

Without conjunctions sentences sound silly

You use 'and', 'or' and 'but' all the time when you're speaking English — if you don't use them when you speak Spanish, you'll sound weird. But don't confuse 'si' (if) and 'sí' (yes).

Articles ('The' and 'A')

'The' and 'a' are essential words. They're tricky in Spanish, because there are different ones for masculine, feminine or plural words (see page 138).

'A' — un, una

These are called 'indefinite articles'.

Masculine: UN	Feminine: UNA
Tengo un hermano.	*Tengo una hermana.*
= I have a brother.	= I have a sister.

In Spanish 'a' is often left out:

a) after the verb 'ser' when talking about someone's occupation or nationality:

e.g. *I'm a student* → Soy estudiante

b) after a negative word:

e.g. *I haven't got a cat.*
→ No tengo gato.

c) in front of 'otro/a':

e.g. *Do you want another coffee?*
→ ¿Quieres otro café?

When you make 'un' or 'una' plural, they mean 'some' or 'a few'.

Pasé unos días en la playa.
= I spent a few days on the beach.

Tengo unas fotos muy buenas.
= I have some very good photos.

'The' — el, la, los, las

These are called 'definite articles'.

1) Spanish 'the' changes for masculine, feminine or plural:

El chico. = The boy. ***La chica.*** = The girl. ***Los hombres.*** = The men. ***Las mujeres.*** = The women.

masculine singular	feminine singular	masculine plural	feminine plural
el	la	los	las

2) But remember 'el' is used before feminine nouns which start with a stressed 'a':

e.g. *The water is cold.* → El agua está fría.

3) 'El' also changes with 'a' (to) and 'de' (of).

4) You can't say 'a el', 'de el'. ***voy a*** + ***el café*** = ***Voy al café.*** = I go to the café.

	el
+ a	al
+ de	del

5) Sometimes you need a definite article in Spanish when you wouldn't use one in English.

a) with nouns used in a general sense:

e.g. *I don't like coffee.*
→No me gusta el café.

b) in front of days of the week and times:

e.g. *Every Monday at five o'clock.*
→ Todos los lunes a las cinco.

c) in front of weights and measurements:

e.g. *2 euros a kilo.*
→ Dos euros el kilo.

d) when you talk about a person and give their title:

e.g. *How is Mr Jiménez?*
→ ¿Cómo está el señor Jiménez?

6) There's also a neuter article 'lo' for things that aren't masculine or feminine. You'll mostly come across it in phrases:

Lo mejor/peor = *the best/worst thing* Lo que = *what/that which*
No sé lo que quiere = *I don't know what he wants.*

*And one more thing — you don't normally need to say '**any**' in Spanish*

This is well worth remembering — you don't need a special word for 'any'. If you want to say 'Have you any apples?', it's just '¿Tienes manzanas?' Finally, something simple...

Quick Questions

To practise your grammar knowledge here's a bumper section of Quick Questions.

Quick Questions

1) Put the correct Spanish word for 'the' in front of the following words which are all in the singular:
   a) perro b) hermana c) padre d) canción e) gente f) ciudad g) autobús
   h) viaje i) carne j) Atlántico
2) Look up the Spanish for the following words and put an appropriate form of 'the':
   a) water b) egg c) music d) climate e) poet f) day g) planet
   h) north i) street j) map k) hand l) salt
3) Make the following plural by saying that there are two of each rather than one:
   a) una naranja b) un hombre c) una mujer d) un helado e) un español
   f) una flor g) un café h) un joven i) una habitación j) un francés
   k) un lápiz l) una semana m) un jueves n) un guitarrista andalúz
   o) una actriz andaluza
4) Make the following words plural:
   a) el actor b) la hermana c) el agua d) la pared e) la ley f) el día
   g) la clase h) el mes i) la nariz
5) Use the Spanish word for 'and' to join the sentence on the right to the sentence on the left so that you have one complete sentence with no repetition.
   a) Tengo una hermana. Tengo dos hermanos.
   b) Tengo el pelo rubio. Tengo los ojos azules.
   c) Quisiera un chocolate. Quisiera dos churros.
   d) Me da un kilo de tomates. Me da una lechuga.
   e) Voy a visitar la catedral. Voy a visitar el museo.
   f) Estudio alemán. Estudio italiano.
6) Use the Spanish for 'or' to join the sentence on the right to the sentence on the left so that there is no repetition.
   a) Los martes voy al gimnasio. Los martes voy a la ciudad.
   b) Quisiera ser periodista. Quisiera ser cantante.
   c) Mañana vamos a jugar al fútbol. Mañana vamos a jugar al tenis.
   d) Puedo enviarle una carta. Puedo enviarle una postal.
   e) Cuesta siete euros. Cuesta ocho euros.
7) Join the following pairs of sentences with the correct Spanish word for 'but'.
   a) Me gusta el esquí. No me gusta el fútbol.
   b) Me encantaría ir al cine. No puedo llegar antes de las nueve.
   c) Tengo sed. No tengo hambre.
   d) Mi amiga no es sudamericana. Mi amiga es española.
   e) Como muchas ensaladas. No como muchas patatas fritas.
   f) No quiero la sal. Quiero la pimienta.
8) Tell your friend, in Spanish...
   a) that you like the film because the actors are very good.
   b) that you don't watch the television because the programmes are bad.
   c) that you are very tired because you worked for ten hours yesterday.
9) Translate the following sentences into English:
   a) Podemos ir al cine si quieres.
   b) Voy de compras con mi amiga.
   c) Manuel es un hombre contento porque siempre canta mientras trabaja.
   d) Isabel quiere ser periodista como su padre.
   e) No me gusta fregar los platos así que vamos a comprar un lavaplatos.

Quick Questions

I know it looks like there's a lot of Quick Questions in this section, but look on the bright side — there are no practice exam questions in the grammar section, so at least you don't have to face those as well. Grammar is very boring to learn, but it's so important that the time you spend doing these questions could make a difference to what mark you get in your exam.

Quick Questions

10) Write the Spanish for 'a' for the following words:
a) camiseta b) hombre c) agua mineral d) turista e) día f) perro
g) clima h) mano i) calle j) canción k) viaje l) uva

11) How would you tell your friend, in Spanish…
a) that you and some English friends are going to spend a few days in Barcelona,
b) that you are going to visit some monuments,
c) that you are going to take a few traveller's cheques and
d) that you are going to have some excellent photos.

12) Using "Vamos a…" write a short sentence to suggest that you all go to each of the following places:
a) la cafetería b) el cine c) las tiendas d) una discoteca e) el bar f) casa g) la playa
h) los toros i) Correos

13) How would you tell your friend, in Spanish, that you are going to the following places:
a) the bank b) the town hall c) a concert d) the café e) the supermarket
f) the Post Office g) the United States h) home

14) Join the following words by using the Spanish for 'of':

a) el centro	la ciudad
b) la hora	el día
c) un mapa	la región
d) la estación	trenes
e) el comedor	el hotel
f) el hermano	Juan

15) Put the following into Spanish:
a) the days of the week b) the months of the year c) a member of a club
d) the band's music e) the walls of the bedroom

16) Translate the following sentences into English:
a) Lo importante es el precio.
b) Lo peor es el problema del efecto invernadero.
c) No sé lo que va a hacer Luisa en el futuro.
d) Lo mejor sería no decir nada.

17) Translate the following sentences into English:
a) Buenas tardes, señor Gómez. ¿Cómo está la señora Gómez?
b) Los viernes termino el trabajo a las cuatro.
c) Los tomates cuestan tres euros el kilo.
d) En invierno hacemos esquí y en verano vamos de vacaciones a la costa.
e) ¡Qué lástima!

18) Translate the following conversation into Spanish:
A: Have you got any sweets?
B: Of course. How many would you like ... a hundred grammes?
A: Yes, and I'd like a few grapes.
B: They cost 4 euros a kilo. Anything else?
A: No. I'm going to the hospital while my mother does the shopping with my sister. My Dad is there and he likes grapes.
B: I hope that it's nothing serious.

Adjectives

Gain more marks and show what an interesting person you are by using some describing words. Make sure you understand what you're saying as well.

Adjectives must 'agree' with the thing they're describing

1) In English, you can use the same describing word (adjective) for whatever you like — like big bus, big buses, big boy, big girl...
2) In Spanish, the describing word has to change to match whether what it's describing is masculine/feminine, singular/plural. Look at these examples where 'pequeño' has to change:

Masculine Singular	Masculine Plural	Feminine Singular	Feminine Plural
el chico pequeñ**o** *(the small boy)*	los chicos pequeñ**os** *(the small boys)*	la chica pequeñ**a** *(the small girl)*	las chicas pequeñ**as** *(the small girls)*

The rules are:

1. The describing word ends in '-a' if the word being described is feminine (see page 138).
2. The describing word ends in an '-s' or an '-es' if the word being described is plural (see page 139).

(Of course, that means if it's feminine plural, then you end up with '-as'.)

IMPORTANT NOTE:
When you look an adjective up in the dictionary it's listed in the masculine singular form. Don't ask me why — it must have been a load of single blokes who wrote the dictionary.

3) Some colours never change at all, because they are actually the names of *things*, and are not real adjectives. The commonest ones are:

beige, naranja, rosa, violeta, crema, púrpura, turquesa

See page 79 for more colours.

e.g. *Three orange hats.*
→ Tres sombreros naranja.

You'll need adjectives if you want to describe things

More things to learn, but you'll have very boring conversations with people if you never use any adjectives. And if you don't use any in your exam, you won't get good marks.

More on Adjectives

This is a really handy page. It gives you a nice list of important adjectives. Learn them and use them and you won't have any trouble describing things to the examiner. They're vital.

Learn these important adjectives

Here are 22 describing words — they're the ones you really have to know.

Top 22 Describing Words

good: bueno/a
bad: malo/a
pretty/nice: bonito/a
happy: feliz
old: viejo/a
young: joven
easy: fácil
difficult: difícil
new: nuevo/a
fast: rápido/a
slow: lento/a
big/great: grande
tall: alto/a
sad: triste
nice (character): simpático/a
interesting: interesante
boring: aburrido/a
strange: raro/a
long: largo/a
handsome/pretty: guapo/a
small: pequeño/a
short (height): bajo/a

*Adjectives that don't end in '-o' follow a different rule to the one on page 144. They don't have a feminine form:

un libro interesante = an interesting book

una asignatura interesante = an interesting subject

You make the plural for these adjectives by adding '-s' or '-es':

niños felices = happy children

chicas jóvenes = young girls

Most describing words go after the word they describe

It's the opposite of English — in Spanish most describing words (adjectives) go after the word they're describing (the noun).

Tengo un coche rápido. = I have a fast car.

The red dress:

Some adjectives lose the final 'o' before masculine nouns

Some adjectives lose the final 'o' when they go in front of a masculine noun:

good: bueno/a
first: primero/a
third: tercero/a
some: alguno/a
none: ninguno/a
bad: malo/a

Un buen día. = A good day.

Be aware that 'alguno' and 'ninguno' both drop an 'o' and add an accent:

No hay ningún taxi libre. = (literally) There isn't any taxi free.

Learn the top 22 adjectives and you're off to a good start

Aaaargh — more tables to learn, but then that's the nature of Spanish grammar. You'll need to learn these adjectives and use them in the exam, or everything you say or write will sound very dull.

More Adjectives

Here are even more adjectives for you. Some of them are a bit more tricky.

Two totally odd adjectives

grande = *big, great* ciento = *100*

1) 'Grande' is the only adjective that drops 'de' in front of both masculine and feminine words.

e.g. *A great lady.*
→ Una gran señora.

e.g. *A great day.*
→ Un gran día.

2) 'Ciento' drops '-to' when it comes in front of anything that isn't another number (but not before 'mil' or 'millón').

e.g. *one hundred euros.*
→ cien euros.

There are some odd ones out that always go in front

cada = *each, every*
mucho/a = *a lot of*
otro/a = *another*
poco/a = *little (not much)*
pocos/as = *few*
tanto/a = *so much*

e.g. *Every day Felipe eats another omelette.*
→ Cada día Felipe come otra tortilla.

Some change what they mean depending on their position

Some adjectives change their meaning according to whether they are before or after the noun. Here are some important ones — learn them carefully.

adjective	meaning if before	meaning if after
grande	great, e.g. un gran hombre = a great man.	big, e.g. un hombre grande = a big man.
mismo	same, e.g. el mismo día = the same day.	self, e.g. yo mismo = me myself.
nuevo	new (different), e.g. tengo un nuevo coche = I have a new [to me] car.	(brand) new, e.g. tengo un coche nuevo = I have a brand new car.
viejo	old (longstanding), e.g. un viejo amigo = an old friend	old (elderly), e.g. un amigo viejo = an elderly friend.

You can also add 'ito/ita' to lots of adjectives to make things seem smaller or cuter, or 'ísimo/a' to make the meaning stronger:

e.g. *My little sister is beautiful.*
→ Mi hermanita es guapita.

e.g. *The book is absolutely awful.*
→ El libro es malísimo.

Learn how to use the tricky adjectives like 'grande'

You need to learn these tricky adjectives really well. Otherwise you'll just make embarrassing mistakes, like calling your best friend your 'elderly friend' instead. It doesn't look good.

Possession

My, your, our — who things belong to

You must be able to use and understand these words to say that something belongs to someone:

You have to choose masculine, feminine or plural to match the thing it's describing (NOT the person who owns it).

	masculine singular	feminine singular	masculine plural	feminine plural
my	mi	mi	mis	mis
your (singular, familiar)	tu	tu	tus	tus
his / her / its / your (singular, polite)	su	su	sus	sus
our	nuestro	nuestra	nuestros	nuestras
your (plural, familiar)	vuestro	vuestra	vuestros	vuestras
their / your (plural, polite)	su	su	sus	sus

Mi hermano es alto, mis padres son bajos. = My brother is tall, my parents are short.

Mine, yours, ours — other belonging words

These words always come after the noun ('nuestro' and 'vuestro' etc. are the same as above).

	masculine singular	feminine singular	masculine plural	feminine plural
mine	mío	mía	míos	mías
yours	tuyo	tuya	tuyos	tuyas
his / hers / yours / theirs	suyo	suya	suyos	suyas

¿Esa casa es tuya? = Is that house yours?

This page shouldn't be too hard to learn

You need to learn all this stuff off by heart though. It won't get itself learnt. Make yourself a blank table for the 'mine, yours, ours' words, and try to fill it in without looking. That's the best way to learn it.

Quick Questions

Check you've understood everything in the section so far by answering these quick questions. It'll be easy, long, difficult, tall, young, interesting, happy, boring, sad, and lots of other adjectives too.

Quick Questions

1) Put the Spanish word for 'little' after the following words making them agree with the noun they describe:
a) un pueblo… b) una casa... c) dos perros… d) unas chicas…

2) Change the following adjectives from 'masculine' to 'feminine':
a) inteligente b) difícil c) guapo d) joven e) feliz f) inglés

3) Beginning with "son", use the following adjectives to describe Mary and Elizabeth:
a) inteligente b) difícil c) guapo d) joven e) feliz f) inglés

4) How would you say in Spanish:
"María is wearing a red skirt with a red T-shirt. She has red gloves, a red hat and red boots. Red is very fashionable this year!"

5) For each of these phrases write the correct form of the adjective to agree with its noun:
a) una canción (triste) b) una historia (raro) c) una decisión (difícil)
d) una mujer (feliz) e) unas clases (aburrido) f) una amiga (francés)
g) unos pantalones (azul) h) la gente (simpático) i) las novelas (interesante)
j) los bailes (andaluz) k) las cafeterías (español)

6) Write a short paragraph to describe three of your Spanish friends:
Pedro is tall, with short black hair and brown eyes. You think that he is very handsome. Pablo and his brother are short with brown hair and green eyes. You think that they are kind but a bit strange because they both wear orange T-shirts.

7) For each of these phrases write the correct form of the adjective to agree with its noun:
a) La habitación está en el (tercero) piso.
b) Hoy hace muy (malo) tiempo.
c) ¿Hay (alguno) taxi libre?
d) "(Bueno) días", me dijo.
e) Colón fue un (grande) marinero.
f) El (primero) hombre fue Adán.
g) Cuesta (ciento) euros.
h) Estoy de muy (bueno) humor hoy.
i) La (tercero) semana de agosto.
j) El restaurante está en la (primero) planta.
k) (Alguno) chicas sufren de anorexia.
l) No tenemos (ninguno) habitación libre para esta noche.
m) Tenemos un apartamento en el (primero) piso.

8) Translate the following sentences into Spanish:
a) The weather is fine.
b) Is there a supermarket round here?
c) Some songs are sad.
d) She has no problem with her parents.
e) It's a bad day for playing tennis.
f) The apartment is on the third floor.
g) It is going to cost more than a hundred and fifty pounds.
h) Good luck!
i) They have no rooms on the first floor.
j) "Good afternoon", said Manuel.

Quick Questions

OK, you probably think that these questions are really dull and boring. That's true, but the only way to learn this grammar is to do lots of dull practice sentences. I wish there was another way, really I do.

Quick Questions

9) Translate the following sentences into Spanish:
   a) Each day you must eat a lot of fruit but few chips.
   b) There are few people on the beach today because the weather is bad.
   c) There are so many things to do in Spain.
   d) "Another day, another cathedral!", said the American tourist.

10) Differentiate between the following two sentences:
   a) Salvador Dalí fue un gran pintor.
   b) Salvador Dalí no fue un pintor grande.
   c) Fue un viejo amigo de Gala Breton.
   d) No fue un amigo viejo de Gala Breton.

11) What do the following sentences mean?
   a) Mi hermano es una persona grande.
   b) Pablo Picasso fue un gran pintor.
   c) Fuimos a España con una vieja amiga de mis padres.
   d) Tenemos una nueva profesora de español.
   e) Yo mismo vi el accidente.
   f) Los Pirineos son unas montañas grandes entre Francia y España.
   g) La Semana Santa es una gran fiesta en Sevilla.
   h) Mi padre compró un coche nuevo.
   i) El vecino de al lado colecciona coches viejos.
   j) Vamos a salir para España el mismo día que vosotros.
   k) Fernando e Isabel fueron grandes monarcas españoles.
   l) ¡Mi hermanito es malísimo!

12) How would you say to your Spanish friend, in Spanish:
   a) We have a brand new dishwasher.
   b) It is a big dishwasher.
   c) It cost more than a hundred pounds.
   d) The old dishwasher was awful.

13) To whom would the following things belong:
   a) mis hermanos b) su coche c) nuestra casa
   d) tu ropa e) vuestra profesora f) sus dientes
   g) su madre h) sus padres

14) Put the following into Spanish:
   a) my dog b) your house c) her dress
   d) his trousers e) our shoes f) my parents
   g) their car h) our friend i) their bedrooms
   j) your sister

15) Translate the following dialogue into English:
   A: Este lápiz no es mío.
   B: No, es mío, no es tuyo.
   A: No es tuyo tampoco. Creo que es el de María.
   B: ¿Es suyo, pues?
   A: Sí, es suyo. Pero estos libros no son suyos.
   B: ¿De quién son, pues?
   A: De Manuel.

Adverbs

This page is about describing things you do, e.g. I speak Spanish perfectly, and about adding more info, e.g. the bus is very red or I speak Spanish almost perfectly.

Make your sentences better by saying how you do things

1) In English, you don't say 'We talk slow', you have to add a 'ly' on the end to say 'We talk slowly'.

These are 'adverbs'.

2) In Spanish, you have to add a 'mente' on the end, but first you have to make sure the describing word is in the feminine form (see page 144).

Habla lentamente. = He speaks slowly.

quickly: rápidamente
rarely: raramente

The Spanish word for 'slow' is 'lento', but the feminine form is 'lenta'. Add 'mente' and you get 'lentamente' = slowly.

3) Unlike normal describing words (see page 144) you don't ever have to change these words — even if what it's about is feminine or plural.

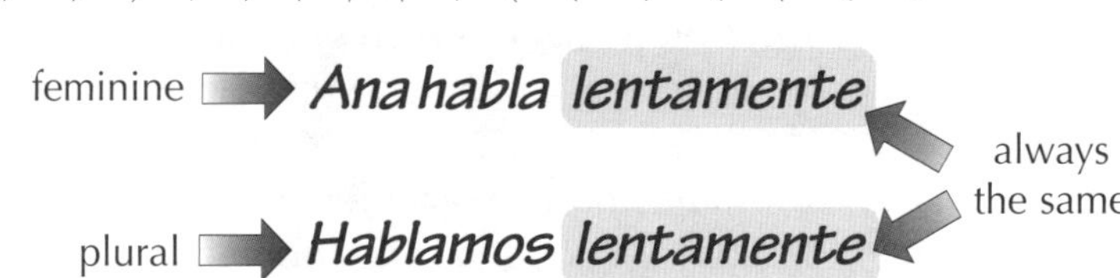

Learn these odd ones out off by heart

Just like in English there are odd ones out — for example, you don't say I sing 'goodly'...

English		Spanish	
good →	well	bueno/a →	bien
bad →	badly	malo/a →	mal

MORE EXAMPLES OF ADDING DESCRIBING WORDS:

Canto. = I sing.

Canto bien. = I sing well.

Canto mal. = I sing badly.

Use one of these four words to give even more detail

Stick one of these four words in front of the describing word in a sentence to add extra detail and impress the examiners.

very: muy
almost: casi
quite: bastante
too: demasiado

You can use them for sentences saying how something is done...

Ella habla casi perfectamente el español. = She speaks Spanish almost perfectly.

...and for sentences about what something is like.

Bob está muy feliz. = Bob is very happy.

These details make your Spanish sound great

This is a bit like English — you have a set ending (-mente) to learn and stick on, and it's not too tricky either. Make sure you really know the standard rule and all the exceptions.

Comparatives and Superlatives

Often you don't just want to say that something is tasty you want to say that it's the tastiest...

How to say more brave, most brave

In Spanish you can't say 'braver' or 'bravest', it's got to be 'more brave' or 'the most brave':

Dave es valiente. = Dave is brave.

Dave es más valiente. = Dave is more brave / braver.

Dave es el más valiente. = Dave is the most brave / bravest.

old: viejo	*older:* más viejo	*oldest:* el más viejo
tall: alto	*taller:* más alto	*tallest:* el más alto

From tall to taller, add 'más'.
From tall to tallest add 'el más'.

You can do this with almost any describing word. Try it with the adjectives on page 145.

BUT, just like in English, there are odd ones out:

good: bueno	*better:* mejor	*best:* el mejor
bad: malo	*worse:* peor	*worst:* el peor
big / old: grande	*bigger / older:* mayor	*biggest / oldest:* el mayor
young / small: pequeño	*younger / smaller:* menor	*youngest / smallest:* el menor

El gorro azul es el mejor. = The blue cap is the best.

Tricky Stuff

It's 'la más...' for feminine, 'los/las más...' for plural

Instead of 'el más' you have to use 'la más' or 'los/las más' to match the word you're describing. *(see p. 141).*

Liz es la más alta. = Liz is the tallest.

Ed y Jo son los más altos. = Ed and Jo are the tallest.

You also have to change the describing word — usually add an 'a' for feminine, and/or an 's' or 'es' for plural (see p.144). NB — you only do this for adjectives, NOT adverbs (see below).

More or most bravely is pretty much the same...

When you're saying that someone does something more or most ...ly, you follow the same pattern as above, but instead of adjectives (see pages 144-146), you use adverbs (see page 150).

Dave actúa valientemente. = Dave acts bravely.

Dave actúa más valientemente. = Dave acts more bravely.

Dave actúa el más valientemente. = Dave acts the most bravely.

There are two odd ones out you need to know:

well: bien → *better:* mejor   *badly:* mal → *worse:* peor

Learn these three great ways of comparing things

You just stick the words in purple on either side of the describing word, like this:

Ed es más joven que Tom. = Ed is younger than Tom.

Ed es menos joven que Tom. = Ed is less young than Tom.

Ed es tan joven como Tom. = Ed is as young as Tom.

This page is the bestest in the book

Make sure you learn how to say bigger or biggest, and how to say bigger than, as big as and less big than. And don't just learn the rule, learn all those exceptions to it as well.

Prepositions

You've got to learn these if you want tip-top marks. They're really useful words anyway.

TO — a

Where we use 'to', they usually use 'a':

Va a Madrid. = He's going to Madrid. ***Voy a casa.*** = I'm going (to) home.

For things like to go, to do, just use the infinitive (see page 164) — you don't need an extra word for 'to'. E.g. ir = to go, hacer = to do/make.

ON — sobre / en

For 'on top' of, it's 'sobre' or 'en': ***Sobre la mesa.*** = On the table.

When it's not 'on top', it's usually 'en': ***Lo vi en la tele.*** = I saw it on TV.

For days of the week, it's left out: ***Me voy el lunes.*** = I'm leaving on Monday.

IN — en, dentro de

'En' is just 'in', 'inside' is usually 'dentro'.

Está en / dentro de la caja. = It's in / inside the box.

If it's in a town, it's 'en': ***Vivo en Málaga.*** = I live in Malaga.

Don't forget to add 'en' when going into a place: ***Teresa entra en la tienda.*** = Teresa enters (into) the shop.

FROM — de, desde or a partir de

Where we use 'from', they usually use 'de': ***Soy de Cardiff.*** = I come from Cardiff.

'Desde' is used where there is a starting and finishing point: ***Desde Londres hasta Madrid.*** = From London to Madrid.

For dates, it's 'a partir de': ***A partir del 4 de junio.*** = From the 4th of June.

Be careful to use the right Spanish preposition

You've probably seen a lot of these words before, so it's not too scary. Just concentrate on using them in the right way, or you'll lose easy marks. Practise plenty of sentences and you'll be fine.

Prepositions

Yes, there's even <u>more</u> prepositions to learn.

OF — de

Where we use 'of', they usually use '<u>de</u>': ***Una botella <u>de</u> leche.*** = A bottle <u>of</u> milk.

'Made of' is '<u>de</u>': ***Es un cinturón <u>de</u> cuero.*** = It's a leather belt.

Be careful — sometimes it's hard to spot the <u>de</u> in a sentence, because de + el = <u>del</u>.

Salgo <u>del</u> supermercado. = I go out <u>of</u> the supermarket.

AT — en, a

Very few English phrases with 'at' in them use '<u>a</u>' in Spanish — most use '<u>en</u>':

<u>A</u> las seis. = <u>At</u> six o'clock.

Ella *está <u>en</u> el colegio.* = She is <u>at</u> school.

<u>En</u> casa. = <u>At</u> home.

Don't forget — a + el = <u>al</u>. Sometimes it can be tricky to spot.

Learn these words for saying where something is

You need these little words a lot, for saying where things are in your <u>town</u> or your <u>house</u>.

El banco está enfrente del hotel y del café. = The bank is <u>opposite</u> the hotel and the cafe.

next to/beside: al lado de
behind: detrás de
in front of: delante de
between: entre
under/below: bajo/debajo de
on/upon: en, sobre
above: encima de
against: contra
in/into: en
at the end of: al final de
at the back of: al fondo de
here: aquí
there: allí, ahí, allá
inside: dentro de
outside: fuera de

Don't forget to use <u>está</u> / <u>están</u> for describing where things are / go.

Prepositions are important little words

Prepositions have loads of <u>different</u> meanings in English — it's important to remember they do in Spanish <u>too</u>, just <u>not</u> the same ones. You have to learn the words from a <u>Spanish perspective</u>.

Quick Questions

You need to practise all this tricky grammar stuff, or you'll forget it. So do these questions NOW.

Quick Questions

1) Change the following adjectives into adverbs by adding "-mente" to the feminine form:
a) lento b) rápido
c) raro d) fácil
e) triste f) feliz
g) perfecto h) especial.

2) How would you say in Spanish:
a) My teacher speaks Spanish very well.
b) Unfortunately we rarely go on holiday to the north of Spain.
c) We understand perfectly what they say.

3) In an e-mail your Spanish friend writes:
"Mi hermano canta bien pero baila mal mientras que mi hermana baila bien y canta mal."
What is your friend telling you?

4) Translate the following dialogue into English:
A: Las entradas al museo son muy caras.
B: ¿Cuánto son?
A: Casi treinta y cinco euros cada una.
B: Ah sí, es demasiado caro especialmente después de haber pagado las entradas al castillo.
A: Sí. ¡Hoy ya hemos gastado bastante dinero en visitas!

5) How would you say the following in Spanish:
a) My Spanish friend speaks too quickly.
b) These shoes are quite expensive.
c) Marta and her sister are very intelligent girls.

6) Describing your friends at school, tell your Spanish friend, in Spanish, that Helen and Sonia are tall, Kay and Debbie are taller but Kerrie is the tallest.

7) A: Me gusta la chaqueta azul.
B: Sí, es buena, pero me gusta menos que la chaqueta negra …
la negra es mejor para ti.
A: Estoy de acuerdo. ¡Pero mira! La chaqueta blanca es la mejor de todas.
Put the jackets in A's order of preference.

8) Your Spanish friend writes to you:
"Mi hermana menor tiene trece años y mi hermano mayor tiene veintidós años. Pero el menor de toda la familia es mi hermanito que tiene siete años."
What is your friend telling you?

9) Place these students in order of intelligence:
Pedro es más inteligente que Ana.
Ana es menos inteligente que Nuria.
Nuria es tan inteligente como Ricardo.
Ricardo es menos inteligente que Pedro.

10) How would you say in Spanish:
"Spanish is less difficult than French. ICT is more interesting than maths and business studies are as easy as geography"?

11) How would you tell your friend in Spanish:
"I am going home. I'm going back to Bolton"?

Quick Questions

Here's another beautiful page of hand-crafted questions for you to enjoy. ¡Qué suerte!

Quick Questions

12) Your friend phones you and says:
"Ahora estoy en Londres estudiando inglés en una escuela de idiomas. ¿Puedo ir a Leeds a verte después del curso?"
What are you being told and what question does your friend ask?

13) How would you tell your friend that you are at home today but that tomorrow you are going to go to York?

14) Your Spanish friend produces a matchbox and says:
"¿Quieres ver lo que tengo dentro de esta cajita?"
What are you being asked?

15) How would you say to your friend:
"What is there inside the box?"

16) In a bar in Spain you order the following in Spanish:
a) a cup of coffee with milk
b) a glass of orange juice
c) a bottle of mineral water

17) Your friend asks you what your trousers are made of. You reply in Spanish that the trousers are made of leather but the belt is made of plastic.

18) Translate the following sentences into Spanish:
a) Your cup is on the table.
b) I saw that programme on television.
c) I'm going to Spain on Friday.

19) How would you tell your friend, in Spanish, that you come from Bristol?

20) How would you tell your friend, in Spanish, that the flight from London to Málaga leaves the airport at 10 o'clock, but that from 1st April it's going to leave at 9.30?

21) What is being advertised?
"Por la tarde, aquí, Real Madrid contra Celta de Vigo a las ocho."

22) There's a panic as your friend's mother asks: "¿Dónde está el gato?"
Make the following suggestions in Spanish:
a) outside in the garden?
b) under the table?
c) behind the sofa?
d) inside the microwave?
e) at the back of the wardrobe?

23) Translate the following dialogue into English:
A: ¡Por favor! ¿Dónde está la Oficina de Turismo?
B: Está detrás del ayuntamiento, al lado de la estación de autobuses.
A: ¿Delante de los grandes almacenes?
B: No, no, entre el banco y la farmacia central.
A: ¿No está al final de una calle?
B: No, ésa es la estación de trenes.
A: Ah, sí, entiendo. Gracias.

24) You see a sign in a shop window:
"Rebajas de hasta cincuenta por ciento en todo."
What does it say?

Por and Para

'Por' and 'para' are two nightmare words for English-speakers because they both mean 'for' — but in different ways. This bit's tricky I'm afraid, but it's really important — it's worth learning.

Use **Para** for...

1) To say who or what something is for: ***Este dinero es para ti.*** = This money is for you.

Una habitación para dos personas. = A room for two people.

El tren para Buenos Aires. = The train for Buenos Aires.

2) When you want to say 'to' / 'in order to':

Se fue de vacaciones para descansar. = He went on holiday in order to rest.

Pon más sal para darle más sabor. = Put in more salt to give it more flavour.

3) When you want to say 'by' in time phrases:

Para mañana. = By / for tomorrow.

Para entonces. = By / for then.

4) 'For' in sentences 'for X days...' ***Quiero el coche para tres días.*** = I want the car for three days.

5) 'In...view': ***Para mí, ella es la chica más atractiva de todas.*** = In my view she's the most attractive girl of all.

6) 'On the point of' (confusingly, in Latin America they use 'por'): ***Está para llover.*** = It's about to rain.

Use **Por** for...

1) Time sentences:

Vivió en Málaga por un año. = He lived in Malaga for a year.

Por la mañana. = In the morning.

2) Direction / place sentences: ***El tren va por el túnel.*** = The train goes through the tunnel.

3) Number phrases:

Dos veces por día. = Twice a day.

Veinte por ciento. = Twenty per cent.

4) Exchange: ***Pagó diez euros por el libro.*** = He paid 10 euros for the book.

5) On behalf of: ***Lo hace por ti.*** = He does it for you.

NB with 'gracias' it's always 'por': ***Gracias por todos los peces.*** = Thanks for all the fish.

You need to use 'por' and 'para' correctly

This is one of the hardest things of all in Spanish, I'm afraid — but if you can get it right, it'll seriously impress the examiners and boost your marks. So get practising.

Pronouns

Pronouns are words that replace nouns — like 'you' or 'them'.

Dave has a new job at the poodle parlour.
He likes shaving poodles.

'He' is a pronoun. It means you don't have to say 'Dave' again.

Yo, tú, él, ella — I, you, he, she

'I', 'you', 'he', etc are not usually needed in Spanish — unless you want to emphasise or make it clear exactly who you're talking about. You definitely need to know them though — or you'll end up getting seriously confused.

The subject pronouns

I:	yo	*we:*	nosotros/as
you (informal singular):	tú	*you (informal plural):*	vosotros/as
he / it:	él	*they (masc. or mixed masc. & fem.):*	ellos
she / it:	ella	*they (all fem.):*	ellas
you (formal singular):	usted	*you (formal plural):*	ustedes
one:	se		

THE FOUR YOUs

Remember — there are four ways of talking to 'you'. 'Tú' is for one person who's your friend, a member of your family or about your age. For a group of people you know, use 'vosotros/as'. You use 'usted' to be polite to one person (for older people who aren't your family or friends), or 'ustedes' if there's more than one of them.

Me, te, lo, la — me, you, him, her

These are for the person/thing in a sentence that's having the action done to it (the direct object).

The direct object pronouns

me:	me	*us:*	nos
you (inf. sing.):	te	*you (inf. plu.):*	os
him / it / you (form. sing. masc.):	lo	*them / you (formal plu. m.):*	los
her / it / you (form. sing. fem.):	la	*them / you (formal plu. f.):*	las

Dave lava el perro. = Dave washes the dog. *Dave lo lava.* = Dave washes it.

Learn how to use pronouns correctly

The best way to learn how to use these is to do lots of practice sentences. Translate these: Sharon hates French. She hates it. The dog eats bacon. He eats it. Now make up some more.

Pronouns

Yes, there's another page of pronouns for you. This section seems never-ending.

There are special words for to me, to her, to them

For things that need 'to', 'for' or 'by', e.g. writing to someone, use the indirect object pronouns:

The indirect object pronouns

to me:	me	*to us:*	nos
to you (inf. sing.):	te	*to you (inf. plu.):*	os
to him / her / it / you (form. sing.):	le	*to them / you (form. pl.):*	les

El perro da el cepillo a Dave. = The dog gives the brush to Dave.

These pronouns usually come before the verb, but when you tell someone to do something they are tacked on to the end of the verb.

El perro le da el cepillo. = The dog gives the brush to him.

¡Escríbele! = Write to him / her!

¡Dígame! = Tell me!

You'll also definitely need these pronouns for saying you like something. You have to say 'it is pleasing to me' etc.

Me gusta la música. = I like music.

Watch out — it doesn't matter if the person is singular or plural. You need 'gusta' if the thing you like is singular, or 'gustan' if it's plural.

No nos gusta el pulpo. = We don't like octopus.

¿Te gustan los árboles? = Do you like trees?

No les gustan las flores. = They don't like flowers.

Tricky Stuff

Special words for me, you, him, her...

There are some pronouns which change when they come after a preposition:

The prepositional pronouns

me:	mí	*us:*	nosotros/as
you (informal sing.):	ti	*you (inf. plu.):*	vosotros/as
him / it:	él	*them (m. or mixed m. & f.):*	ellos
her / it:	ella	*them (all fem.):*	ellas
you (formal sing.):	usted	*you (formal plu.):*	ustedes

¿Hablas de mí? = Are you talking about me?

El regalo no es para ti, es para ella. = The present isn't for you, it's for her.

'With me' and 'with you'(fam. sing.) have their own special words:

Va conmigo. = He's going with me.

Voy contigo. = I'm going with you.

You need to know all these special words

There's a lot to learn on these pages. But actually you've seen a lot of it before. You learnt how to say you like something when you learnt about sports and hobbies. It's not too hard, really.

Pronouns

The Personal — 'a'

Extra preposition alert — you need to put an extra 'a' in before the word for any human being after every single verb except 'tener'.

Veo a mi hermano. *BUT* ***Veo el árbol.***

= I see my brother. = I see the tree.

Estoy buscando a Juan. *BUT* ***Estoy buscando un taxi.***

= I'm looking for Juan. = I'm looking for a taxi.

Tengo dos hermanos.

= I have two brothers.

Que — that, which, who

'Que' is a special kind of pronoun (a relative pronoun). It can mean 'which', 'who', 'what' or 'that' — and it can't be left out of sentences.

Dice que va a llover. = He says that it's going to rain.

It's not like English — you can't leave out the 'that'.

La persona que vive aquí. = The person who lives here.

Fui a Menorca, que es una isla preciosa. = I went to Menorca, which is a lovely island.

Getting the Order Right

1) These pronouns usually go before the verb — though they can go before OR on the end of an infinitive or a present participle:

Le voy a hablar. / Voy a hablarle. = I'm going to speak to him.

Lo estamos mirando. / Estamos mirándolo. = We are watching it.

...and they must go on the end of a command to do something:

Déme su pasaporte, por favor. = Give me your passport please.

2) Whenever there are two object pronouns in the same sentence, the indirect ones always go first:

Me los da. = He gives them to me.

Te la enviaré. = I'll send it to you.

3) But, if the indirect pronoun is 'le' or 'les', then it changes to 'se' when it comes in front of lo, la, los or las (even though the final meaning may not be very clear!)

Se las da. = He gives them to him / her / them / you (sing.) / you (plu.)

Se lo regalé. = I gave it to him / her / them / you (sing.) / you (plu.)

It could be any one of these — you need to look at the sentences around to work out who it's on about.

Just cover and scribble

You should have the hang of this by now. These grammar pages are pretty hard going, so don't do too many at once. In fact, it's probably time for a cup of tea and a TV programme by now.

Pronouns

This page is about pointing things out, and generally making it clear which thing you're on about.

How to say this, that or the other

Use 'este', etc... for saying things like 'this man', 'these apples' — i.e. when you're using 'this' as a describing word.

	masculine singular	feminine singular		masculine plural	feminine plural
THIS THAT THAT	este ese aquel	esta esa aquella	THESE THOSE THOSE (further away)	estos esos aquellos	estas esas aquellas

Examples:

este pájaro = *this bird*

aquella casa = *that house*

estos bolis = *these pens*

esas manzanas = *those apples*

Use the neuter when you're not talking about a particular thing:

neuter	
THIS THAT	esto eso

¿Qué es esto? = What's this?

¡Eso es! = That's it!

It's different when the 'this' or 'these' is a noun

When you say things like 'this is mine', you're using 'this' as a noun.
That means you need to stick an accent on the 'this' word: e.g. éstos, ése etc...

Tengo dos perros; éste es simpático, pero ése es malo.

= I've got two dogs; this one here is nice, but that one there is nasty.

Algo — Something Alguien — Someone

There's nothing very special about these, you just need to be able to understand and use them:

¿Quiere algo?

= Do you want something?

Alguien ha llevado el dinero.

= Someone has taken the money.

Hay algo en mi bolso.

= There's something in my bag.

Buscan a alguien muy gordo.

= They're looking for someone very fat.

You're nearly half-way — keep going

None of this stuff is too tricky — as long as you're absolutely sure you've got it clear.
Remember — 'este', 'esa' and the others always go with another word, like 'este hombre'.

Quick Questions

Don't skip over the pages on pronouns — they're important. Check you can remember all that vital pronoun information by doing these Quick Questions.

Quick Questions

1) Tell your friend, in Spanish, that you are going to book a room for two people. Last year you paid thirty five euros for an apartment.

2) As your friend is about to leave you say:
"This present is for your parents."

3) Your friend says:
"Para mí, eres el más simpático de todos mis amigos ingleses".
What are you being told?

4) How would you say to your friend:
"We went on holiday to relax but Dad hired a car for four days. We went to Gibraltar along the road that passes through Marbella. We left in the morning. We arrived at night. The traffic was awful."

5) All the following mean 'you'. What is the difference between them?
a) tú b) Vd./usted c) vosotros/as d) Vds./ustedes

6) Replace the direct object (underlined) by the correct pronoun and put it in the correct place:
a) Vi <u>el partido</u> en la tele.
b) Odio <u>los animales domésticos</u>.
c) Quiero mucho <u>las canciones viejas</u>.
d) Visité <u>la catedral</u> ayer.
e) Nuestros amigos vieron <u>a Teresa y a mí</u> en el supermercado.

7) How would you say the following sentences in Spanish?
a) The sweets? We ate them all on Wednesday!
b) The girls? We saw them this morning!
c) Eduardo and I? They saw us in the disco!

8) How would you say the following in Spanish?
a) I like Spanish wine but I don't like Spanish olives.
b) We like squid but we don't like octopus.
c) They like chocolate but they don't like biscuits.
d) She likes tomatoes but she doesn't like lettuce.

9) In the following sentences change the named person into a pronoun and put the pronoun into the correct position. (Be careful about stress marks.)
a) ¡Escribe una carta <u>a Juan</u>!
b) ¡Manda <u>a Teresa</u> un regalo!
c) ¡Envía una postal <u>a Juan y Teresa</u>!

10) Explain to your friend, in Spanish, the seating arrangements at the table in your class.
"To the right of me is Emma, opposite her is Lucy and to the right of her is Daniel. On the other side of me is Jason and opposite him is Tom."

11) How would you say in Spanish:
a) with me, b) with them, c) with her, d) with you?

12) Replace the pronoun with the named people in brackets.
a) Lo ven todos los días. (Pablo)
b) La estoy buscando. (Teresa)
c) Las quiero mucho. (mis hermanas)
d) Los visitamos cada fin de semana. (mis tíos)
e) ¿Los vas a encontrar en la discoteca? (tus amigos)
f) La quiero muchísimo. (Elena)
g) Lo buscan por todas partes. (nuestro profesor)

Quick Questions

Yes, you've guessed it — there's another page of questions for you to do. It shouldn't take all that long to do them. Don't forget to check the answers to see which bits you're not sure on.

Quick Questions

13) Link the two sentences by replacing the word underlined with the Spanish for 'who':
   a) Aquí está la persona. La persona lo hizo.
   b) Busco a mi hermanito. Mi hermanito solamente tiene tres años.
   c) Vamos a ver a nuestros tíos. Nuestros tíos viven en Nueva York.
14) Link the two sentences by replacing the word underlined with the Spanish for 'which/that':
   a) Te doy las flores. Las flores costaron diez libras.
   b) Vamos a vender los libros. Los libros están en la mesa.
   c) Va a la playa. La playa está a cien metros del hotel.
15) How would you say to your friend, in Spanish:
   a) "They say it's going to rain",
   b) "They say we are going to win the match",
   c) "I think it's true".
16) Replace the noun underlined with a pronoun and put it in the correct position. Remember to include a stress mark where necessary.
   a) ¿Te presto el libro?
   b) Nos enviaron la postal desde Málaga.
   c) Te mandamos los sellos la semana pasada.
   d) ¿Me escribes las cartas?
   e) Voy a prestarte el libro.
17) Replace the underlined indirect object with a pronoun and put it in the correct position. Remember the stress marks!
   a) Lo presto a Manuel.
   b) La enviaron a sus padres desde Málaga.
   c) Los mandamos a Teresa ayer.
   d) ¿Las escribiste a tus primos y primas?
   e) Voy a prestarlo a mi mejor amiga.
18) Put the right Spanish word for 'this' or 'these' in front of these nouns:
   a) perro, b) chica, c) canción, d) decisiones.
19) How would you say in Spanish:
   a) This actress is great!
   b) These shoes are too expensive.
   c) This book is interesting.
   d) These T-shirts are cheap!
20) Put the right Spanish word for 'that' or 'those' in front of these nouns:
   a) hombre, b) mujer, c) viajes, d) calle.
21) Translate the following dialogue into English: (hacer juego means 'to go with' for colours)

   A: ¿Qué te parece estos pantalones?

   B: Prefiero aquéllos en el escaparate.

   A: ¿No te gusta tampoco esta camiseta roja?

   B: Sí, pero aquélla en el escaparate es blanca y es mejor. ¿Por qué no los pruebas con aquel sombrero azul?

   A: Pero ¡éste no hace juego con aquellos pantalones!

   B: Claro, pero si tomas aquella camiseta, sí que hará juego. Y si llevas estas gafas de sol, ¡no vas a ver la diferencia de colores!

Revision Summary

We're about half-way through the grammar section here, so it's a good moment for a bit of quiet reflection, and a summary of what you should have leant by now. Take a look at the questions below, and make sure that you can answer them before you go any further.

1) What are the words for 'the' and 'a' that go with each of these words?
a) 'pie' (masculine) b) 'flor' (feminine)

2) Make these Spanish words plural: a) una manzana b) el jueves c) un joven

3) What are the Spanish words for a) and, b) or, c) but, d) because?

4) Use the Spanish word for 'and' to turn these two phrases into one sentence that says 'I have a bird and a carrot': 'Tengo un pájaro.' = I have a bird. 'Tengo una zanahoria.' = I have a carrot.

5) How would you say in Spanish a) a red dress b) a green apple c) a pretty girl?

6) What is the difference between 'una gran señora' and 'una señora grande'?

7) What are the Spanish words for a) my horse, b) our house, c) his clothes, d) her house?

8) This sentence means 'I speak Spanish' — 'Hablo español'.
How would you change the sentence to mean 'I speak Spanish well'?
How would you change the sentence to mean 'I speak Spanish very well'?

9) How do you say 'Bob is taller than me' in Spanish? How do you say 'Bob is the tallest'?

10) This sentence means 'I speak slowly' — 'Hablo lentamente'.
How would you say 'I speak the slowest'?

11) How would you say in Spanish a) He's going to London b) I'm from Grimsby

12) How would you say in Spanish a) The dog is under the table b) The milk is in the fridge

13) How would you say in Spanish a) The bus for Granada b) I earn 50 euros a day

14) What are the Spanish words for:
'I', 'you' (informal, singular), 'he', 'she', 'we', 'you' (formal, plural) and 'they'?

15) What do these Spanish words mean? a) 'me' b) 'te' c) 'le' d) 'les'

16) How would you say these in Spanish: a) This dog is green. b) These cats are blue.

17) What do these sentences mean? a) Me gustan las manzanas, pero no me gusta ésta.
b) ¿Tiene pantalones rojos? Ésos son naranja.

Verbs

You just can't get away from this stuff, I'm afraid. But think about this — if you learn it now, it'll make the whole of Spanish GCSE easier...

Verbs are action words — they tell you what's going on

These are verbs.

Ethel plays football every Saturday.

Alex wished his grandma preferred knitting.

And so is this.

There's a lot you need to know about verbs, but it all boils down to these two things...

1) The verb is different for different times

You say things differently if they happened last week, or aren't going to happen till tomorrow.

Has already happened:
I went to Tibet last year.
I have been to Tibet.
I had been to Tibet.

PAST

Happening now:
I go to Tibet.
I am going to Tibet.

PRESENT

Hasn't happened yet:
I go to Tibet on Monday.
I will go to Tibet.
I will be going to Tibet.

FUTURE

These are all different tenses, in case you're interested.

2) The verb is different for different people

You'd say 'he plays', but never 'I plays' — it'd be daft. The verb changes to fit the person.

happening to me:
I am miserable.

happening to you:
You are miserable.

happening to her:
She is miserable.

OK, you get the picture — verbs are really important. You use them all the time, after all.

The infinitive means 'to...'

In Spanish infinitives always end in 'r'.

When you look up a verb in the dictionary, this is what you get:

(to) give: dar
(to) go: ir

Most of the time, you won't want the verb in its raw state — you'll have to change it so it's right for the person and time you're talking about.

BUT: if you want to use two verbs together, the second one usually needs to be infinitive.

Quiero comer. = I want to eat.

Preferimos bailar. = We prefer to dance.

Learn this right now

I'm not kidding. Over the next few pages there's loads of stuff on verbs because there's loads you need to know. Some of it's easy, some of it's tricky, but you need to learn it.

Present Tense

Sadly, this is nothing to do with Christmas gifts — it's the easiest of the verb forms in Spanish. That doesn't mean you can skip it though — you've still got to get it right.

The present tense is what's happening now

You'll use it more than anything else, so it's really important.

It's all about sticking 'endings' onto the main bit of the word (the 'stem'). For the present tense, the 'stems' that you stick the endings onto are dead easy:

Formula for Present Tense Stems

stem = infinitive – last two letters

Example of Present Tense Stems

infinitive	hablar	vivir	comer
stem	habl	viv	com

Endings for **-er** verbs

To form the present tense of regular '-er' verbs, add the following endings to the verb's stem — for example:

comer = to eat

I eat	como	*we eat:*	com**emos**
you (informal sing.) eat:	com**es**	*you (informal plu.) eat:*	com**éis**
he / she / it / one eats:	com**e**	*they eat:*	com**en**
you (formal sing.) eat:	com**e**	*you (formal plu.) eat:*	com**en**

The first bit ('com') is the stem and doesn't change.

See page 157 for when to use each one of the four forms of 'you'.

he, she, it and you (formal. sing.) always have the same ending.

Verbs really are vital

There's a lot of stuff about verbs on the next few pages. That's because there's a lot you need to know. If you don't learn the stuff on these pages before you move on, you'll find it tough.

Present Tense

Here's some more info about the present tense. Get this lot learned and you're well away.

Endings for -ir verbs

To form the present tense of regular '-ir' verbs,
add the following endings to the verb's stem — for example:

vivir = to live

I live	viv**o**	*we live:*	viv**imos**
you (informal sing.) live:	viv**es**	*you (inf. plu.) live:*	viv**ís**
he / she / it / one lives:	viv**e**	*they live:*	viv**en**
you (formal sing.) live:	viv**e**	*you (formal plu.) live:*	viv**en**

The first bit ('viv') is the stem and doesn't change.

they and you (formal plural) always have the same ending.

Endings for -ar verbs

To form the present tense of regular '-ar' verbs, add the following endings to the verb's stem — for example:

hablar = to speak

I speak	habl**o**	*we speak:*	habl**amos**
you (informal sing.) speak:	habl**as**	*you (inf. plu.) speak:*	habl**áis**
he / she / it / speaks:	habl**a**	*they speak:*	habl**an**
you (formal sing.) speak:	habl**a**	*you (formal plu.) speak:*	habl**an**

So if you want to say something like 'He talks a lot', it's dead easy:

hablar = to speak

1) Start by knocking off the 'ar':

hablar

2) Then add on the new ending:

habl ← a

3) And — ta da...

Habla mucho.

= He talks a lot.

Learn these common endings for the present tense

All you have to do is learn the endings for '-ar', '-er' & '-ir' verbs. They aren't too bad, really, because a lot of them are the same — especially the '-er' and '-ir' ones. Learn them and practise them.

Present Tense (Irregular)

OK, on the last two pages you got nice regular verbs. Now you get the horrible irregular ones.

Some Spanish verbs are almost irregular

Some verbs change their spelling (but only in the present tense).
These are called stem or radical changing verbs, and they change the 'e' in the stem to an 'ie' and the 'o' or 'u' in the stem to a 'ue'.

The stem doesn't change in the 'we' and 'you' forms.

(1) Example of 'e' to 'ie' verbs: 'Querer' means 'to want'.

querer = to want

I want:	quiero	*we want:*	queremos
you (informal sing.) want:	quieres	*you (informal plural) want:*	queréis
he / she / it wants / you (formal sing.) want:	quiere	*they / you (formal plural) want:*	quieren

Other important verbs that go like this are:

INFINITIVE	'I' PERSON	INFINITIVE	'I' PERSON
cerrar (to close)	cierro	sentarse (to sit down)	me siento
comenzar (to begin)	comienzo	sentir (to feel)	siento
empezar (to begin)	empiezo	tener (to have)	tengo (tú tienes)
pensar (to think)	pienso	venir (to come)	vengo (tú vienes)
preferir (to prefer)	prefiero		

These two are irregular in the 'I' person too.

(2) Example of 'o' to 'ue' verbs: 'Poder' means 'to be able to'.

poder = to be able to

I can:	puedo	*we can:*	podemos
you (informal sing.) can:	puedes	*you (informal plural) can:*	podéis
he / she / it / you (formal sing.) can:	puede	*they / you (formal plural) can:*	pueden

Other important verbs that go like this are:

INFINITIVE	'I' PERSON	INFINITIVE	'I' PERSON
acostarse (to go to bed)	me acuesto	jugar (to play)	juego
almorzar (to have lunch)	almuerzo	llover (to rain)	llueve (it rains)
costar (to cost)	cuesta (it costs)	morir (to die)	muero
doler (to hurt)	duele (it hurts)	volver (to return)	vuelvo
dormir (to sleep)	duermo		

These verbs are a bit trickier, but don't panic

Don't think that the present tense is so easy that you don't need to bother learning it. Once you've got these endings learnt, you'll be able to move on to the more complicated tenses.

Present Tense (Irregular)

These irregular verbs can be a pain, but there's no getting round it — you've got to learn them.

Some of the most useful verbs are totally irregular

Here are the most useful irregular verbs:

1. **ir = to go**

I go:	voy	*we go:*	vamos
you (informal sing.) go:	vas	*you (informal plural) go:*	vais
he / she / it goes / you (formal sing.) go:	va	*they / you (formal plural) go:*	van

'Ser' and 'estar' both mean 'to be' — they're probably the two most important Spanish verbs in the whole world.

2. **ser = to be**

I am:	soy	*we are:*	somos
you (informal sing.) are:	eres	*you (informal plural) are:*	sois
he / she / it is / you (formal sing.) are:	es	*they / you (formal plural) are:*	son

3. **estar = to be**

I am:	estoy	*we are:*	estamos
you (informal sing.) are:	estás	*you (informal plural) are:*	estáis
he / she / it is / you (formal sing.) are:	está	*they / you (formal plural) are:*	están

'Ser' and 'estar' both mean 'to be' but are used differently.
It takes plenty of practice to use the right one all the time.

Use 'ser' for pretty permanent things, such as nationality, height, occupation:

Julio es español, es alto y moreno. = Julio is Spanish, he is tall and dark.

Use 'estar' for either fairly temporary things:

Estamos tristes hoy. = We are sad today.

OR for saying where things are:

Madrid está en España. = Madrid is in Spain.

Keep going and learn these as well

It always seems unfair that the verbs you use most often are irregular. But once you've learnt them, you can use them over and over again, so it's well worth a little bit of effort.

Quick Questions

There aren't any practice exam questions in this section, so you'll need to concentrate extra hard on the Quick Questions instead. There's plenty here to keep you busy, and make sure that you've really understood the grammar. Don't ignore this section, though it probably is the most boring one in the book. If you can't use the grammar correctly, you won't get many marks in the exam, even if you've memorised the contents of the dictionary at the back of this book.

Quick Questions

1) How would you say the following in Spanish:
   a) I eat b) we eat c) she eats d) you (informal, singular) eat
   e) you (informal, plural) eat f) they eat g) you (formal plural) eat
   h) you (formal, singular) eat?

2) Match up the people named in the first column with the correct form of the Spanish verb 'to drink' on the right. You may use each answer more than once.

a) He	i) beben
b) They	ii) bebe
c) We	iii) bebéis
d) You (informal, singular)	iv) bebes
e) I	v) bebo
f) You (formal, plural)	vi) bebemos
g) She	
h) You (informal plural)	
i) You (formal singular)	

3) Put the "-ir" verb in brackets into the correct form of the present tense:
   a) Mi familia ... (vivir) en una casa pequeña.
   b) Los ascensores ... (subir) al décimo piso.
   c) El tendero ... (abrir) el supermercado a las siete.
   d) (Tú) ... (escribir) una postal de Valencia.
   e) (Yo) ... (vivir) en el norte de Inglaterra.
   f) (Nosotros) ... (subir) al primer piso.
   g) Mis padres ... (leer) el periódico por la mañana.
   h) (Vds.) ... (escribir) muchas cartas.

4) Put the following sentences into Spanish:
   a) You (informal, singular) write often.
   b) I go up to the fifth floor on foot.
   c) They open the bar at five pm.
   d) Do you (informal, plural) live near Manchester?
   e) We live in an apartment.

5) Using the Spanish verb 'to speak', how would you say the following:
   a) I speak Spanish.
   b) Do you (familiar, plural) speak Spanish?
   c) We speak to our teacher.
   d) Your parents speak too quickly.
   e) Do you (formal, singular) speak English?

6) Put the verb in brackets into the correct form of the present tense.
   a) Vd. (ayudar) con mis deberes.
   b) Nosotros (mirar) la ropa nueva en el escaparate.
   c) El tren no (llegar) siempre con retraso.
   d) Paco y María Dolores (estudiar) inglés en el instituto.
   e) María Dolores e Isabel siempre (escuchar) con atención.

Quick Questions

Yes, I'm afraid there's even more of these questions to do. There's no point in pretending that they're interesting, or even exciting. The only good thing is that they will tell you if you've learnt the stuff in this section. Make sure you go back over the bits you got wrong.

Quick Questions

7) Translate the following sentences into Spanish:
   a) We learn nothing at school because we understand nothing.
   b) They open their books and write the perfect answer.
   c) When you get home do you rest in front of the telly?
   d) I always listen when my teacher speaks to me.

8) How would you say the following in Spanish:
   a) I am English.
   b) You are a kind boy.
   c) Elena is great!
   d) The children are awful.
   e) We are marvellous.
   f) You are intelligent girls.
   g) Are you the chemist?
   h) He's a doctor.

9) Using "estar" fill in the gaps with the correct form of the verb.
   a) Nosotros ... en casa.
   b) ¿ ... tú enferma?
   c) Hoy yo ... de buen humor
   d) Mi casa no ... cerca del instituto.
   e) ¿Dónde ... vosotros?
   f) ¡Vds. ... sentados en nuestras plazas reservadas!

10) Translate the following sentences into Spanish. Remember the difference between "ser" and "estar".
   a) Julio is tall, dark and handsome and he's here.
   b) London is in England. It's the capital.
   c) Tom is English but he's in Spain at the moment.
   d) What time is it? It's ten fifty-two and today is Thursday.
   e) Where is the nearest bank? It's in the square. It's the Banco Atlántico.

11) Using "ir" fill in the gaps with the correct form of the verb in the present tense.
   a) ¿ ... Vds. de vacaciones a Inglaterra?
   b) Nosotros ... al instituto juntos.
   c) Las chicas ... de tiendas los sábados.
   d) Yo ... al cine.
   e) ¿ ... vosotros a la discoteca?

12) Insert the verb "querer" or "poder" as indicated and put the original verb into the infinitive.
   a) No lavo los platos. (querer)
   b) Mi padre no compra un lavaplatos. (querer)
   c) ¿Se cambia moneda extranjera aquí? (poder)
   d) Empezamos mañana. (poder)
   e) ¿Por qué no estudian la geografía? (querer)

13) What do the following sentences mean in English?
   a) Las tiendas cierran a las cuatro los domingos.
   b) Mi tío comienza el trabajo a las cinco de la mañana pero mi padre empieza a las nueve menos cuarto.
   c) ¿Qué piensas de María Dolores? Viene a vernos mañana.
   d) Mis amigos juegan en ordenadores que cuestan mil libras cada uno.

The Future

You'll need to talk about things that are going to happen at some point in the future. There are two ways you can do it — and the first one's a piece of cake...

1) You can use 'I'm going to' to talk about the future

This is pretty easy, so there are no excuses for not learning it.

voy = I am going This is a bit of 'ir' (see page 168). It changes depending on whether it's "I am going", "you are going"...	+	 ***a*** This is just one of those things — you have to stick it in.	+	*Another Verb* (infinitive — see p.164) ***bailar*** = to dance	=	*Easy sentence about the future:* ***Voy a bailar.*** = I am going to dance.

Examples:

Ella va a jugar al tenis.
= She is going to play tennis.

Put in phrases to say when you're going to do it (see pages 4-5):

El sábado, vamos a ir a Francia.
= On Saturday, we are going to go to France.

2) You have to understand the proper Future Tense

This is another of those tenses where it's all about sticking endings onto something (the 'stem').

Future Tense Endings

I:	-é	*we:*	-emos
you (informal sing.):	-ás	*you (informal plural):*	-éis
he / she / it / you (formal sing.):	-á	*they / you (formal plural):*	-án

The conditional tense uses the same 'stems', but different endings.

Luckily, the 'stems' that you stick the endings onto are pretty easy:

1) For most verbs, you just stick the ending onto the infinitive (see page 164).

Jugaré al tenis. = I will play tennis.

Dormirás. = You will sleep.

Cogerá el autobús. = He will take the bus.

Venderemos el perro. = We will sell the dog.

2) These verbs don't follow the pattern. You have to learn them off by heart.

These are the most important ones:

VERB	STEM
decir	dir
haber	habr
hacer	har

VERB	STEM
poner	pondr
querer	querr
saber	sabr
venir	vendr

VERB	STEM
salir	saldr
tener	tendr
poder	podr

The first way of talking about the future is really easy

The proper future tense is harder than the top way of talking about the future — but it'll win you more marks. Make sure you can understand it, as it could turn up in the exam.

The Past (Perfect Tense)

Uh oh, it's the first of several past tenses now. The main thing is you need to make sure you can tell it apart from the future (page 171) and the present (page 165) tenses. You don't want to be stuck not knowing whether something has happened, is happening or is going to happen.

¿Qué has hecho? — What have you done?

You have to be able to make and understand sentences like this:

This is the perfect tense.

= I have played tennis.

There are two important bits:

1) You always need a bit to mean 'I have' — see the next page.

2) This bit means 'played'. It's a special version of 'jugar' (to play). In English, most of these words end in '-ed'. See below.

jugado = played: special past tense words

Learn the patterns for making the special past tense words like 'jugado' (played).

These are the past participles.

-ar verbs

FORMULA:

Remove '-ar', then add '-ado'

EXAMPLES:

jugar → jugado
to play — *played*

esperar → esperado
to wait — *waited*

-er/-ir verbs

FORMULA:

Remove '-er' or '-ir' then add '-ido'

EXAMPLES:

vender → vendido
to sell — *sold*

salir → salido
to leave — *left*

beber → bebido
to drink — *drunk*

elegir → elegido
to choose — *chosen*

Learn the perfect tense right now

This page isn't easy, but it's dead important — in the exams, you'll definitely need to talk or write about something that's happened in the past. Practise by writing these endings down until you know them.

The Past (Perfect Tense)

You've probably guessed by now that there'd be exceptions to the rule:

Some verbs don't follow the patterns

It's dead annoying when verbs don't follow the patterns, because a lot of the most useful verbs are irregular — you just have to learn them off by heart:

VERB	PAST TENSE VERSION*	TRANSLATION
abrir:	abierto	*opened*
cubrir:	cubierto	*covered*
decir:	dicho	*said*
descubrir:	descubierto	*found out / discovered*
escribir:	escrito	*written*
hacer:	hecho	*done / made*
poner:	puesto	*put*
romper:	roto	*broken*
ver:	visto	*seen*
volver:	vuelto	*returned*

* ie the past participle.

I have played: for 'have' use 'haber'

For the 'have' bit of these past tense phrases, you use the present tense of 'haber'.

haber = to have

I have:	he	*we have:*	hemos
you have (informal sing.):	has	*you have (informal plural):*	habéis
he / she / one has:	ha	*they / you have (formal plural):*	han
you have (formal sing.):	ha		

When 'haber' is used like this, it's called an auxiliary verb.

EXAMPLES: ***He ido al cine.*** = I have gone / been to the cinema.

(Ella) ha jugado al tenis. = She has played tennis.

Te has puesto muy feo. = You have become very ugly.

You just have to learn the irregular ones

Sit down and get this list of irregular verbs learnt. Test yourself by looking at the verb, then writing down its past tense version (past participle) and its meaning as well. Try it now, and see how well you do.

Another Past Tense — Did

Don't be scared by this tense — it looks scary but it's not too bad really.

¿Qué hiciste después? — What did you do next?

This is like saying 'I did', rather than 'I have done' — just take the stem of the infinitive, and add the following endings onto it:

This is the PRETERITE.

Preterite Endings for '-ar' verbs

I:	-é	*we:*	-amos
you (inf. sing.):	-aste	*you (inf. plu.):*	-asteis
he / she / it / you (form. sing.):	-ó	*they / you (form. plu):*	-aron

Preterite Endings for '-er' / '-ir' verbs

I:	-í	*we:*	-imos
you (inf. sing.):	-iste	*you (inf. plu.):*	-isteis
he / she / it / you (form. sing.):	-ió	*they / you:*	-ieron

Pasó toda la vida en Badajoz. = He spent all his life in Badajoz.

Watch out: The accents are really important. They can change the meaning of words — e.g. *'hablo'* = I speak, to *'habló'* = he spoke!

Nací en Portsmouth. = I was born in Portsmouth.

Bailamos hasta medianoche. = We danced until midnight.

There are four vital irregular verbs in the preterite

Typical — the words you'll need most often are the irregular ones.

Ser — to be / Ir — to go (they have the same preterite)

I was / went:	fui	*we were / went:*	fuimos
you were / went:	fuiste	*you were / went:*	fuisteis
he / she / it was / went you were / went:	fue	*they / you were / went:*	fueron

Estar — to be

I was:	estuve	*we were:*	estuvimos
you were:	estuviste	*you were:*	estuvisteis
you were /he / she / it was:	estuvo	*they / you were:*	estuvieron

Hacer — to do or make

I did / made:	hice	*we did / made:*	hicimos
you did / made:	hiciste	*you did / made:*	hicisteis
you / he / she / it did / made:	hizo	*they / you did / made:*	hicieron

Here are some other common irregular ones:

Infinitives	yo	el/ella/Vd.
dar	di	dio
decir	dije	dijo
poder	pude	pudo
poner	puse	puso
querer	quise	quiso
tener	tuve	tuvo
traer	traje	trajo
venir	vine	vino

EXAMPLES:

No dijeron nada. = They didn't say anything.

Dijiste que no te gustó. = You said you didn't like it.

¿Dónde pusiste el queso? = Where did you put the cheese?

If you've cracked the preterite, you're doing well

If you've got the hang of this, then you're well on your way to a top grade in the exam. Make sure that you learn the irregular ones — once again, they're all really common verbs, so you need to know them.

Quick Questions

Here's another lovely set of Quick Questions to test what you've learnt so far.

Quick Questions

1) Using the construction with "ir", fill in the gaps to show what these people will be doing.
   a) Tom y James … jugar para City.
   b) ¿Tú … bailar con María?
   c) Yo … hacer mis deberes.
   d) ¿Vds. … ir de vacaciones a Inglaterra?
   e) Paco … salir con Nuria.
2) Send an e-mail to your friend, in Spanish, to tell him/her what you will be doing during the holidays. Use the construction with "ir".
   Explain that you are going to go to Spain with your family, and that you are going to rent an apartment on the coast. You are going to go by plane and the flight is going to last two hours. You are going to be there for two weeks and your Dad is going to rent a car because you are all going to visit Gaudí's cathedral in Barcelona.
3) Put the verb in brackets into the correct form of the future tense.
   a) James y Tom (dormir) en el autocar.
   b) Eduardo y tú (coger) el autobús.
   c) Mi padre (vender) el perro.
   d) Tú y yo (ir) a la discoteca.
   e) Yo te (telefonear) mañana por la mañana.
4) Put the verb in brackets into the correct form of the future tense.
   a) Vd. (poner) un suéter.
   b) Nosotros lo (saber) más tarde.
   c) El tren no (salir) con retraso.
   d) Paco y María Dolores (venir) a la fiesta.
   e) María Dolores e Isabel (querer) ir también.
5) Write the past participles of the following verbs:
   a) mandar b) estudiar c) comer d) subir e) cerrar
6) Replace the infinitive with the correct past participle.
   a) ¿Has (abrir) todos tus regalos?
   b) ¿Qué ha (hacer) Vd. con mi toalla?
   c) No me han (escribir) una carta.
   d) Mis padres han (volver) del trabajo.
7) Answer the following questions by saying that you have already carried out the action suggested. Begin with the Spanish for 'already'.
   a) ¿Vas a ir a Mallorca?
   b) ¿Verás la Alhambra?
   c) ¿Comerás calamares?
   d) ¿Conocerás a Tomás?
8) Put the following sentences into Spanish:
   a) I have seen Gibraltar.
   b) We have already been to Barcelona.
   c) You have become very ugly whilst your sister has become very beautiful.

Quick Questions

You can't have too much practice when it comes to things like the past tense. Have a go at these Quick Questions as well, until you're really sure what you're doing when it comes to the perfect and the preterite tenses.

Quick Questions

9) Put the following sentences into Spanish:
   a) They have returned from their holiday.
   b) Have you told María Dolores that you have already bought the tickets?
   c) Excuse me, sir. Have you found my bracelet?

10) Put the verb in brackets into the correct form of the preterite tense.
   a) Eric y Bobby (jugar) al fútbol para United.
   b) ¿Tú (bailar) en la discoteca?
   c) Yo (pasar) quince días en España.
   d) ¿(Tomar) Vd. el tren?
   e) Paco (estudiar) medicina.
   f) Elena y yo (cenar) juntos.
   g) Pedro y tú (escuchar) la radio.
   h) Nuria e Isabel (comprar) sandalias nuevas.

11) How would you say the following in Spanish?
   a) We had lunch.
   b) He studied.
   c) I danced.
   d) She sang.
   e) You (formal, plural) listened.
   f) You (formal, singular) swam.
   g) You (informal, singular) and Nuria bought a bag.
   h) He spoke.

12) How would you say the following in Spanish?
   a) The waiter understood.
   b) I wrote to my family.
   c) Isabel opened the door.
   d) They went up to the fifth floor.
   e) We ate fried squid.

13) Put the following into English:
   a) Fuimos niños horribles pero fuimos a un buen instituto.
   b) Fue médico y fue a los Estados Unidos, donde estuvo durante doce años.
   c) Estuve diez años en el norte y en aquel entonces fui un chico trabajador pero cuando fui a la universidad me hice perezoso.
   d) ¿No fuiste de vacaciones? No, estuve enferma así que no fui. Aquel verano fue un desastre para mí.
   e) Fueron a ver a Natalia pero no estuvo en casa.

14) Send an e-mail to your friend, in Spanish, to tell him/her what you did during the holidays.
   Explain that you went to Spain with your family, and that you rented an apartment on the coast. You went by plane and the flight lasted two hours. You were there for two weeks but your Dad didn't rent a car because he got frightened of the traffic. So you caught the train. But he lost the tickets and he had to pay again. He was in a very bad mood that day and it was a disaster. He said that he would never return to Spain.

Imperfect Tense

...And another page of verbs. ...And another tense for talking about the past — you lucky thing!

What you were doing or used to do

This is the imperfect tense.

This is another dead useful one. There are 3 easy steps to making this tense:

1) Get the infinitive of the verb you want to use (see page 164).
2) Knock the '-ar', '-er' or '-ir' off the end to find the stem.
3) Add the correct ending from the 1st or 2nd list:

Imperfect Tense Endings for '-ar' verbs			
I:	-aba	*we:*	-ábamos
you (inf. sing.):	-abas	*you (inf. plu.):*	-abais
he / she / it / you (form. sing.):	-aba	*they / you (form. plu.):*	-aban

Imperfect Tense Endings for '-er'/'-ir' verbs			
I:	-ía	*we:*	-íamos
you (inf. sing.):	-ías	*you (inf. plu.):*	-íais
he / she / it / you (form. sing.):	-ía	*they / you (form. plu.):*	-ían

EXAMPLES: *I was doing / used to do*: hacer → hacía
He was speaking / used to speak: hablar → hablaba
We were / used to be: estar → estábamos

SOME GOOD NEWS: there are only 3 verbs that don't follow the pattern — ser, ir, and ver.

Ir = to go	
I used to go =	iba
you (inf. sing.) used to go =	ibas
he / she / it used to go =	iba
you (form. sing.) used to go =	iba
we used to go =	íbamos
you (inf. plu.) used to go =	ibais
they / you (form. plu.) used to go =	iban

Ser = to be	
I used to be =	era
you (inf. sing.) used to be =	eras
he / she / it used to be =	era
you (form. sing.) used to be =	era
we used to be =	éramos
you (inf. plu.) used to be =	erais
they / you (form. plu.) used to be =	eran

VER is almost regular, just add normal '-er' endings onto 've-', e.g. 'veía'.

Había... — There was... Era... — It was...

'Había' is the imperfect version of 'hay'. And instead of using 'es' (it is), you can use 'era' (it was).

Hay un mono en el árbol. = There is a monkey in the tree.

Había un mono en el árbol. = There was a monkey in the tree.

Es demasiado caro. = It is too expensive.

Era demasiado caro. = It was too expensive.

WHEN TO USE THE IMPERFECT

1) What you used to do by habit / repeatedly in the past: ***Iba al cine cada jueves.*** = I used to go to the cinema every Thursday.

2) Descriptions about something in the past, including what was going on when something else happened:

Hacía mucho calor. = It was very hot.

Saqué una foto mientras dormía. = I took a photo while she was sleeping.

Use the preterite tense for the key event, and the imperfect tense for the on-going situation.

Can there be any more past tenses to learn?

By now you're probably getting a bit fed up. There's a lot to learn here, and you're probably wishing the Spanish had invented a simpler language. Don't panic, just learn the endings, and it'll be ok.

The Conditional Tense

You've probably been using the conditional tense quite a lot without realising it.

The Conditional Tense: What would you do?

The conditional tense (for saying 'would') uses the stems from the future tense (see page 171) and adds the imperfect endings like '-ía' (see page 177).

For regular verbs: **INFINITIVE + IMPERFECT 'ía' endings = CONDITIONAL**

EXAMPLES:

hablaría — *I would speak.*

beberían — *They would drink.*

viviríamos — *We would live.*

Compraría un helado. = I would buy an ice-cream.

Deberías escribirme. = You should write to me.

Nos gustaría salir. = We would like to go out.

Some verbs don't follow the regular pattern, so you need:

FUTURE STEM + IMPERFECT 'ía' endings = CONDITIONAL

EXAMPLE:

¿Podría usted ayudarme?
= Could you help me?

Just go back and learn the list of stems on page 171 — 'dir', 'habr', 'har' etc. Write them out with the new endings here to get a list of conditional verbs to learn.

Two really common verbs often get replaced in the conditional by a different form.

querría = quisiera.

habría = hubiera.

EXAMPLES:

Quisiera reservar una mesa para tres personas. = I would like to reserve a table for three.

Te hubiera ayudado antes. = I would have helped you sooner.

Don't lose your concentration — this is important

Don't get confused between the conditional and the future or the imperfect. Watch out for 'quisiera' — you'll use this one quite a lot, and it's a bit unusual. Just learn it and use it.

Reflexive Verbs

Sometimes you'll have to talk about things you do to yourself — like 'washing yourself'.

Talking about yourself — me, te, se...

'Se' means 'oneself'. Here are all the different ways to say 'self':

myself:	me	*yourself (form. sing):*	se
yourself (inf. sing.):	te	*ourselves:*	nos
himself:	se	*yourselves (inf. plu.):*	os
herself:	se	*themselves, each other:*	se
oneself:	se	*yourselves (form. plu.):*	se

You can tell which verbs need 'self' by checking in the dictionary — they're the ones that end in 'se'. If you look up 'to wash', it'll say 'lavarse'.

Me lavo — I wash myself

These verbs are useful for talking about daily routine stuff... All you've got to do is learn the pattern:

lavarse = to wash oneself

I wash myself =	me lavo	nos lavamos	*= we wash ourselves*
you wash yourself (inf. sing.) =	te lavas	os laváis	*= you wash yourselves (inf. plu.)*
he washes himself / she washes herself / one washes oneself / you wash yourself (form. sing.) =	se lava	se lavan	*they wash themselves / = you wash yourselves (form. plu.)*

There are lots of these verbs, but here are the ones you should know for the exam:

8 IMPORTANT REFLEXIVE VERBS	EXAMPLES
to go to bed: acostarse	Me acuesto a las once. = *I go to bed at 11 o'clock.*
to get up: levantarse	Me levanto a las ocho. = *I get up at 8 o'clock.*
to feel: sentirse	¿Te sientes mal? = *Do you feel ill?*
to be called (literally = to call oneself): llamarse	Me llamo Bob. = *I'm called Bob. (literally = I call myself Bob)*
to wake up: despertarse	Me despierto muy temprano. = *I wake up very early.*
to be spelt: escribirse	¿Cómo se escribe? = *How is that spelt?*
to go away: irse	Se va por la mañana. = *He's leaving in the morning.*
to wear: vestirse	Siempre se viste de negro. = *She always wears black.*

Perfect tense reflexive verbs are pretty easy

When you want to use reflexive verbs in the perfect tense, you just put the 'me', 'se' or whatever, in front of all the bits of the verb as usual:

Ponerse (to put on): ***Me he puesto el sombrero.*** = I've put the hat on.

Stick the 'me' at the start. Then put the whole of the perfect tense verb (see page 172).

¿Se habla español?

Here's another use of 'se' — to be impersonal. Instead of saying someone does something, it says that things have something done to them. It can also mean 'one' — e.g. 'Can one come in?'

Las puertas se abren a las nueve. = The doors are opened at nine.

¿Se puede entrar? = Can one come in?

Even more grammar to get to grips with here

Reflexive verbs are pretty common in Spanish. If you don't learn them, you're going to look a bit silly when you can't talk about things like washing, getting up, or what you're wearing.

Negatives

This stuff's easy enough. Well, most of it is...

Use 'no' to say not

In English you change a sentence to mean the opposite by adding 'not'. For example, 'I am Bob' → 'I am not Bob'. In Spanish, you put 'no' in front of the action word (verb).

Soy Bob. = I am Bob. *No soy Bob.* = I am not Bob.

This is the verb. The 'no' goes in front, easy.

Tricky Stuff

You do the same with all the tenses. For example, the perfect tense goes:

No lo he visto. = I have not seen that.

Ella no ha llegado. = She has not arrived.

Tricky Stuff

No, I don't!

'No' in Spanish means both 'no' and 'not', so answering a question, you may need to say 'no' twice:

No, no quiero pulpo, gracias. = No, I don't want any octopus, thanks.

No, prefiero no ver una película. = No, I prefer not to see a film.

No ... nunca — never, no ... nada — nothing

There are more negatives you need to understand, and for top marks you should use them too.

No voy más a York. = I don't go to York any more. (I no longer go to York.)

No voy nunca a York. = I never go to York. (I don't ever go to York.)

No voy ni a York ni a Belfast. = I neither go to York nor to Belfast.

not any more: no ... más *(no longer)*

not ever: no ... nunca *(never)*

neither ... nor: no ... ni ... ni

not anybody: no ... nadie *(nobody)*

not anything: no ... nada *(nothing)*

not any, not one: no ... ningún / ninguna *(not a single...)*

No hay nadie aquí. = There isn't anybody here. (There is nobody here.)

Aquí no hay nada. = There isn't anything here. (There is nothing here.)

No hay ningún plátano. = There aren't any bananas. (There is not a single banana.)

No, nobody, never, nothing and not — don't be too negative

Good news — it's nowhere near as bad as it looks. It seems confusing because you need 'no' with everything — but it actually helps you spot negative sentences. Write them down and see.

Present Subjunctive

OK, I'll admit it. This is tricky stuff. But it's very important if you want a top grade.

Quisiera — I would like

Remember this? It's handy for being polite, instead of saying 'I want' all the time.

Quisiera leche. = I would like some milk.

Quisiera ir al hospital. = I would like to go to the hospital.

The subjunctive is more like a mood than a tense

This isn't another tense, but a different mood, and Spanish speakers are really keen on it. In fact, there's so much to learn, I can only try and give you an idea of it here. If you can manage to use it a bit, it could add the * to your 'A'. Just use the 'I' person and add the endings:

	hablar (hablo – I speak)	comer (como – I eat)	vivir (vivo – I live)	tener (tengo – I have)
I	hable	coma	viva	tenga
you (inf. sing.)	hables	comas	vivas	tengas
he / she/ it / you (form. sing.)	hable	coma	viva	tenga
we	hablemos	comamos	vivamos	tengamos
you (inf. plur.)	habléis	comáis	viváis	tengáis
they / you (form. plur.)	hablen	coman	vivan	tengan

When a sentence has two linked subjects, the verb belonging to the second subject is often put into the subjunctive.

Elena quiere que Jorge lave los platos. = Elena wants Jorge to wash the dishes. (i.e. Elena wants that Jorge should wash the dishes.)

The rules and reasons are too tricky to go into — just learn these common examples:

1. Trying to get someone else to do something, or trying to stop them: ***Espero que me escribas pronto.*** = I hope (that) you will write to me soon.
2. After expressing an emotion or opinion about something : ***Me alegro de que podáis venir mañana.*** = I'm pleased that you can come tomorrow.
3. After any doubts: ***Dudamos que el tren llegue a tiempo.*** = We doubt that the train will arrive on time.
4. When there is a need or requirement: ***Necesito a un amigo que sepa cocinar.*** = I need a friend who knows how to cook.
5. When talking about a vague future: ***Cuando sea mayor, quiero ser bombero.*** = When I'm grown up, I want to be a fireman.
6. After the phrases 'para que' (so that), 'antes de que' (before), 'como si' (as if) and 'aunque' (even if):

   Vamos a la playa para que veas el mar. = We're going to the beach so that you can see the sea.

Tricky Stuff Tricky Stuff Tricky Stuff Tricky Stuff

Now it's getting more complicated, but you can still do it

Things like the subjunctive sound really scary, but a lot of that is to do with the name. The endings aren't hard, and you can learn when you need to use it quite easily. Just don't panic.

Quick Questions

You're not far from the end now, but there's still some important grammar left to learn.

Quick Questions

1) What does 'había' mean in English?

2) Put these sentences into the imperfect tense.

   a) Hay un cine en el pueblo.
   b) Aquellos zapatos son demasiado caros.
   c) Es muy duro estudiar.
   d) Hay mucha gente en la calle.

3) Put the verb in brackets into the correct form of the imperfect tense.

   a) Mis abuelos (vivir) en Londres.
   b) ¿Qué tiempo (hacer)?
   c) Tú y yo (telefonear) a nuestros padres todos los días.
   d) Mi abuela me (hablar) de su pasado.
   e) Cuando yo (ser) joven (ayudar) a mi madre.
   f) ¿(Salir) tú con mi amiga?
   g) A veces mi familia y yo (ir) al zoo donde (mirar) los monos que (comer) los cacahuetes que nosotros les (lanzar).
   h) Nuestros abuelos nos (dar) siempre regalos estupendos que nosotros (abrir) muy rápidamente.

4) What do the following mean in English?

   a) Yo diría que sí. b) Saldríamos todos juntos. c) Podrían venir en agosto.
   d) Tendrías que llevar tu pasaporte. e) Me pondría ropa de lana.

5) Put the verb in brackets into the correct form of the conditional tense.

   a) Mi hermano no (lavar) los platos.
   b) Mi padre no (comprar) un coche nuevo.
   c) Yo (cambiar) moneda extranjera en el banco.
   d) Elena y yo (empezar) otra vez mañana.
   e) Yo no (beber) el agua.

6) Write down the Spanish for:

   a) to wake up b) to get up c) to go to bed

7) Put the correct form of the reflexive pronoun in the following sentences:

   a) Yo … siento mal.
   b) Tú … despiertas temprano.
   c) Tu hermana y tú … vais por la mañana.
   d) Mi prima y mi hermana … llaman Teresa.
   e) Mi familia y yo … acostamos tarde.
   f) Mi abuela siempre … viste de negro.

8) What do the following sentences mean in English?

   a) Voy a acostarme tarde.
   b) Mi amiga española se fue el martes pasado.
   c) Todos los días nos levantábamos temprano.
   d) ¿Os vais a duchar ahora?
   e) Mi padre se despertó tarde esta mañana, no se afeitó pero se fue al trabajo.

Quick Questions

This page has scary things like the subjunctive on it. Remember to go back and re-read the section if you get the answers wrong. It's not too scary once you've learnt it.

Quick Questions

9) Write an e-mail in Spanish to your friend describing your daily routine. Say what time you wake up, when you get up, whether you have a wash or shower, when you have breakfast, what time you go off to school, what time you return home, when you have your evening meal and what time you go to bed.

10) What do the following sentences mean in English?
   a) Se puede aparcar en la plaza.
   b) Aquí se habla inglés.
   c) El banco se abre a las nueve y media y se cierra a las doce del mediodía.
   d) No se puede entrar.
   e) ¡Se dice que es loca!
   f) En España se cena a eso de las diez.

11) Turn these sentences into the negative:
   a) Mi hermano lavó los platos. b) Mi padre ha comprado un coche nuevo.
   c) Cambié mis cheques de viaje en el banco. d) Bebió mucho.
   e) Van a ir a la piscina con nosotros.

12) Your friend is feeling rather miserable and tells you:
   "No voy más a la discoteca porque no hay ningún autobús después de las diez. No voy al cine porque no hay nada interesante. No voy ni a la discoteca ni al cine así que no veo a nadie."
   Why is your friend so miserable?

13) You want to moan to your friend in Spain. Say:
   "There's nothing to do here. There's nobody interesting. I never see my friends. I would like a sandwich but there's neither bread nor butter and there's not a single chocolate in the house."

14) Put the infinitive into the correct form of the subjunctive:
   a) Elena quiere que yo (pasar) la aspiradora.
   b) Me alegro de que tú y yo (poder) salir juntos.
   c) Dudo que la discoteca (estar) abierta ahora.
   d) Necesitamos una persona que (saber) conducir un camión.
   e) Cuando (ser) rica, compraré una pulsera de oro.
   f) Vamos a España para que yo (mejorar) mi español.
   g) No creo que Nuria y tú (tener) problemas.
   h) Espero que Vds. (hablar) mucho español.

15) Translate the following dialogue into English:
   A: Me alegro de que seamos amigos, pero espero que cuando tengas mucho dinero no me olvides.
   B: ¡Claro que no! Pero no creo que eso sea posible y dudo que suceda, sobre todo porque, antes de que yo pueda ganar, es necesario que compre un billete de la lotería.

Imperative

You need to understand this, and for top marks you need to be able to do it yourself too.

You need this stuff for bossing people about

This is called the imperative.

The single informal bit's easy — it's just like the 'tú' part of the present tense but without the 's' at the end.

hablas = you speak *bebes* = you drink. *escribes* = you write. *¡Escucha esto!* = Listen to this!

¡Habla! = Speak! *¡Bebe!* = Drink! *¡Escribe!* = Write!

There are a few common irregular ones:

decir	hacer	ir	oír	poner	salir	tener	venir
di	haz	ve	oye	pon	sal	ten	ven

It seems really odd, but if you want to tell several people what to do, you take the infinitive and change the final 'r' to a 'd', even with the irregular ones:

hablar ➡ *¡Hablad!* *salir* ➡ *¡Salid!* *hacer* ➡ *¡Haced!* *escribir* ➡ *¡Escribid!* *beber* ➡ *¡Bebed!*

¡Terminad vuestros deberes! = Finish your homework!

Politely telling people what to do

This can be more difficult. You have to take the 'I' person of the verb in the present tense, and change the last 'o' to an 'a' or an 'e', whichever is the opposite ending to the one you would expect. Confused? The examples should help: *hablo* ➡ *¡Hable!* *como* ➡ *¡Coma!* *escribo* ➡ *¡Escriba!*

Siga todo recto. = Continue straight on.

(seguir ➡ sigo)

Coja la primera a la derecha. = Take the first on the right.

(coger ➡ cojo)

At least the polite plural is easy — just add an 'n' as usual:

¡Hablen! ¡Coman! ¡Escriban!

And the only real exceptions are:

dar	haber	ir	saber	ser
dé	haya	vaya	sepa	sea

If you tell someone to do something, any pronouns (me, it, them etc.) are stuck on the end, in the normal word order:

Te levantas. = You get up. *¡Levántate!* = Get up! *Me lo trae.* = You bring it to me. *¡Traígamelo!* = Bring it to me!

Add 'no' for saying what not to do

Orders where you say no are in the subjunctive.

Also, change the normal endings to their opposites in all cases: *¡No escuches!* = Don't listen!

And move any pronouns from the end to the beginning: *¡Tócalo!* = Touch it! *¡No lo toques!* = Don't touch it!

It's imperative that you learn this

Seriously, you do need to be able to order people around. Spanish people use the imperative quite a lot. You can do it politely though — no need to sound like you're badly brought up.

Saber, Conocer and Poder

Here are three really useful verbs that people are always getting wrong — make sure you don't.

'To know information' is 'Saber'

1) Saber means 'to know', in the sense of having learnt something (like how to play the piano), or knowing information (eg knowing what time the bus leaves).

   Have a look at these examples:

Ella sabe la respuesta a la pregunta.	*She knows the answer to the question.*
No sé si tenemos plátanos.	*I don't know if we have any bananas.*
¿Sabe usted cuándo llega el tren?	*Do you know when the train arrives?*

2) Saber followed by an infinitive means *'to know how to do something'*, in the sense of a skill, for example:

   Sabe esquiar. = He knows how to ski.

   No sabe leer. = She cannot read.

   Sé conducir. = I can drive.

IMPORTANT: '**saber**' is a regular verb in the present tense, except for the '**I**' **person**, which is '**sé**'.

'To be familiar with' is 'Conocer'

Conocer means to know a person or place — 'to be familiar with'.
If someone asks you if you know their mate Gertrude, this is the one to use.

Conozco Madrid. = I know Madrid.

No conoce esta ciudad. = He doesn't know this town.

¿Conoces a mi amigo? = Do you know my friend?

IMPORTANT: like 'saber', '**conocer**' is also a **normal verb** with an **odd** '**I**' **person** = '**conozco**'.

'To be able to' is 'Poder'

Poder (*to be able to / can*) has three very important meanings:

1) Being able to do something (not knowing how to do it, but just being able to — like 'Yes, I can come tomorrow').

   Si quieres, puedo llevar el equipaje. = I can carry the luggage if you like.

2) Permission to do something. ***Se pueden sacar fotos aquí.*** = You can take photos here.

3) Possibility — something could be the case. ***Eso puede pasar.*** = That can happen.

Learn these three verbs and learn how to use them

Three mega-handy verbs that you need to sort out. Don't forget the difference between saber and conocer, and make sure that you know the three meanings of poder. Wonderful stuff...

Pluperfect, Present Participle and Acabar de

Three more bits to learn — you may come across them in the listening or reading papers.

Había hecho — 'I had done'

This is the pluperfect tense.

1) You need to be able to understand this if it comes up in the reading or listening exams.
2) It's similar to the perfect tense (see page 172) — that's for saying what you have done, but this is for saying what you had done.
3) It's still made of a bit of haber + a past participle, but the bit of 'haber' is in the imperfect tense.

For stuff on the imperfect tense, see p. 177.

Imperfect tense of haber + past participle

Betty había llegado. = Betty had arrived.

Había escrito una carta. = I had written a letter.

Doing, saying, thinking are present participles

Most of the time you'd translate things like 'I am doing' and 'I was doing' with normal tenses — those two would be 'hago' (present tense), and 'hacía' (imperfect tense). But sometimes you want to stress that something is ongoing at the moment, or was ongoing in the past.

For example: ***Estoy almorzando.*** = I'm having my lunch.

Estaba durmiendo cuando sonó el teléfono. = He was sleeping when the phone rang.

There are two bits to this:

a) the correct part of 'estar' (to be) in the present or the imperfect tense, and

b) the special word to describe the 'ing' bit — called the present participle.

'-ar' verbs e.g. hablar	'-er' verbs e.g. comer	'-ir' verbs e.g. vivir
stem (e.g. habl) + ando	stem (e.g. com) + iendo	stem (e.g. viv) + iendo
hablando	comiendo	viviendo

There are only a few irregular ones:

1) caer → estoy cayendo (I'm falling).
2) leer → estamos leyendo (we're reading).

Also worth remembering are:

servir → sirviendo
dormir → durmiendo
pedir → pidiendo
morir → muriendo

Acabo de... — 'I have just...'

To say what's just happened, use the present tense of 'acabar' + 'de' + the verb you want in the infinitive.

acabar: to finish

acabo	acabamos
acabas	acabáis
acaba	acaban

Acabo de ducharme. = I have just taken a shower.

Acaba de salir. = She has just left.

This is the last page of things to learn — hurrah!

Don't relax just yet, though. We've slotted in quite a few important things on this last page. Don't skip straight on to the Quick Questions until you're sure you've absorbed these last vital bits.

Quick Questions

This is the final set of Quick Questions in the entire book. Keep going, you're nearly there.

Quick Questions

1) What do you do in order to obey these commands?
Which are formal and which informal?
a) ¡Levante la mano! b) ¡Abre la ventanilla! c) ¡Escuchen!
d) ¡Ven aquí! e) ¡Haced vuestros deberes! f) ¡Pon la mesa!

2) Make these "tú" form commands into "vosotros" commands.
a) ¡Sal de aquí en seguida! b) ¡Ven con nosotros!
c) ¡Levanta la mano! d) ¡Termina los deberes!
e) ¡Ten cuidado! f) ¡Espera en la parada de autobús!

3) Turn these infinitives into formal commands using "Vds."
a) Dejar las llaves en Recepción. b) Coger la segunda a la izquierda.
c) Seguir todo recto. d) Ir con Dios.
e) Hablar más despacio. f) Aprender los verbos.

4) What do the following mean?
a) ¡Viva el Rey! b) ¡Aparque el coche en la plaza!
c) ¡Pague cuando se vaya! d) ¡Dé este paquete a sus padres!

5) How would you make these commands negative? Tell the person not to do it.
a) ¡Hable! b) ¡Coman en clase! c) ¡Escriban en la mesa!
d) ¡Arrojen papeles! e) ¡Duerma aquí!

6) Tell your friend not to do the following:
a) ¡Habla! b) ¡Come en clase! c) ¡Vende el gato!
d) ¡Escucha! e) ¡Nada en el río! f) ¡Duerme aquí!

7) Convert the following questions into commands. Be careful because you may need a stress mark.
a) ¿Te levantas? b) ¿Te vas? c) ¿Te acuestas?
d) ¿Me ayudas? e) ¿Te pones un suéter? f) ¿Le llamas?
g) ¿Le escribes una carta? h) ¿Me dices la verdad?
i) ¿Me das tu número de teléfono?

8) How would you say the following in Spanish, using the "tú" form? You may need some stress marks.
a) Go away! b) Phone me! c) Tell me when!
d) Leave me your phone number! e) Send me a message!

9) "¿Sabes cuándo sale el tren?" asks your friend.
Say that you don't know but that your mother knows.

10) "¿Cómo se dice 'London' en español?" asks your teacher.
Reply: 'We all know that.'

11) Your friend sends you an e-mail.
"Yo sé esquiar pero en este momento no puedo porque me he roto la pierna … ¡esquiando!" What are you being told?

12) Tell your friend that you can swim but you can't at the moment because you have flu.

13) "¿Conoces a mi amiga Elena?" asks your friend. Reply that you don't know her but say "Pleased to meet you, Elena."

14) Translate this conversation, putting your part into Spanish and your friend's into English:
You: Ask your friend if (s)he knows Madrid.
Friend: No conozco Madrid pero conozco muy bien La Coruña.
¿Conoces Londres?
You: Say that you know it very well.

Quick Questions

Don't skip these questions just because they're the last ones. It won't take you long to do them, honest.

Quick Questions

15) A friend asks:
"¿Puedes ir a la discoteca esta tarde?"
What are you being asked?

16) Ask your friend's mother if you and María Dolores can go out clubbing tonight.

17) Her mother replies: "Pues no, no podéis, porque hemos reservado una mesa en el restaurante para toda la familia esta tarde para celebrar el cumpleaños del hermano de María Dolores."
What has María Dolores' mother just told you?

18) Your friend asks:
"¿Puedes ayudarme con mis deberes de inglés?"
What are you being asked?

19) Say to your friend: "I can help you if you want."

20) Write a short passage in Spanish explaining that you could go to Ibiza in the summer but that you know Ibiza very well. You could go to Italy but that you can't speak Italian.

21) Translate the following sentences into English:
a) Sonia había llegado.
b) Habíamos terminado.
c) Yo todavía no había comido pulpo.
d) Mis amigos ya se habían ido.
e) ¿Le habías llamado a Elena por teléfono?

22) Translate the following into Spanish:
We had arrived very late because we had had a terrible journey. It had rained all day and we had stopped at a service station but I hadn't eaten anything. A journey that normally lasts two hours had lasted six.

23) "¿Dónde está Pedro? ¿Qué hace?"
Where is he? What is he doing? Translate these sentences.
a) Está comiendo.
b) Está durmiendo.
c) Está leyendo el periódico.
d) Está sirviendo en el bar.
e) Está jugando al fútbol en la playa.

24) You are asked "¿Qué estás haciendo?" Reply that:
a) you are having your lunch.
b) you are talking to Ricardo.
c) you are doing your Spanish homework.
d) you are washing up.

25) What do the following mean in English?
a) Estábamos buscando el apartamento.
b) Elena estaba escribiendo una carta cuando llegó Ricardo.
c) Mis amigos estaban pasándolo bien cantando y bailando.

26) Translate the following sentences:
a) Acabo de lavarme.
b) Pedro e Isabel acaban de salir.
c) Acabamos de dar un paseo.
d) María Dolores acaba de coger el vuelo de regreso para Madrid.

27) How would you say, in Spanish?
a) I have just phoned Isabel.
b) She has just left.
c) They have just come back.
d) We have just finished all the exercises!

Revision Summary

The stuff in this section really helps you to put words together to say what you want to. The way to make sure you've learnt it is to check you can do all these questions. Try them all, and look up any you can't do. Then try them all again. Keep doing that until you can answer all of them. THEN you'll really know your Spanish grammar.

1) How do you say these in Spanish?
a) I have b) she has c) they have d) I am e) he is f) we are

2) What letter do Spanish infinitives end in?

3) What do each of these phrases mean? a) 'Como un pastel' b) 'He comido un pastel'
c) 'Comí un pastel' d) 'Comía un pastel' e) 'Voy a comer un pastel f) 'Comeré un pastel'
g) 'Comería un pastel'.

4) How would you say these in Spanish?
a) 'I like to eat a cake.' b) 'I will eat a cake next year.' c) 'I had eaten a cake.'

5) Fill in the missing Spanish words (past participles). I've done the first one for you.
a) to make/do = hacer; made/done = hecho
b) to buy = comprar; bought = ? c) to ask = pedir; asked = ?
d) to finish = terminar; finished = ? e) to sell = vender; sold = ?

6) How do you say these in Spanish? a) I have gone. b) I have come.

7) This means 'I'm called Jim' — 'Me llamo Jim'. How would you say these in Spanish?
a) She's called Sarah. b) You're called (informal singular) Marigold.
c) We're called Hopkins. d) You're called (formal) Fitzgerald.

8) How do you say these in Spanish? a) I don't go out. b) I never go out.

9) How do you say these in Spanish? a) Get out! b) Let's go out! c) Come here!

10) How do you say in Spanish that you don't know how to ride a horse?

11) For each word, write out a sentence in Spanish that includes it: a) nada b) ni...ni.

12) How do you say in Spanish 'I had eaten 3 loaves of bread'?

13) How do you say these in Spanish? a) I'm swimming in the sea. b) I'm eating a sandwich.

14) What does this sentence mean? 'Acabo de llegar.'

15) Write out these sentences in Spanish:
a) I have just left. b) She has just said 'hello'. c) We have just started.

Practice Exam

Once you've been through all the questions in this book, you should feel pretty confident about the exam. As final preparation, here's a **practice exam** to prepare you for the real thing. It's split into **four papers** — listening, speaking, reading and writing. It's designed to give you the best exam practice possible for all the different question styles, whichever syllabus you're following. If you're doing Foundation you won't have learnt every bit, but it's still good practice.

General Certificate of Secondary Education

CGP Practice Exam Paper GCSE Spanish

GCSE
Spanish

Centre name					
Centre number					
Candidate number					

Listening Paper

Surname
Other names
Candidate signature

Time allowed: 40 minutes approximately
+ 5 minutes reading time before the test

Instructions to candidates

- Write in black or blue ink or ballpoint pen.
- Before the CD is started, you will be allowed **five** minutes during which you may read through the questions. You may make notes in this time.
- Answer **all** questions in the spaces provided.
- Answer the **section A** questions in **Spanish.**
- Answer the **section B** questions in **English.**
- Give all the information you are asked for, and **write neatly**.
- The marks are shown by each question.
- The maximum mark for this paper is 40.

This is what you should do for each item:

- Before each new question, please read through the relevant instructions and question parts.
- Listen carefully to the recording. There will be a pause to allow you to read the questions again, make notes, or write down your answers.
- Listen to the recording again. There will be another pause to allow you to complete or check your answers.
- You may write at any time.
- You will hear a single tone at the end of each item.

The use of dictionaries is not permitted.

Instructions for person working the CD

- One track on the CD = one question.
- There are 9 questions, covered on the CD by tracks 21-29.

Question No.	1	2	3	4	5	6	7	8	9
CD Track No.	21	22	23	24	25	26	27	28	29

- Please give students 5 minutes at the start to read through the exam. Then allow students to read the instructions and question parts for Question 1.
- You may then begin to play the CD, one track at a time, stopping the CD after each track.
- Please play each track through twice, allowing a short pause between each playing.

Leave blank

SECCIÓN A

Preguntas y respuestas **en español**.

1 La compra. ¿Adónde va Carla, y qué problema tiene su padre?

Escribe las letras correctas en las casillas.

a) Primero se va:
A a la panadería
B a la carnicería
C al mercado
D a la pescadería

☐

(1 mark)

b) Después se va:
A al supermercado
B a la tienda de ropa
C a la zapatería
D a la heladería

☐

(1 mark)

c) Finalmente se va:
A a la librería
B al estanco
C a la farmacia
D a la pastelería

☐

(1 mark)

d) ¿Dónde le duele a su padre?

A **B** **C** **D**

Escribe la letra correcta en esta casilla. ☐

(1 mark)

Turn over

Lea
blar

2 El tiempo libre.

¿Por qué Alvaro no puede salir el sábado por la noche?

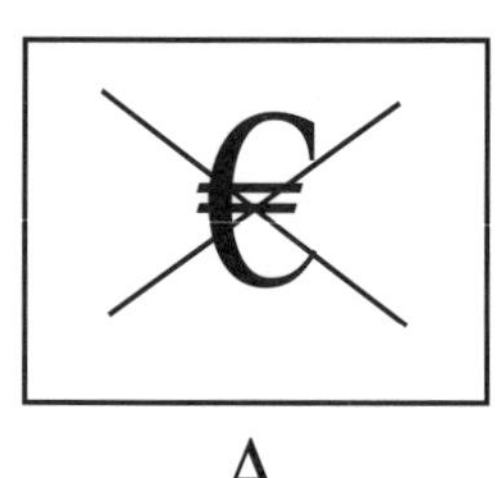
A

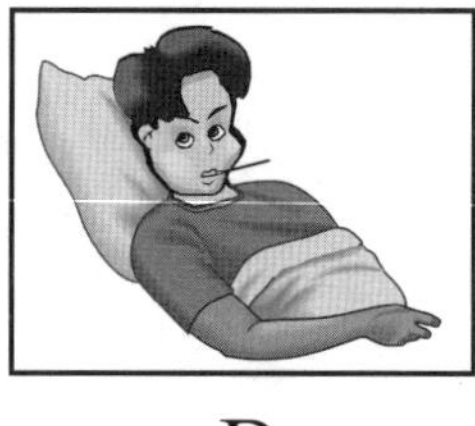
B

C

D

Escribe la letra correcta en esta casilla. ☐ *(1 mark)*

3 En el restaurante.
¿Cuál es la opinión de los jóvenes sobre el restaurante?

Escribe **P** (Positiva)
N (Negativa)
P+N (Positiva y Negativa)

Ejemplo	**Emilia**	**N**
a)	**Alicia**	
b)	**Manuela**	
c)	**Carlos**	

(3 marks)

Leave blank

4 Unos amigos españoles están haciendo planes.
¿Cuándo se encontrarán? ¿A qué hora? Y, ¿cuáles son sus números de teléfono?
Rellena la tabla **en español**.

	¿Cuándo?	**¿A qué hora?**	**Número de teléfono**
Ejemplo	**4 de febrero**	**9.30**	**92 21 33**
a)			
b)			
c)			

(9 marks)

5 ¿Qué piensan los alumnos de sus asignaturas? Rellena la tabla **en español**.

	¿Le gusta?	**¿Por qué?**	**¿No le gusta?**	**¿Por qué?**
Encarna	historia			muy complicadas
Raúl		la profesora es buena	ciencias	
Elena		le encanta el baloncesto		inútil
Rosa	informática			

(9 marks)

Turn over

Leave blank

6 ¿Dónde está?

Mira el mapa. Estás en la cruz. ¿Dónde está:

Ejemplo **A** la oficina de turismo?
B el castillo?
C el mercado?
D la biblioteca?

Escribe las letras correctas en cada casilla.

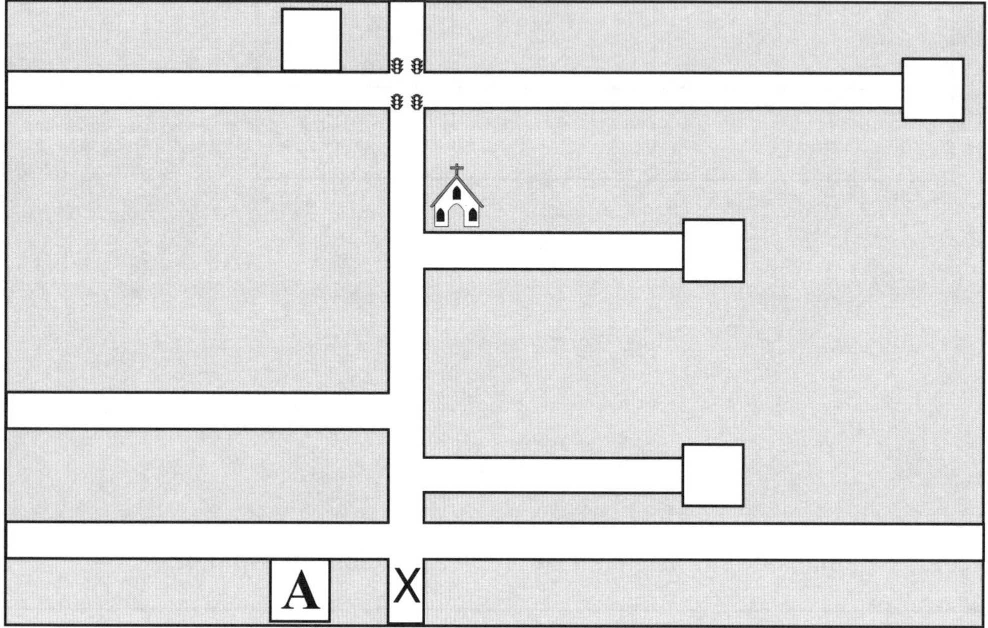

(3 marks)

Leave blank

7 En la estación de ferrocarril.

Escribe la letra correcta en cada casilla.

a) El tren llega a Madrid:

A a las tres
B a las diez y veinte
C a las ocho
D a las doce y media

☐ *(1 mark)*

b) El señor quiere:

A un billete sencillo
B dos billetes de ida y vuelta
C dos billetes de ida
D un billete de primera clase

☐ *(1 mark)*

c) En total cuesta:

A 9,40 €
B 5,50 €
C 1,20 €
D 4,90 €

☐ *(1 mark)*

d) El señor busca:

A los servicios
B la sala de espera
C un teléfono
D la cafetería

☐ *(1 mark)*

Turn over

SECTION B

Questions and answers **in English**.

Leave blank

8 Víctor and María are discussing what teenagers eat.

a) i) What does Víctor think of teenagers' diets today?

....

(1 mark)

ii) Give a reason for your answer.

....

....

(1 mark)

b) Does María agree? .... *(1 mark)*

Give a reason for your answer.

....

....

(1 mark)

Leave blank

9 Puri is talking about where she lives.

a) Which word best describes Puri's town?

A boring
B dirty
C pretty
D interesting

Write the correct letter in this box. ☐

(1 mark)

b) i) What does Puri think her town will be like in the future?

....

(1 mark)

ii) Give a reason for your answer.

....

....

(1 mark)

END OF TEST

General Certificate of Secondary Education

GCSE Spanish

Speaking Paper

Centre name					
Centre number					
Candidate number					

Surname
Other names
Candidate signature

- This paper contains 2 role-plays and 1 list of topics for general conversation.

Instructions to candidates for role-plays
- Find a friend or parent to read the teacher's parts for you.
- You will have a few minutes to read through your task before the role-play begins.
- Make sure you answer the questions asked by your teacher.
- Try and be as clear as possible in your answers.
- The use of dictionaries is not permitted.

Instructions to candidates for conversation
- The teacher has a list of questions to ask you in conversation.
- You will not have the opportunity to prepare answers for this conversation.
- Try to answer all the questions asked by your teacher.
- Try and be as clear as possible in your answers.

Instructions to teachers
- It is essential that you give the student every opportunity to complete their tasks.
- You may change the target language phrases if the student's response makes this necessary, but you must remember not to provide students with any key vocabulary.
- In the general conversation, questions have been given as a suggestion, and the conversation should be allowed to flow naturally if the occasion arises.

Leave blank

ROLE PLAY 1 (HIGHER TIER)

CANDIDATE'S ROLE

You are discussing holidays with a Spanish friend who wants to go skiing with you at Christmas, but you cannot go then.

- Tu problema y tu razón
- !
- Tus vacaciones del año pasado (**dos** detalles).
- Tus planes para septiembre (**dos** detalles).

When you see this –!– you will have to respond to something which you have not prepared.

Your teacher will play the part of your friend and will speak first.

(16 marks)

AQA, 2004

Leave blank

ROLE PLAY 1 (HIGHER TIER)

TEACHER'S ROLE

- Because the candidate's role is unstructured, it is essential that you are clear about the tasks which the candidate must accomplish.
- You may change the target language phrases given below if necessary, for example if the candidate's response makes them inappropriate.
- Remember that **if you supply key vocabulary, candidates cannot be rewarded for it**.

---

1 Begin the conversation by introducing the situation and then ask the candidate if he/she wants to go skiing at Christmas.

Estás hablando con tu amigo español/tu amiga española. Yo soy tu amigo/amiga. ¿Quieres hacer esquí durante las vacaciones de Navidad?

2 ! Allow the candidate to say that he/she cannot go skiing at Christmas and to say why not. Say that is a pity. Ask if he/she likes skiing and why (not).

¡Qué lástima! ¿Te gusta esquiar? ...¿Por qué (no)?

3 Allow the candidate to say if he/she likes skiing and to say why (not).
Say okay and ask him/her to tell you about his/her holidays last year. Elicit **two** details.

Vale. Háblame de tus vacaciones del año pasado.

4 Allow the candidate to give **two** details of last year's holidays.
Ask what his/her plans are for September. Elicit **two** details.

¿Y qué planes tienes para septiembre?

5 Allow the candidate to give **two** plans for September.
End the conversation by saying that you are going to study in another school.

Yo voy a estudiar en otro instituto.

NB You should address the candidate as '*tú*' throughout this role play.

AQA, 2004

Leave blank

ROLE PLAY 2 (HIGHER TIER)

CANDIDATE'S ROLE

You witness a person robbing a jeweller in Spain. The police are taking statements. The Examiner will play the part of the policeman / policewoman and will begin the conversation.

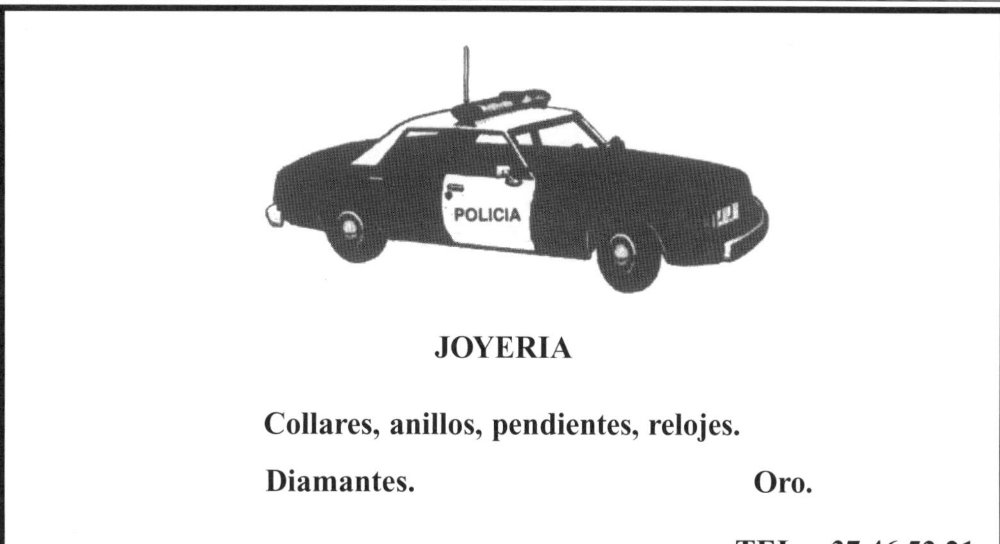

1. **Describe lo que viste.**
2. !
3. **Cómo se escapó.**
4. **Tu alojamiento.**
5. !

(20 marks)

Edexcel, 2004

Leave blank

ROLE PLAY 2 (HIGHER TIER)

TEACHER'S ROLE

Introduction to be read by the Examiner.

Has visto un robo en una joyería en España. Yo soy el / la policía.

Exam: **Gracias por su ayuda. ¿Qué vio usted exactamente?**

Cand: Task 1

Exam: ***¿Puede darme una descripción del ladrón?***

Cand: *Candidate responds to unpredictable*

Exam: **Muy bien. ¿Cómo se escapó?**

Cand: Task 3

Exam: **Vale. Y ¿dónde está usted alojado/a?**

Cand: Task 4

Exam: **Y *¿qué planes tiene para mañana?***

Cand: *Candidate responds to unpredictable*

Exam: **Muchas gracias. Estaremos en contacto.**

Edexcel, 2004

Leave blank

TOPICS

GENERAL CONVERSATION

- Teachers should conduct a conversation on at least **two** of the following topics. Only these topics may be used. Suggested questions are given as a guide only.
- For Foundation Tier, the conversation should last for **not less than four minutes and not more than six minutes.**
- For Higher Tier, the conversation should last for **not less than six minutes and not more than eight minutes.**

Education/Work

Dime algo de tu colegio.
¿Qué asignatura te gusta menos? ¿Por qué?
¿Has hecho prácticas laborales? ¿Qué hiciste?
¿Qué planes tienes para el septiembre que viene?
¿Cuáles son las ventajas de ir a la universidad?

Personal Relationships

Háblame un poco de ti.
Dime algo de tu familia.
¿Cómo celebraste tu cumpleaños el año pasado?
¿Tienes animales domésticos? ¿Cómo es/son?
Si tienes hijos en el futuro, ¿qué tipo de padre/madre vas a ser?

The Environment

¿Vives en un piso o en una casa? ¿Cómo es?
¿Qué sitios de interés recomendarías visitar en tu región?
¿En qué país preferirías vivir? ¿Por qué?
¿Qué haces para mejorar el medio ambiente?
¿Qué cambios has visto en tu pueblo/ciudad en los últimos años?

(20 marks)

AQA, 2003

General Certificate of Secondary Education

GCSE
Spanish

Centre name					
Centre number					
Candidate number					

Reading Paper

Surname
Other names
Candidate signature

Time allowed: 50 minutes

Instructions to candidates

- Write in blue or black ink or ballpoint pen.
- Write your name and other details in the spaces provided above.
- Answer **all** questions in the spaces provided.
- Answer the **section A** questions in **Spanish.**
  Answer the **section B** questions in **English.**
- Give all the information you are asked for and **write neatly**.

Information for candidates

- The marks available are given in brackets at the end of each question.
- There are 10 questions in this paper.
- The use of dictionaries is not permitted.

Total = 35 marks

Leave blank

SECCION A — Preguntas y respuestas **en español.**

En el instituto.

1 Las notas de Pepe.

	Asignatura	**Observaciones del profesor**
A	Música	Flojo. Necesita trabajar más.
B	Lengua española	No escucha al profesor.
C	Inglés	Alumno inteligente.
D	Alemán	Siempre llega a tiempo a clase.
E	Educación física	Siempre olvida sus cosas.

Escribe la letra de la asignatura correcta en cada casilla.

¿En qué asignatura es Pepe ...

Ejemplo

... puntual?	**D**
... perezoso?	
... capaz?	

(2 marks)

AQA, 2003

2 Las observaciones del tutor.

Pepe tiene muchas dificultades de comprensión. Necesita participar más en clase. Nunca hace los deberes.

Termina la frase.

El tutor piensa que Pepe es un alumno ...

A	... excelente.
B	... bueno.
C	... regular.
D	... malo.

Escribe la letra correcta en esta casilla. ☐

(1 mark)

AQA, 2003

Leave blank

3 Opiniones sobre las vacaciones de camping.

Tengo dos trabajos - soy profesora y ama de casa.
Cuando hago camping dejo de ser profesora pero no dejo de ser ama de casa. ¿Es divertido? ¡Qué va! No tengo ni lavaplatos ni lavadora y tengo que preparar las comidas sin cocina.
Mamá.

Para mí, ir de camping es estar lejos de la ciudad, lejos de la contaminación y lejos del ruido. Es estar junto a la naturaleza y junto a la tranquilidad. Es la manera perfecta de relajarse.
Papá.

Si hace mal tiempo no recomiendo hacer camping. El año pasado hicimos camping en los Pirineos y fue una experiencia desagradable porque llovió todos los días. Si hace buen tiempo no hay nada mejor.
Nina.

Cuando vamos de camping tenemos mucha libertad. No hay horario de comida como en los hoteles. No hay que tomar parte en las actividades organizadas. Siempre vamos con otras familias y los padres nos dejan jugar mientras descansan.
Laura.

¿Cuál es la opinión de la familia Ferrol sobre las vacaciones de camping?

Escribe **P** (Positiva)
N (Negativa)
P + N (Positiva y negativa)

Ejemplo

Mamá	**N**
Papá	
Nina	
Laura	

(3 marks)

(the photos reproduced here are not the original images from the exam question)

AQA, 2004

Turn over

Leave blank

La salud.

4 Ordenadores en los hospitales.

Miles de niños son hospitalizados a diario. Muchas organizaciones han decidido instalar ordenadores en los hospitales porque los niños enfermos se aburrían, veían demasiados programas de televisíon y engordaban. Sobre todo han comprobado que estos pacientes jóvenes se mejoran más rápidamente que otros. Estos niños pueden seguir estudiando desde su cama. También pueden tener contacto con sus amigos por Internet.

(a) ¿Qué les pasaba a los niños enfermos con respecto al peso?

....

(1 mark)

(b) ¿Cuál es la razón **más importante** para instalar ordenadores en los hospitales?

....

(1 mark)

(c) ¿Por qué estarán contentos los profesores con esta iniciativa?

....

(1 mark)

(Total 3 marks)

AQA, 2004

Leave blank

5 Carmen y Pedro escriben sobre la comida y la bebida.

Cuando estudiaba no tenía mucho dinero para comprar comida de calidad y por eso tenía que comprar comida barata. Ahora trabajo y tengo suficiente dinero para comprar buena comida pero no tengo tiempo para prepararla. Tomo mucha comida rápida. El mes que viene iré de vacaciones a Colombia. Dicen que los postres colombianos son muy ricos pero nunca me ha gustado la comida dulce. Por eso quisiera probar la comida picante en los restaurantes típicos de Colombia.

Quiero hacer una vida más sana. Antes tomaba lo que quería: zumos, refrescos y gaseosas, siempre muy fríos. No aguanto las bebidas calientes. Ahora sólo tomo bebidas sin gas. Por supuesto, me están prohibidas las bebidas alcohólicas y las bebidas con gas. Sin embargo, voy a celebrar mi cumpleaños con unas copas de champán. Serán las primeras bebidas alcohólicas de mi vida. ¡Espero que me gusten!

¿Qué toman?

Rellena la tabla.

	Tomaba	Toma	Tomará
Carmen		Comida rápida	
Pedro	Bebidas frías		Bebidas alcohólicas

(3 marks)

(the photos reproduced here are not the original images from the exam question)

AQA, 2003

Turn over

Leave blank

LA DROGA Y EL CRIMEN

6 Lee este artículo.

> El famoso criminal de los años noventa, 'El Birlar', se enfrenta a una nueva temporada de 20 años de cárcel por su participación en diez robos cometidos cuando se escapó en marzo de 2003. Ya ha pasado quince de sus treinta y ocho años en la cárcel. Cuando se presentó el ladrón al tribunal, se mostró arrepentido, y aseguró no ser el mismo que hace un año. 'Robar no está bien' dijo, y admitió haber cometido los robos 'bajo los efectos de la droga'. 'Ahora lo único que quiero hacer es asumir mis responsabilidades' añadió, y también prometió que va a someterse a una cura de desintoxicación.

Rellena los espacios con las palabras más adecuadas de la lista:

pasaba	robaba	dejar
drogas	**criminal**	más
robos	menos	siente
tomar		

Ejemplo: 'El Birlar' es un ....**criminal**.......... bien conocido en España.

(a) 'El Birlar' .... tiempo en la cárcel cuando se escapó. **(1)**

(b) Cometió otros .... **(1)**

(c) Ahora tiene veinte años .... en la cárcel. **(1)**

(d) Esta vez, dice que lo .... mucho. **(1)**

(e) También dice que va a .... las drogas para siempre. **(1)**

(Total 5 marks)

Edexcel, 2004

Leave blank

7 Lee este artículo.

Tragedia en los Pirineos durante la Vuelta a España[1]

En la etapa[2] de las montañas, tres fotógrafos murieron y dos resultaron heridos cuando el conductor perdió el control del Range Rover en el que viajaban. Según testigos, el accidente no fue debido al mal estado de las carreteras ni a las lluvias recientes. Los frenos fallaron. Un fotógrafo muerto era primo de un ciclista del equipo español, Juan Fernández. El entrenador del equipo español comentó:

"Me enteré de lo que había sucedido en plena carrera por las emisoras de radio. Decidí no decir nada a los ciclistas para evitar ponerles nerviosos. Se lo diré a Juan camino al hotel."

Tras la cuarta etapa, ya hay nuevo líder. Santiago Zabel, como es la costumbre, se puso el jersey oro. Sólo cuenta con cuatro segundos de ventaja con el británico David Johnson, diferencia que tratará de aumentar mañana en la próxima etapa. Zabel se ha especializado en conseguir triunfos en alta sierra. Comentó: "Para mí es un premio y me quita el sabor amargo del primer día." En la primera etapa Zabel se quedó a sólo un segundo de ser líder tras una caída.

[1] **La Vuelta a España** — a cycle race through Spain over several days
[2] **etapa** — a day-long stage of the race.

OCR, 2004

Turn over

Contesta a las preguntas **en español**.

Ejemplo:	¿Dónde tuvo lugar el accidente?
	En las montañas

a) ¿En qué trabajaban las víctimas?

.... (1)

b) ¿Por qué perdió el control el conductor?

.... (1)

c) ¿Por qué el entrenador no habló con Juan Fernández en seguida?

.... (1)

d) ¿Cuándo aprendió Fernández de lo sucedido?

.... (1)

e) ¿Por qué Zabel cambió de jersey?

.... (1)

f) ¿Qué terreno prefiere Zabel?

.... (1)

g) ¿Por qué no ganó Zabel el primer día?

.... (1)

(total 7 marks)

OCR, 2004

Leave blank

SECTION B

Questions and answers in **English**.

8 The problem page.

Problema

Querido Juan:
Te escribo porque tengo un problema muy raro. En el colegio mis notas son siempre estupendas, tengo muchos amigos, estoy enamorada de un chico y me entiendo perfectamente con mis padres. En total, todo me va de maravilla, sin embargo me siento infeliz. ¡Ayúdame!
Ana.

(a) Why is Ana's problem so unusual?

....

(1 mark)

Explicación

Querida Ana:
Es raro considerar como problema el que las cosas vayan bien. Al contrario, todo el mundo quisiera estar en tu lugar. Lo que pasa es que piensas que todo es perfecto, pero en realidad falta algo importante en tu vida.

(b) How does Juan explain how Ana feels?

....

(1 mark)

Solución

Dedícate a hacer felices a los otros. Cuidar a otras personas que no tienen tu misma suerte, acompañar a algún enfermo o anciano que lo necesite son algunas de las muchas actividades que pueden hacer que tu vida tenga más sentido.
Juan.

(c) How does Juan suggest that Ana solves her problem?
Mention **one** thing **only**.

....

(1 mark)

AQA, 2004

Leave blank

9 An article about living on a 'Floating Island' in the future.

Vivir en medio del océano es un sueño cada vez más cercano. Dentro de poco podremos vivir en ***'Islas flotantes'***.

La estructura general de la isla estará compuesta de estructuras metálicas. La parte habitada estará a quince metros por encima del nivel del mar. Allí se alojarán los habitantes y en la parte sumergida habrá un aparcamiento, almacenes y un acuario para ver la flora y la fauna marinas.

En las magníficas playas de la isla los turistas podrán broncearse antes de volver a la habitación de su hotel. Se podrá llegar a la isla por diferentes medios de transporte: en barco o en helicóptero para los que quieren aprovechar el tiempo.

Which of these questions have been answered in the article?

A	Would you be able to feel the island moving?
B	What would the island be built on?
C	How would the island protect itself from storms?
D	Would the houses be below sea level?
E	Is it the sort of place you could go for a holiday?
F	Would it be expensive to buy a house there?
G	How would people get to the island?

Write the letters of the correct answers in the boxes.

Example

B			

(3 marks)

AQA, 2004

Leave blank

Answer the following questions in **English**.

10 **SPRING CELEBRATIONS IN SEVILLE**

- La famosa feria de abril es una cita imprescindible para cualquier amante de Sevilla.
- Empezó a celebrarse en 1847 cuando el ayuntamiento decidió crear una feria de ganado a las afueras de la ciudad, de tres días de duración.
- La feria comienza de verdad cuando se encienden las luces del Palacio.
- En cuanto a la música, vayas donde vayas, escucharás las típicas sevillanas, y ¡acabarás bailando!
- Los caballos también tienen su parte en las fiestas. Más de 3000 asistirán cada día, o tirando carros o montados.
- Y se dedicarán las tardes a los toros, como siempre, en la famosa plaza de toros, hogar tradicional del toreo en España.

(a) For whom are these fiestas essential?

....

(1 mark)

(b) Where did the fiestas originally take place?

....

(1 mark)

(c) What marks the opening ceremony?

....

(1 mark)

(d) What effect does the music have on visitors?

....

(1 mark)

(e) What is special about the bullring?

....

(1 mark)

(Total 5 marks)

END OF TEST

Edexcel, 2004

General Certificate of Secondary Education

GCSE
Spanish
Writing Paper

Centre name					
Centre number					
Candidate number					

Surname
Other names
Candidate signature

Time allowed: 60 minutes

Instructions to candidates
- Write in black or blue ink or ballpoint pen.
- Write your name and other details in the spaces provided above.
- Answer **all** questions in the spaces provided, **in Spanish.**
- If you need more space for rough work or answers, use the blank page(s) in this booklet, or ask for more paper.
- Before the end of the test, cross out **all** rough work.
- Give all the information you're asked for, and **write neatly.**

Information for candidates
- The marks available are given in brackets at the end of each question
- There are two questions in this paper.
- To get the highest marks, you must answer each part of the question fully, developing your answers where appropriate.
- The use of dictionaries is not permitted.

Leave blank

1 You see this article in a Spanish magazine.

El Fin de Curso

Los años en el colegio son los más felices de tu vida - según dicen. Ya se acerca el fin de curso. Muchos jóvenes de dieciséis años van a buscar trabajo, otros van a seguir estudiando.

Escríbenos con tus ideas. Queremos las opiniones de nuestros lectores.

Escribe una carta a la revista, en **español**. Menciona **todos** los detalles.

Menciona:

- tus memorias de los años en el colegio;
- los problemas que existen en nuestra sociedad para los jóvenes hoy en día;
- quiénes ayudan más con los problemas, los padres y la familia o los amigos y por qué;
- tus planes para el futuro.

(20 marks)

Don't worry about the number of marks — different exam boards use different systems for these writing questions.

AQA, 2003

Leav
blan

AQA, 2003

2 **Pasaste quince días en Valencia el verano pasado. Describe tu visita allí.**

Escribe unas **150** palabras **en español**.

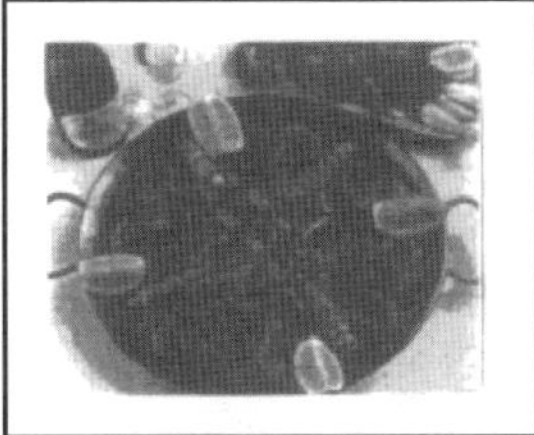

cocina tradicional valenciana

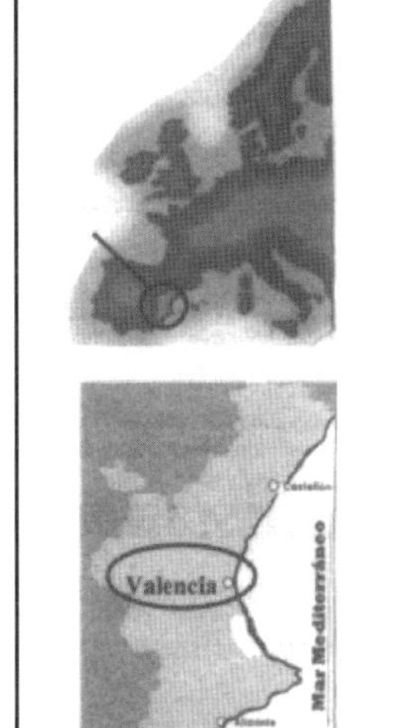

playas bonitas

hoteles de todo tipo

a orillas del Mediterráneo

museos y galerías de arte

CIUDAD MODERNA Y DINÁMICA

Menciona:

- la ciudad y la región
- lo que había de interés turístico
- lo que hiciste y lo que viste <u>durante el día</u>
- si recomendarías una visita a Valencia y por qué (no)

(30 marks)

Don't worry about the number of marks — different exam boards use different systems for these writing questions.

Edexcel, 2004

Leave blank

Edexcel, 2004

Page 6 (Quick Questions)

1) once, doce, trece, catorce, quince, dieciséis, diecisiete, dieciocho, diecinueve, veinte
2) veintiuno, veintitrés, veinticinco, veintisiete, veintinueve
3) veintiséis, treinta y uno, cuarenta y cinco, cincuenta y cuatro, sesenta y seis, setenta y ocho, ochenta y siete, noventa y nueve, ciento uno, dos mil cinco
4) veintiuna manzanas, treinta y un discos compactos, ciento un perros, cien euros
5) 1989.
6) mañana, ayer, esta noche, cada día/todos los días, mañana por la mañana.
7) 3rd. Mi habitación está en el primer piso.
8) 2nd on the right, 4th house on the left.
9) Todas las botellas. Todos los coches.
10) Los martes voy al cine, los miércoles hago mis deberes de español y los fines de semana hago las compras/voy de compras.
11) I went to the swimming baths yesterday, today I'm going clubbing and tomorrow I'm going out with my friends.
12) See example.
13) They're arriving on Thursday, 12th August at 11.20 am and catching the return flight on the 28th at 12 noon/midday.
14) Llego el sábado veinticinco de julio a las tres de la tarde y tomo el vuelo de regreso el diez de agosto.
15) A: ¿Qué haces esta tarde?
    B: Voy a la piscina.
    A: ¿Vas a menudo?
    B: Sí, todas las semanas/cada semana.
    A: ¿Cada/Todos los miércoles por la tarde?
    B: No siempre. ¿Quieres venir?
    A: No puedo esta semana porque voy a una fiesta esta noche. ¿Qué haces mañana por la mañana?
    B: A veces hacemos las compras/vamos de compras los jueves.
    A: Pues, ¿un día de la semana próxima?
    B: Vale. Pero no el fin de semana próximo porque toda la familia va a visitar a mis tíos. ¿El viernes próximo por la mañana?
    A: ¡Estupendo!

Page 11 (Quick Questions)

1) por favor; gracias; de nada; lo siento; encantado/a
2) How are you - informal
3) a) ¿Qué tal?/¿Cómo estás? b) ¿Cómo está (usted)?
   c) ¿Cómo está (usted)? d) ¿Qué tal?/¿Cómo estás?
4) ¡Por favor/Perdone, señor!
5) Con permiso.
6) What do you want to do? Quisiera telefonear a mis padres.
7) ¿Qué piensas de Madonna? ¿Cuál es tu opinión de Madonna? ¿Qué te parece Madonna?
8) ¿Quién va a la fiesta? Everyone is going except Elena. ¿Cuándo es la fiesta? ¿Qué día es? ¿A qué hora empieza/comienza? ¿Cómo vamos? ¿Por qué no va Elena?
9) ¿Cuántas habitaciones hay en la casa? ¿Cuántos discos compactos tienes?
10) Me interesan los idiomas, encuentro los ordenadores estupendos pero no me interesa el tenis de mesa y creo/pienso/me parece que el fútbol es horrible.
11) She likes your T-shirt but thinks your shoes are awful.
12) Do you prefer (a) tea or (b) coffee? Me da igual.
13) Me encanta el tenis de mesa pero no me gustan los plátanos.
14) Me gusta el español pero no me gusta la biología.
15) amable; agradable; horrible; bueno; malo; maravilloso
16) No me gusta esta película porque los actores son terribles.
17) Sally es preciosa, Emma es simpática y Carlos es malo.
18) Por qué 19) Porque
20) I think that Elena is amazing but I think her friend Raúl is boring because he doesn't like football.

Page 12 (Listening Questions)

1) a) 3 b) 5 c) 4
2) a) 2 de octubre b) 16 de septiembre
   c) 5 de diciembre d) 20 de abril
3) a) F b) F c) V d) F

Page 14 (Reading Question)

1) a) (el chalet cuesta) 150.000 euros
   b) (el teléfono de la inmobiliaria es el) 963 47 65 89
   c) 13-5-1985 or el trece de mayo de mil novecientos ochenta y cinco
   d) (vive en) Valladolid
   e) (toma vacaciones) en agosto

Page 15 (Writing Question)

Sample answer:

¡Hola Vicente!

Estudio en un colegio privado que está en el sur de Londres. Las clases empiezan a las ocho y media y terminan a las tres y cuarto de la tarde. Después podemos realizar actividades extra-escolares, si queremos, pero yo prefiero jugar con mis amigos porque me parece que las actividades extra-escolares son aburridas. De lunes a jueves tenemos siete clases al día, que duran cuarenta y cinco minutos. Tenemos un descanso de quince minutos a las diez de la mañana y la comida es de doce a una. A mí tampoco me gusta mucho la comida de mi colegio y prefiero las hamburguesas y las pizzas.

Por las tardes, tenemos tres clases más. Los viernes sólo tenemos las tres clases de la tarde porque hacemos deporte toda la mañana. Lo que más me gusta de mi colegio es que hay muy buenas instalaciones deportivas y una piscina cubierta. Yo también pienso que el deporte es bueno para mantenerse sano. Lo malo de mi colegio es la comida y que tenemos que llevar uniforme. Llevamos un traje negro, con camisa blanca, corbata verde y zapatos negros.

Estudio siete asignaturas en total. Me encanta el español porque la profesora que tenemos es nativa y muy simpática; es de Segovia y se llama Ana. También me interesa la informática porque me gusta utilizar el ordenador y mandar mensajes a mis amigos.

Cuando termino el colegio, voy a casa en autobús. Me encanta jugar en el ordenador por las tardes, pero mis padres no me permiten jugar más de dos horas; piensan que es malo para la vista. Voy a clases de karate con mi hermano todos los jueves de cinco a seis y mi padre nos recoge cuando sale del trabajo. Me encantan los animales y tengo un gato en casa que se llama Rufino. A veces vamos a visitar a mis abuelos los fines de semana.

Page 21 (Quick Questions)

1) hace frío; hace sol; hace mucho calor; hay tormenta
2) Aquí hace buen tiempo. ¿Qué tiempo hace en España?
3) Tomorrow it will generally be nice throughout the country. In the south the sky will be clear and it will be sunny and hot. In the north it will be a bit cloudy and it will rain on the coast.
4) En el norte de Inglaterra mañana lloverá/va a llover y estará/va a estar muy nublado. En el sur habrá/va a haber tormenta. En (el país de) Gales hará/va a hacer mucho viento y nevará/va a nevar en las montañas escocesas.
5) La semana próxima hará/va a hacer mucho frío y nevará/va a nevar el martes.
6) ¿De dónde eres/vienes?
7) Soy de los Estados Unidos. No soy inglesa.
8) a) una francesa b) un alemán c) dos holandeses d) dos italianas
   e) un escocés f) tres galesas
9) A: Where are you going on holiday? Abroad?
   B: Yes, this year we will (be) go(ing) back/return(ing) to Spain.
   A: Why?
   B: Because you can guarantee there'll be sunshine.
   A: Was there a problem last year?
   B: Yes, last summer my parents decided to (go) camp(ing) and we stayed at a campsite in Belgium. It rained all the time. The pitch was under/

beneath the trees, the tent and the sleeping bags were soaked, there was no drinking water and you couldn't light a fire.

A: What a disaster!

B: And where are *you* going?

A: We're going to a campsite in Belgium. We leave tomorrow morning!

10) a) las vacaciones b) una pensión
c) un albergue juvenil d) una caravana

11) una habitación individual; un aparcamiento; el comedor

12) ¡La cuenta, por favor!

Page 27 (Quick Questions)

1) arriba; abajo; fuera
2) a la izquierda; a la derecha; todo recto / todo derecho
3) ¿Dónde están los servicios?
4) Down there, at the end of the corridor, in the yard, third door on the left.
5) ¿Tiene(n) un aparcamiento y un teléfono?
6) The car park is on the right of the hotel and there's a telephone in every room but the public telephone is here in Reception.
7) ¿A qué hora/Cuándo se sirve la cena?
8) The evening meal is served in the dining room on the first floor between nine o'clock and eleven thirty (pm).
9) ¿Puede darme información sobre los monumentos de la ciudad?
10) A leaflet about the city monuments/sights, museums and the gallery.
11) ¿Cuándo/A qué hora abre el museo?
12) The coach for Granada is leaving from in front of the hotel at quarter to ten. It returns at quarter past six.
13) hace quince días; el verano pasado; este año; dentro de/en dos semanas.
14) A: Hi! You're back from holiday are you?

B: Yes that's right. I only got back two days ago.

A: Where did you go?

B: I spent a week in Miami and then a fortnight in France.

A: Who did you go with?

B: I went to the USA with my family but I travelled to France with some friends.

15) A: Fui a Italia con unos/as amigos/as.

B: ¿Qué tiempo hacía?

A: Hacía sol pero no hacía calor.

B: ¿Qué hiciste allí?

A: Fuimos a la playa, jugué al tenis y fui al mercado a hacer las compras ... me relajé.

Page 28 (Listening Questions)

1) A 2) G 3) E
4) a) en julio b) en avión c) visitar galerías de arte
5) a) doble b) ducha y balcón c) cinco d) 200/doscientos

Page 30 (Reading Question)

1) a) His parents and grandparents. b) Friday
c) i) played cards ii) listened to music
d) They're very nice.
e) **Two** from: it was cold / it was windy / it didn't rain.

Page 31 (Writing Question)

Sample answer:

¡Hola!

Estoy de acuerdo. No es justo que tienes que pasar un mes entero con tus padres en el campo. Normalmente voy de vacaciones al extranjero con mi familia. Vamos a Grecia o a España porque a mi madre le encanta el clima mediterráneo. No me gusta nada hacer camping. Es muy incómodo dormir en un saco de dormir. Yo prefiero dormir en una cama y tomar una ducha, ¡con agua caliente! Me gusta pasar las vacaciones en las ciudades grandes como Barcelona, París o Nueva York porque hay mucho que hacer y la vida nocturna es muy buena. El año pasado fui de vacaciones con un grupo de amigos escolares. Pasamos cuatro días en Londres en un albergue juvenil. Vimos muchos sitios de interés como 'Buckingham Palace' y 'The London Eye'. Lo pasé fenomenal y tengo ganas de volver. En agosto voy a ir a Gales. Voy a visitar a mis tíos que viven allí. Vamos a pasar unos días en la playa y unos días haciendo ciclismo en el campo. Gales es un país muy bonito que a mí me gusta mucho.

Bueno, Sara, te aconsejo que hables con tus padres sobre las vacaciones. ¿Por qué no pasas dos semanas con tus padres y dos semanas con tus amigos en la playa?

¡Escríbeme pronto!

Oliver

Page 37 (Quick Questions)

1) el polideportivo; el ayuntamiento; la biblioteca
2) un estanco
3) Por favor, señor(it)a, ¿hay un banco por aquí?
4) There are two or three but the nearest is just round the corner.
5) ¿Dónde está la catedral?
6) It's near the castle, in the Main Square, in the city centre.
7) Está lejos?
8) It's not far … 200 metres away … a 10-minute walk.
9) ¿Para ir al ayuntamiento?
10) Vivo en un pueblo en el noroeste de Inglaterra.
11) A: Excuse me, how do I get to the museum?

B: Go straight on to/as far as the traffic lights. Turn left, take the first street on the right and it's on the right.

A: Is there a lot to see?

B: Yes, lots. There are lots of interesting things and there's always something to do.

12) A: ¿Cómo es la ciudad donde vives?

B: Pues es un pueblo/una pequeña ciudad y es muy tranquilo/a.

A: ¿Te gusta vivir allí?

B: No mucho. Es aburrido/a.

A: ¿Qué hay en tu pueblo/ciudad?

B: No hay cine, hay una piscina y un mercado los martes. No hay nada que hacer el/los fin(es) de semana.

A: Te gustaría la ciudad donde vivo porque hay mucho que hacer. Hay muchas tiendas, un estadio, un zoo y un parque grande.

Page 41 (Quick Questions)

1) Un billete de ida y vuelta de segunda clase; no fumadores; salidas; sala de espera
2) Quisiera tomar el barco para Palma.
3) ¿Qué autobús va al aeropuerto?
4) Number 33. There's one coming now.
5) Quisiera ir a Barcelona el viernes.
6) Normalmente voy al instituto a pie pero ayer fui en bici(cleta).
7) El año pasado fui(mos) a España en barco pero este verano mi familia y yo vamos (a ir) en avión.
8) Alguien me ha robado el monedero.
9) Quisiera cambiar dinero.
10) How much do you want to change?
11) Treinta libras esterlinas en cheques de viaje.
12) A: Excuse me, when is there a train to Barcelona?

B: One leaves every half hour.

A: What time does the next one leave?

B: 9.50, but the train is about 12 minutes late.

A: When is it going to get to Barcelona?

B: Well, normally at 10.35.

A: I'd like 2 first class returns.

B: Here you are!

A: Which platform does it go from?

B: Platform 2.

A: Thanks.

B: Have a good trip!

13) A: Por favor (señor(a/ita). He perdido mi bolso.

B: ¿Dónde lo perdió?

A: Lo perdí en el parque detrás del ayuntamiento.

B: ¿Cómo es?

A: Es bastante grande, muy viejo, y de cuero negro.

B: ¿Qué había dentro/contenía?

A: Todo mi dinero, mi pasaporte y las llaves del apartamento.

B: De acuerdo/Vale. Telefonearé/Llamaré al ayuntamiento (por teléfono).

Page 42 (Listening Questions)

1) B   2) A   3) 50   4) B   5) 78-45-32

Page 44 (Reading Question)

1) a) Three from: It's close to the mountains and the sea. You can go to both at the weekend. There are good shops, a park, an open air swimming pool, a sports centre and historic monuments.
   b) Two from: You can go to the park with friends/play sport/swim in the open air swimming pool.
   c) There are a lot of tourists./You have to queue to get into some places./ There are traffic problems.

Page 45 (Writing Question)

Sample answer:

¡Hola!

Lo siento, es difícil para tí, pero hay que ser más positivo. Me llevo bien con mis padres, pero dicen que no estoy estudiando bastante.

Como ya sabes, vivo en un pequeño pueblo. Me gusta porque es tranquilo. Para ir a la ciudad, sólo necesito coger el autobús. Todo el mundo se conoce y hay un buen ambiente. El fin de semana pasado, hice camping con mis amigos. ¡Fue fenomenal!

Es verdad que la ciudad tiene cines, teatros, discotecas y restaurantes. Lo malo es que hay ruido, polución y está llena de gente. En el campo, se puede ir en bicicleta y montar a caballo sin peligro.

Estoy en contacto con tres amigos que viven lejos. Me encanta escribirles y enviar fotos. Nos llamamos por teléfono de vez en cuando y nos vemos durante las vacaciones.

Vas a hacerte nuevos amigos muy pronto…estoy segura. Es una nueva experiencia estupenda. No te olvides de coleccionar las direcciones de tus amigos en Valencia antes de irte.

Buena suerte y escríbeme pronto.

Page 51 (Quick Questions)

1) la educación física; la informática; las ciencias; el tercer trimestre; las asignaturas; las reglas.
2) What time do lessons start?
3) Las clases comienzan/empiezan a las nueve.
4) ¿A qué hora terminan tus clases?
5) Me gustan las matemáticas y me gusta la química pero odio la física.
6) What is your favourite subject?
7) E.g. Me gusta(n) el/los/la(s) … porque es/son interesante(s) y el/la profesor(a) es estupendo/a.
8) A: How long have you been going to this school?

B: I've only been going here for two weeks.

A: Do you like the lessons?

B: I don't understand everything and the lessons last an hour … it's a very long time.

A: Yes, but there's break and the lunch break, and we have two and a half months holiday in the summer.

B: How lucky!

A: How much holiday do you have in your country?

9) E.g. Tengo/Tenemos dos semanas/quince días en Navidad y en Semana Santa, una semana en el primer trimestre, una semana en el segundo trimestre, una semana en el tercer trimestre y seis semanas en el verano.
10) They don't wear uniform.
11) E.g. Llevamos pantalones negros/falda negra, zapatos negros, camisa blanca, chaqueta roja y jersey rojo.
12) Normalmente voy al instituto a pie con mis amigos pero a veces vamos en coche. El lunes por la mañana, mi primera clase es español. Aprendo el español desde hace dos años. Después del español estudio música. Me gusta la música porque toco en un grupo en mis ratos libres. Después del recreo estudio ciencias empresariales pero no me gusta el/la profesor(a) y no entiendo/comprendo las ciencias empresariales.
13) ¿Qué haces en tus ratos libres?
14) How do you spell your family name (surname)?
15) Do you speak English?
16) No entiendo/comprendo (bien). ¿Puede(s) repetir (eso), por favor?
17) a) be quiet   b) stand up   c) sit down
18) That's right.

Page 56 (Quick Questions)

1) un trabajo a tiempo parcial
2) la doctora; la contable; la dependienta; la mujer policía; la actriz
3) el ingeniero; el dentista; el mecánico; el actor; el trabajador
4) el carnicero; el panadero; el peluquero; el farmacéutico; el enfermero/el doctor, el cocinero … or any of the feminine forms of these jobs.
5) My father is a plumber and works 39 hours a week and my sister is a secretary and works part-time.
6) An answer similar to answer 5.
7) How much do you earn?
8) Gano cinco libras por hora.
9) A: I have a part-time job in a shop. I work Saturday mornings from 7 to midday and I earn €8.50 an hour.

B: Would you like to work in a shop after school?

A: No way! I haven't yet decided what I want to do in the future but I know that I wouldn't want to be a salesperson. How about you?

B: I would like to do A-levels because afterwards I want to do IT at university.

A: You would have to study hard because it would be difficult, wouldn't it?

B: Yes, but it would be very interesting and I would earn a lot of money!

A: Well, good luck!

10) E.g. Quisiera ser … porque sería muy (interesante) y ganaría mucho dinero.
11) E.g. No quisiera ser … porque sería muy (aburrido/a) y trabajaría muchas horas.
12) A: ¿Qué quisiera/te gustaría hacer después de los exámenes?

B: Quisiera/me gustaría ser contable porque ganan mucho dinero.

Page 57 (Listening Questions)

1)

	lunes	**martes**	**miércoles**	**jueves**	**viernes**
8.30	inglés	*arte*	inglés	arte	inglés
9.20	*matemáticas*	*arte*	*matemáticas*	arte	*matemáticas*
10.10	**recreo**	**recreo**	**recreo**	**recreo**	**recreo**
10.40	*historia*	ciencias	*historia*	*ciencias*	*historia*
11.30	informática	ciencias	*informática*	*ciencias*	*informática*
12.20	**recreo**	**recreo**	**recreo**	**recreo**	**recreo**
12.40	música	*ed. física*	*música*	ed. física	*música*
1.30	*geografía*	*ed. física*	*geografía*	ed. física	*geografía*

2) a) 2   b) 3   c) 4   d) 1

Page 59 (Reading Question)

1) a) (Las clases) terminan a las cinco (de la tarde).
   b) (Antes del recreo hay) dos clases.
   c) (Los alumnos estudian) inglés y alemán.
   d) (Las vacaciones de verano) duran dos meses.
   e) (No se puede llevar pantalones) vaqueros.

Page 60 (Writing Question)

Sample answer:

Hotel 'El Cisne Blanco'
Carretera de Granada s/n
12356 Málaga
Spain

Peter Swan
124 Wokingham Road
Reading
Berkshire
RG2 34T
Reino Unido

Reading, 29 de junio 2005

Estimado señor González:

En respuesta a su anuncio publicado en el periódico 'La Gaviota' el día 24 de junio, quiero solicitar el puesto de camarero en su hotel.

Me llamo Peter Swan, soy de Inglaterra y tengo 21 años. Me he graduado recientemente por la Universidad de Bath, donde estudié historia y español.

Como puede ver en mi curriculum, tengo experiencia previa, pues trabajé como camarero a tiempo parcial en un restaurante en Reading, durante las vacaciones de verano.

Tengo buen conocimiento del español a nivel oral y escrito. Me gustaría pasar un año en España para practicar mi español. Quisiera trabajar en su hotel como camarero pues me gusta el turismo y me encanta conocer a personas nuevas.

Soy un chico trabajador y responsable. Adjunto le envío mi CV y las dos referencias.

En espera de sus noticias, reciba un cordial saludo.

Peter Swan

Page 65 (Quick Questions)

1) Mis padres hacen senderismo cada/todos los fin(es) de semana.
2) En invierno vamos a hacer esquí/esquiar/hacemos esquí/esquiamos.
3) Her parents go out jogging every afternoon/evening.
4) ¿Practicas algún deporte?
5) She's a member of a table tennis club and they play matches twice a month.
6) Me gusta ir al polideportivo/centro de deportes para jugar al bádminton cada/todos los domingo(s) de(sde las) seis (hast)a (las) ocho.
7) Mi hermano es miembro de un club de tenis y mi hermana toca la batería en un grupo.
8) una pista de hielo; un casete; una flauta; Voy a la pesca.
9) Fui al gimnasio.
10) What was it like?
11) A: Do you have a hobby?
    B: Yes, I'm learning (how) to play the guitar because I love music. What about you?
    A: I listen to CDs on my stereo.
    B: Do you have a lot/Have you got many?
    A: Yes, a lot. My father collects old records from the seventies but I don't like that music because I think it's boring. Don't you agree?
    B: Why do you think that?
    A: Well, it's not interesting.
    B: I don't agree/I disagree/I don't think that. That music is exciting because it's got/it has (a) great beat/rhythm.
    A: That's not true.
12) A: ¿Cómo era el concierto anoche?
    B: ¡Estupendo/Fenomenal! El grupo era magnífico/fantástico. Canté y bailé toda la noche.
    A: No podía ir.
    B: ¿Por qué no?
    A: Porque había un partido. Nado para el equipo del instituto. Me encanta nadar/la natación.
    B: No me gusta nadar/la natación porque creo que es peligroso/a.
    A: ¿Por qué?
    B: Porque no sé nadar.

Page 71 (Quick Questions)

1) un espectáculo; una obra de teatro; una sesión; una canción.
2) ¿Cuánto cuesta una sesión de tenis?
3) €5.50 per hour.
4) ¿Cuándo/A qué hora está abierta la pista de hielo? It opens at 7.30am and closes at 1pm.
5) ¿Se puede nadar en el río?
6) ¿Hay una bolera por aquí?
7) Dos entradas para la bolera, por favor.
8) desafortunadamente; preferiría; lo siento.
9) Let's go to the theatre.
10) Lo siento pero desafortunadamente no puedo ir porque no tengo bastante dinero.
11) Vamos a pasear/dar un paseo/paseamos/damos un paseo.
12) It starts at 7.25 (19.25) and ends at 9.50 (21.50)
13) She heard this great song on the radio recently but doesn't know the (female) singer's name.
14) La semana pasada leí la nueva novela de Terry Pratchett.
15) Vamos al cine.
16) Buena idea. Me encantaría.
17) ¿Cuándo nos encontramos/vemos?
18) You will meet on the corner of your street near the number 30 bus stop.
19) a) este programa b) esta revista c) este equipo d) esta película
20) ¿Puedo hacer una llamada telefónica?
21) E.g. Me gusta ver … en la televisión porque es … ¿Qué programas te gusta ver?
22) A: What have you done recently?
    B: Well, I went to the cinema recently.
    A: Was the film good?
    B: Great! It was a horror film. I love this sort/type of film. What about you?
    A: No, I think that these films are boring. I'd prefer to see/watch a romantic film because it's more interesting. Don't you agree?
    B: No way! I don't agree at all.
    A: Well, we're not going out to the cinema together.
    B: Well, let's go ten-pin bowling.
    A: Unfortunately I don't have enough money, I'm sorry.
    B: It doesn't matter, I'll pay.
    A: Great! Thanks!

Page 72 (Listening Questions)

1) a) 4 b) 1 c) 3 d) 2
2) a) siete y media b) 3/tres c) Correos
3) a) she's very silly / stupid
   b) he's ugly / he's a bad actor / he always plays the same parts
   c) watch a DVD

Page 74 (Reading Question)

1) a) Rocío P+N b) Puri N c) Esther P+N

Page 75 (Writing Question)

Sample answer:

¡Hola Beatriz!

A mí me gusta el deporte. Soy miembro de un club de natación y los fines de semana hago senderismo, ciclismo o voy al gimnasio. Depende qué tiempo hace pero prefiero estar en el aire libre.

La semana pasada fui a la piscina martes y jueves, por supuesto. El domingo, afortunadamente, hacía sol así que fui al campo con un grupo de amigos. Anduvimos diez kilómetros y me lo pasé muy bien.

El deporte me relaja. Charlo con mis amigos y puedo mantenerme en buena salud al mismo tiempo. En mi ciudad, hay un polideportivo con una piscina grande. Hay un parque también y una pista de hielo. No vivo lejos del campo y de las colinas.

Como tú, tengo bastante trabajo escolar. Sin embargo, creo que me organizo mejor y hago mis deberes más rápidamente después de practicar deporte y divertirme. Si no te gusta el deporte de equipo, ¿por qué no intentas algo diferente? Hay una gran variedad de actividades para todos los gustos. ¿Cómo es tu región para el deporte?

Un abrazo

Page 82 (Quick Questions)

1) la pastelería; la panadería; la carnicería; la charcutería; la librería; la farmacia.
2) ¿Dónde está la tienda de comestibles más cerca?
3) ¿A qué hora cierra el supermercado?
4) un hipermercado; la farmacia; una papelería; una librería.
5) ¿Tiene pan?
6) Quisiera una barra de pan.
7) Do you want anything else?
8) Quisiera también dos pasteles.
9) She's giving you the cakes.
10) (Eso) Es todo, gracias.
11) "Quinientos gramos de caramelos" and "dos kilos de tomates".
12) There are big (price) reductions today/there's a sale on.
13) (los) juegos de ordenador; la ropa; (los) caramelos.
14) "Quisiera una falda roja y mi talla es la treinta y ocho."
15) A pair of black shoes, size 8 or 9.
16) A: Good morning. What can I do for you?

    B: Do you have/Have you got any T-shirts like these but in other colours?

    A: What size are you?

    B: I don't know exactly!

    A: Well, we have this one in dark blue and white or orange and green. And this other T-shirt in black and white.

    B: Don't you have it in white?

    A: Yes, but there's no reduction/it's not in the sale.

    B: Well, I won't take it because I don't like the colours and the white one is too expensive. Thank you.

    A: Well, I'm sorry.
17) E.g. Recibo 3 libras esterlinas por semana y lo gasto en caramelos y libros.

Page 89 (Quick Questions)

1) las legumbres/las verduras; fuera: la carne de cerdo: un helado de fresa; una botella de agua mineral: un panecillo con un poco de mantequilla y una taza de chocolate caliente; un café con leche.
2) Pass the sugar.
3) ¿Le/te puedo pasar la pimienta?
4) ¿Te gustan los desayunos ingleses?
5) She likes them a lot and thinks they are very good/nice.
6) La comida estaba deliciosa y la tarta estaba muy rica.
7) ¿Me puede(s) pasar la sal, por favor?
8) A: I am a vegetarian.

    B: What do you eat, then?

    A: Lots of things. I have enough with (the) vegetables, eggs, pasta, fruit and, of course, desserts … I like desserts a lot.

    B: Why don't you eat beef, for example, or ham?

    A: Well, I don't like meat.

    B: Aren't you hungry without meat?

    A: Of course not!
9) Fixed price menu.
10) Peach, lemon or apple ice cream.
11) A: ¿Tiene una mesa libre?

    B: ¿Para cuántas personas?

    A: Somos dos. Quisiéramos sentarnos en la terraza.

    B: Muy bien.

    A: ¿Qué es el plato del día?

    B: Tortilla española o paella (valenciana)
12) Quisiera un postre, por favor.
13) ¡Señorita! ¡La cuenta, por favor! ¿Está incluido el servicio?
14) ¡Por favor, señorita! ¿Dónde están los servicios?

Page 90 (Listening Questions)

1)

	¿Qué compra?	¿Cuánto quiere?	¿Cuánto cuesta en total?
Ejemplo i)	tomates	2 kilos	
Ejemplo ii)	jamón	8 lonchas	2,70 euros
a) i)	patatas	*1 kilo*	
ii)	*pan*	1 barra	1,70 euros
b) i)	*naranjas*	*4*	
ii)	agua sin gas	2 botellas	*3,40 euros*
c) i)	*queso*	4 lonchas	
ii)	*cerezas*	500g	*2,60 euros*

2) a) A b) C c) B

Page 92 (Reading Questions)

1) a) A b) D c) B
2) a) D b) A c) C

Page 93 (Writing Question)

Sample answer:

¡Hola Paula!

Pues, es una pena para tí porque, claro, no te diviertes mucho. Es verdad que la vida es cara y para comprar CDs y ropa, se necesita mucho dinero. A mí me encanta ir de compras. Se puede ver a sus amigos, charlar y escuchar sus consejos y ideas sobre, por ejemplo, la moda y los gustos de música. Siempre te dicen si la ropa te va bien o no y se puede tener confianza en ellos….¡mucho mejor que ir con los padres! Se puede tomar el café juntos y hacer planes para ir al cine o a un concierto por la tarde. Antes, no tenía bastante dinero de bolsillo tampoco pero ahora trabajo en casa para ganar un poco más. Mis padres me dan cinco libras por semana. Luego, por ejemplo, si lavo el coche, recibo dos libras. También, en vez de coger el autobús para ir al colegio o a la ciudad, voy a pie y así, ahorro más. Mi madre me da bocadillos por la mañana para llevar a la ciudad. Así, comemos en el parque….es más agradable y mucho menos caro que ir al café. Aquí en mi ciudad, hay un montón de pequeñas tiendas baratas y se puede comprar ropa mucho menos cara que en los grandes almacenes. A mí me encantan las rebajas.

Buena suerte y escríbeme pronto.

Ana

Page 102 (Quick Questions)

1) To spell your surname.
2) To talk about/describe yourself.
3) E.g. Me llamo Kate, tengo 16 años y mi cumpleaños es el 21 de abril.
4) a) delgado/a, b) bajo/a, c) de talla mediana, d) el pelo a media melena.
5) She is tall, red-haired with green eyes. Her boyfriend is tall (too) with fairly short black hair and brown eyes.
6) Soy … tengo el pelo … y los ojos …
7) Brother; grandfather; cousin; father.
   La hermana; la abuela; la prima; la madre.
8) Her name is Antonia, she is 39, short with long straight black hair.
9) Mi … se llama... . Tiene … años, es … y tiene el pelo … y los ojos … .
10) ¿Tienes animales?
11) Tenemos un perro que se llama Spot y un conejo.
12) Can you describe where you live?
13) Vivo en una pequeña casa moderna que no está lejos de las tiendas y hay un parque cerca.
14) Vivo en una gran ciudad industrial/con mucha industria de ciento cincuenta mil habitantes.
15) It's a 3rd floor apartment with 2 bedrooms, lounge, small dining room and a modern bathroom.
16) a) un jardín b) los árboles c) un césped d) las flores
17) Mi dormitorio es (size), tiene (furniture), y hay (more furniture) y es (colour).
18) ¿Cuándo/A qué hora se come?
19) Breakfast at 7.00 or 7.30, lunch at 2pm and evening meal at about10.
20) Todas las semanas mi hermana limpia nuestro dormitorio/cuarto y yo paso la aspiradora.
21) A: Do you have to help around the house?
    B: Yes, I have to make my bed and tidy my room.
    A: Manuel lays the table and sometimes does the washing up.
    B: We don't do the washing-up in our house because we have a dishwasher.
    A: That's lucky! Does your father help around the house?
    B: Yes, he sometimes lays the table or does the vacuum-cleaning.

Page 106 (Quick Questions)

1) How are you?
2) Estoy cansado/a.
3) a) fatal, b) regular, c) maravillosamente bien.
4) How are you? Don't you feel well?
5) Me siento mal.
6) What hurts/Where does it hurt?
7) Me duelen los ojos.
8) a) Tiene una insolación, b) me duele la rodilla, c) me duelen los pies.
9) Something for a headache.
10) Do you want aspirin or paracetamol?
11) a) Dolor de diente, b) dolor de estómago, c) dolor de cabeza, d) dolor de oídos.
12) a) ¡Pasen! b) ¡Pasa! c) ¡Pase!
13) Éste es mi papá y ésta es mi mamá.
14) It's 9 o'clock. Still no breakfast and the person is hungry.
15) A: Hi, Rebeca! How are you/How's things?
    B: Fine, thanks. And you?
    A: Not bad/So so. I have a bit of a cold. Come in, come in! May I introduce my mother? Mum, this is Rebeca.
    B: Pleased to meet you!
    C: Pleased to meet you! (Do) Sit down.
    B: Thank you very much.
16) A: ¡Pase, por favor! ¡Siéntese! ¿Cómo está?
    B: Me duele la cabeza, me duele todo el cuerpo y creo que tengo fiebre.
    A: Creo que tiene la gripe. Debe ir a la farmacia y debe beber mucha agua.
    B: Gracias, doctor. Adiós.

Page 107 (Listening Questions)

1) D

2)

	Remedio
Ejemplo	Beber agua
a)	Meterse en la cama
b)	Tomar aspirinas
c)	Quedarse en casa/no salir

Page 109 (Reading Question)

1) a) i) tiene mucha historia ii) tiene un palacio famoso *(in any order)*
   b) Two from: es de talla mediana/tiene los ojos marrones/tiene el pelo moreno.
   c) No hace su cama/no pasa la aspiradora.

Page 110 (Writing Question)

Sample answer:

¡Hola Miguel!

Pues, haces mucho. No me sorprende que estés cansado. Como ya sabes, vivo en una casa bastante grande con jardín. ¡Por eso, todo el mundo tiene que ayudar! Siempre arreglo mi cuarto y hago mi cama. Es fácil porque intento hacer un poco todos los días. Dos veces por semana, quito la mesa y friego todos los platos después de cenar. A mí me gusta porque pongo la música en la cocina y me divierto. También, salgo con el perro con mis amigos. Así, no es aburrido porque podemos charlar al mismo tiempo.
Mi padre trabaja en el jardín los domingos, mi madre prepara toda la cocina y mi hermano menor pasa la aspiradora de vez en cuando. A veces, mi madre me da más dinero de bolsillo si limpio el garaje o los muebles en el jardín. Sin embargo, creo que es importante compartir las tareas entre cada miembro de la familia. Claro, a veces las tareas son aburridas, pero, son necesarias y todos los que viven en casa tienen la responsabilidad de ayudar. ¡Una tarea compartida es una tarea menos grande! ¿Hay alguien que te pueda ayudar? No puedes hacer todo tú mismo, eso no es justo.
¡Buena suerte y hasta pronto!

Page 117 (Quick Questions)

1) ¿Cuál es tu número de teléfono? 2) 412507
3) You have to say the numbers in pairs. If your number is an odd number of digits, say the first one as a single figure e.g. ocho, veintitrés, cero cero, cincuenta y siete = 8230057
4) There's a phone call for you. 5) ¡Dígame!
6) A: Hello! It's Ana … Is Jaime there/in?
   B: Yes.
   A: Can I speak to him?
   B: Actually/The fact is that he's in the shower.
   A: Oh, right! Well, could he call me back before half nine?
   B: Yes, I'll give him the message.
   A: Thanks. Goodbye, see you soon!
   B: See you later!
7) Soy … ¿Puede llamarme María Dolores después de la comida? Si no estoy (le) puede dar un recado/mensaje a Jaime. El número de teléfono es el veinte, once, dieciséis. Gracias. ¡Hasta luego!
8) ¿Hay una cabina de teléfono por aquí/aquí cerca?
9) una tarjeta postal; un paquete; Correos.
10) She wants to know the price of stamps to send a letter and 4 postcards to Spain. Is there a postbox near your house or must she go to the Post Office?
11) a) Quisiera enviar/mandar estas dos cartas a Inglaterra.
    b) ¿Tiene sellos?
    c) ¿Tiene sellos para mandar/enviar una carta a Inglaterra?
    d) ¿Cuánto cuestan los sellos?
    e) ¿Dónde está el buzón más cerca?
12) Quisiera disculparme por haber dejado …
    a) … mi pasta de dientes en el cuarto de baño.

b) … mi sombrero en el armario.
c) … mi nuevo CD en el equipo de música.

13) a) Muy señor mío, b) Muy señora mía, c) Le saluda atentamente, d) Estimada señorita Gómez, e) Estimado señor Hernández, f) Le saluda atentamente.

Page 118 (Listening Questions)

1) a) 2 b) 4 c) 3

2)

¿Qué quieren mandar?	¿A qué país?	¿Cuánto cuesta?
una carta	Inglaterra	0,60 euros
3 paquetes	*Alemania*	16,36 euros
10 cartas	*Italia*	*5 euros*
una tarjeta postal	Australia	*1,92 euros*

Page 120 (Reading Question)

1) 6,20 € 2) 1,50 €
3) 902 120 120 4) No. (Sólo de lunes a sábados, excepto festivos)

Page 121 (Writing Question)

Sample answer:

El Director
Restaurante 'Los Claveles'
Paseo de Murillo 15, Bajo
Salamanca 23678

Alice Reynolds
12 Arcadia Road
Liverpool
L23 4RG
Reino Unido
Liverpool, 3 de abril de 2005

Muy señor mío:

Le escribo para decirle que cuando estaba de vacaciones en España, fui a cenar a su restaurante; fue el sábado 30 de marzo. Éramos cuatro personas en total y nos sentamos en la mesa número 16, al lado de los servicios.

Disfrutamos mucho de la cena y salimos del restaurante a las once y media. Regresamos al hotel, y al día siguiente vi que no tenía mi bolso. Llamé por teléfono, pero el restaurante estaba cerrado.

Es un bolso marrón de cuero y contenía mi monedero, una cámara de fotos y mis gafas de sol.

Le agradecería que me enviara el bolso por correo si lo ha encontrado. Es un regalo de mi novio y tiene gran valor sentimental.

Dándole las gracias por anticipado. Le saluda antentamente.

Alice Reynolds

Page 126 (Quick Questions)

1) Did you do any work experience?
2) Como experiencia laboral trabajé en la oficina de un contable.
3) What did you do there?
4) El trabajo fue muy aburrido.
5) Trabajé allí durante/Pasé allí una semana.
6) What do you want to do in the future?
7) Quisiera ser abogado/a y ganar mucho dinero.
8) She worked in a bank. She found it very boring because she doesn't like working with numbers, she prefers helping people.
9) A: Where did you do your work experience?
B: I worked for three weeks in a 4-star hotel.
A: Did you like the job?
B: Yes, quite a lot. It was hard work but it wasn't difficult. It was interesting because I met new people, but ten hours a day is a lot, you know.
A: What were your work colleagues like?
B: Well, some were very friendly so I didn't feel lonely but others weren't so friendly.
10) a) cómodo/a, b) maduro/a, c) un/una ayudante, d) una asignatura, e) responsable.
11) Quisiera mejorar mi español.
12) qualifications; (school) subjects; problems.
13) a) Fui al instituto en Stroud. b) Me encanta viajar.
14) A: Buenos días. ¿Cuántos años tiene?
B: Tengo dieciséis años.
A: ¿Qué trabajo le interesa?
B: Quisiera/Me gustaría trabajar en una agencia de viajes en una ciudad grande.
A: ¿Por qué quiere trabajar allí?
B: Me gusta ayudar a la gente y el turismo me interesa mucho.
A: ¿Dónde hizo su experiencia laboral?
B: Trabajé en las oficinas de una compañía de autocares. Trabajé allí durante dos semanas/quince días.
A: ¿Cómo fue el trabajo?
B: El trabajo no fue difícil, fue interesante pero el horario fue muy largo porque los autocares iban al extranjero.
A: ¿Qué hizo usted en el instituto?
B: Mis asignaturas preferidas fueron la informática y las ciencias empresariales.
A: Pues, gracias. Le vamos a enviar una carta. Adiós.
B: Gracias. Adiós.

Page 132 (Quick Questions)

1) a) la contaminación del aire, b) el medio ambiente, c) la naturaleza.
2) a) exhaust fumes, b) the greenhouse effect, c) natural resources.
3) Is the environment important to you?
4) a) Emilio isn't interested in it because he thinks scientists will solve the problems.
b) Alicia lives in a big town/city and thinks emissions from industry and transport are damaging nature and contaminating the air we breathe.
c) Paco is very worried because pollution of the air, sea and land will endanger the planet.
5) Me preocupa la contaminación debido al/a causa del efecto invernadero.
6) un régimen; el ejercicio; las drogas; los cigarrillos.
7) What do you eat?
8) No como patatas fritas todos los días/cada día y voy al gimnasio regularmente.
9) What do you think of people who smoke?
10) No bebo nunca alcohol y creo/pienso/me parece que los cigarrillos son horribles.
11) a) un héroe, b) los medios de comunicación, c) un cantante, d) una actriz, e) la gente famosa.
12) Celebrities are often role models for young people. You can admire them because they are very successful but they are not normal people.
13) Pienso que … es … porque es … .
14) Llevo ropa de moda.
15) There is a lot of unemployment in my area, especially among young people who have a lot of problems getting a job. I think it's unfair, it seems discriminatory and it annoys me.
16) A: What do you do to stay so slim?
B: I eat healthy things. For example, I eat lots of salads and fruit, but I'm not thin, you know.
A: Some girls have dietary problems like anorexia because they want to be successful like their heroines, the 'Supermodels'.

B: I think these 'Supermodels' have a bad influence on young people.

Page 133 (Listening Questions)

1) a) supermercado b) las seis de la tarde
c) mecánico d) tazas de té y café e) pagado

2) a) i) Industrial pollution ii) Traffic fumes
b) i) They're not interested in nature or animals / the environment.
ii) They drop litter / don't use rubbish bins.
c) To protect it for our children / for future generations.

Page 135 (Reading Question)

1) a) australiana b) Neighbours
c) 'The Delinquents' y 'Moulin Rouge' d) Dolce & Gabbana
e) Love Kylie

Page 136 (Writing Question)

Sample answer:

Hoy en día muchas personas abandonan las ciudades y se van a vivir en el campo. Hay cada vez más coches en las ciudades y, por tanto, más tráfico y más contaminación en la atmósfera, mientras que el aire que se respira en el campo es limpio y fresco, sin polución.

El tráfico genera problemas de aparcamiento y mucho ruido, que no es bueno para nuestra salud. Se dice que las personas que viven en el campo viven más años que las que viven en la ciudad; esto es porque llevan una vida más sana y sufren menos enfermedades.

Algunos piensan que una de las desventajas de vivir en el campo es que los niños reciben una peor educación, pues no hay muchos colegios donde estudiar y, por tanto, menos elección. Yo opino que los niños que viven en el campo aprenden las cosas más elementales porque están en contacto directo con la naturaleza.

Una de las desventajas de vivir en el campo es que la gente tiene menos acceso a la cultura; en el campo no hay cines, teatros o museos y por tanto, es más aburrido. Pero en el campo se pueden practicar deportes y actividades al aire libre que normalmente no se pueden practicar en las ciudades.

En las ciudades hay delincuencia y problemas con las drogas. En el campo la vida no es tan impersonal como en las ciudades, ya que conoces a todos tus vecinos.

Page 142-143 (Quick Questions)

1) a) el perro, b) la hermana, c) el padre, d) la canción, e) la gente, f) la ciudad, g) el autobús, h) el viaje, i) la carne, j) el Atlántico.

2) a) el agua, b) el huevo, c) la música, d) el clima, e) el poeta, f) el día, g) el planeta, h) el norte, i) la calle, j) el mapa, k) la mano, l) la sal.

3) a) dos naranjas, b) dos hombres, c) dos mujeres, d) dos helados, e) dos españoles, f) dos flores, g) dos cafés, h) dos jóvenes, i) dos habitaciones, j) dos franceses, k) dos lápices, l) dos semanas, m) dos jueves, n) dos guitarristas andaluces, o) dos actrices andaluzas.

4) a) los actores, b) las hermanas, c) las aguas, d) las paredes, e) las leyes, f) los días, g) las clases, h) los meses, i) las narices.

5) a) Tengo una hermana y dos hermanos.
b) Tengo el pelo rubio y los ojos azules.
c) Quisiera un chocolate y dos churros.
d) Me da un kilo de tomates y una lechuga.
e) Voy a visitar la catedral y el museo.
f) Estudio alemán e italiano.

6) a) Los martes voy al gimnasio o a la ciudad.
b) Quisiera ser periodista o cantante.
c) Mañana vamos a jugar al fútbol o al tenis.
d) Puedo enviarle una carta o una postal.
e) Cuesta siete u ocho euros.

7) a) Me gusta el esquí pero no me gusta el fútbol.
b) Me encantaría salir al cine pero no puedo llegar antes de las nueve.
c) Tengo sed pero no tengo hambre.
d) Mi amiga no es sudamericana sino española.
e) Como muchas ensaladas pero no como muchas patatas fritas.
f) No quiero la sal sino la pimienta.

8) a) Me gusta la película porque los actores son buenos.
b) No veo la televisión porque los programas son malos.
c) Estoy muy cansado porque trabajé diez horas ayer.

9) a) We can go to the cinema if you want/wish.
b) I'm going shopping with my friend.
c) Manuel is a happy man because he always sings while he works.
d) Isabel wants to be a journalist like her father.
e) I don't like doing the washing up so we are going to buy a dishwasher.

10) a) una camiseta, b) un hombre, c) un agua mineral, d) un/una turista, e) un día, f) un perro, g) un clima, h) una mano, i) una calle, j) una canción, k) un viaje, l) una uva.

11) a) Unos amigos ingleses y yo vamos a pasar unos días en Barcelona,
b) vamos a visitar unos monumentos,
c) vamos a llevar unos cheques de viaje y
d) vamos a tener unas fotos excelentes.

12) a) Vamos a la cafetería. b) Vamos al cine. c) Vamos a las tiendas. d) Vamos a una discoteca. e) Vamos al bar. f) Vamos a casa. g) Vamos a la playa. h) Vamos a los toros. i) Vamos a Correos.

13) a) Voy al banco. b) Voy al ayuntamiento. c) Voy a un concierto. d) Voy a la cafetería. e) Voy al supermercado. f) Voy a Correos. g) Voy a los Estados Unidos. h) Voy a casa.

14) a) el centro de la ciudad, b) la hora del día, c) un mapa de la región, d) la estación de trenes, e) el comedor del hotel, f) el hermano de Juan.

15) a) los días de la semana, b) los meses del año, c) un miembro de un club, d) la música del grupo, e) las paredes del dormitorio.

16) a) The important thing is the price.
b) The worst thing is the problem of the greenhouse effect.
c) I don't know what Luisa is going to do in the future.
d) The best thing would be to say nothing.

17) a) Good afternoon/evening, Mr. Gómez. How is Mrs Gómez?
b) On Fridays I finish work at four o'clock.
c) Tomatoes cost three euros a kilo.
d) In winter we go skiing and in summer we go on holiday to the coast.
e) What a pity!

18) A: ¿Tiene caramelos?
B: Claro/Por supuesto. ¿Cuántos quiere … cien gramos?
A: Sí, y quisiera unas uvas.
B: Cuestan cuatro euros el kilo. ¿Algo más?
A: No. Voy al hospital mientras mi madre va de compras/tiendas con mi hermana. Mi papá está allí y le gustan las uvas.
B: Espero que no es nada grave.

Page 148-149 (Quick Questions)

1) a) un pueblo pequeño b) una casa pequeña
c) dos perros pequeños d) unas chicas pequeñas

2) a) inteligente, b) difícil, c) guapa, d) joven, e) feliz, f) inglesa

3) a) Son inteligentes, b) Son difíciles, c) Son guapas, d) Son jóvenes, e) Son felices, f) Son inglesas.

4) María lleva una falda roja con una camiseta roja. Tiene guantes rojos, un sombrero rojo y botas rojas. ¡El rojo es muy de moda este año!

5) a) una canción triste, b) una historia rara, c) una decisión difícil, d) una mujer feliz, e) unas clases aburridas, f) una amiga francesa, g) unos pantalones azules, h) la gente simpática, i) las novelas interesantes, j) los bailes andaluces, k) las cafeterías españolas.

6) Pedro es alto, con el pelo corto y negro y ojos marrones. Creo que es muy guapo. Pablo y su hermano son bajos con el pelo moreno y los ojos verdes. Creo que son simpáticos pero un poco raros porque los dos llevan camisetas naranja.

7) a) La habitación está en el tercer piso.
b) Hoy hace muy mal tiempo.
c) ¿Hay algún taxi libre?
d) "Buenos días", me dijo.
e) Colón fue un gran marinero.
f) El primer hombre fue Adán.
g) Cuesta cien euros.
h) Estoy de muy buen humor hoy.
i) La tercera semana de agosto.
j) El restaurante está en la primera planta.
k) Algunas chicas sufren de la anorexia.
l) No tenemos ninguna habitación libre para esta noche.
m) Tenemos un apartamento en el primer piso.

8) a) Hace buen tiempo.
b) ¿Hay algún supermercado por aquí?

c) Algunas canciones son tristes.
d) No tiene ningún problema con sus padres.
e) Es un mal día para jugar al tenis.
f) El apartamento está en el tercer piso/la tercera planta.
g) Va a costar más de ciento cincuenta libras.
h) ¡Buena suerte!
i) No tienen ninguna habitación en el primer piso/la primera planta.
j) "Buenas tardes", dijo Manuel.

9) a) Cada día debes comer mucha fruta pero pocas patatas fritas.
b) Hay poca gente/pocas personas en la playa hoy porque hace mal tiempo.
c) Hay tantas cosas que hacer en España.
d) "¡Otro día, otra catedral!", dijo el/la turista norteamericano/a.

10) a) Salvador Dalí was a great painter.
b) Salvador Dalí was not a big (in size) painter.
c) He was an old friend (of long standing) of Gala Breton.
d) He was not an old (aged) friend of Gala Breton.

11) a) My brother is a big (in size) person.
b) Pablo Picasso was a great (famous) painter.
c) We went to Spain with an old friend (of long standing) of my parents.
d) We have a new (different) Spanish teacher.
e) I myself saw the accident.
f) The Pyrenees are big (extensive) mountains between France and Spain.
g) Holy Week is a great (important) festival in Seville.
h) My father bought a (brand) new car.
i) The next door neighbour collects old (ancient) cars.
j) We are going to leave for Spain on the same day as you.
k) Fernando and Isabel were great Spanish monarchs.
l) My little brother is awful!

12) a) Tenemos un lavaplatos nuevo.
b) Es un lavaplatos grande.
c) Costó más de cien libras.
d) El viejo lavaplatos fue malísimo.

13) a) me, b) him, her, you (polite) or them, c) us, d) you (singular, familiar) e) you (plural, familiar), f) him, her, you (polite) or them, g) him, her, you (polite) or them, h) him, her, you (polite) or them.

14) a) mi perro, b) tu/vuestra/su casa, c) su vestido, d) sus pantalones, e) nuestros zapatos, f) mis padres, g) su coche, h) nuestro/a amigo/a, i) sus dormitorios, j) tu/vuestra/su hermana.

15) A: This pencil isn't mine.
B: No, it's mine, it's not yours.
A: It's not yours either. I think that it's María's.
B: It's hers then?
A: Yes, it's hers. But these books aren't hers.
B: Whose are they then?
A: Manuel's.

Page 154-155 (Quick Questions)

1) a) lentamente, b) rápidamente, c) raramente, d) fácilmente e) tristemente, f) felizmente, g) perfectamente, h) especialmente

2) a) Mi profesor(a) habla español muy bien.
b) Desafortunadamente vamos raramente de vacaciones al norte de España.
c) Entendemos perfectamente lo que dicen.

3) His/her brother sings well but dances badly whilst his/her sister dances well and sings badly.

4) A: Tickets to the museum are very expensive/dear.
B: How much are they?
A: Almost 35 euros each.
B: Oh yes, it's too expensive, especially after having paid for the tickets to the castle.
A: Yes. Today we've already spent enough money on visits!

5) a) Mi amigo español habla demasiado rápido.
b) Estos zapatos son bastante caros.
c) Marta y su hermana son chicas muy inteligentes.

6) Helen y Sonia son altas, Kay y Debbie son más altas pero Kerrie es la más alta.

7) White best; black next best; blue least.

8) His/her younger sister is 13 and his/her elder brother is 22. The youngest in the family is his/her little brother who is 7.

9) Pedro = 1; Nuria and Ricardo = 2; Ana is the least intelligent.

10) El español es menos difícil que el francés. La informática es más interesante que las matemáticas y las ciencias empresariales son tan fáciles como la geografía.

11) Voy a casa. Vuelvo a Bolton.

12) I'm in London at the moment, studying English at a language school. Can I come to Leeds to see you after the course?

13) Estoy en casa hoy pero mañana voy a ir a York.

14) Do you want to see what I've got in this (little) box?

15) ¿Qué hay en la caj(it)a?

16) a) una taza de café con leche.
b) un vaso de zumo/jugo de naranja
c) una botella de agua mineral

17) Los pantalones son de cuero pero el cinturón es de plástico.

18) a) Tu/Su taza está en la mesa. b) Vi ese programa en la tele.
c) Voy a España el viernes.

19) Soy de Bristol.

20) El vuelo desde Londres hasta Málaga sale del aeropuerto a las diez (de la mañana) pero a partir del primero de abril va a salir a las nueve y media.

21) Real Madrid against Celta Vigo here at 8 pm.

22) a) ¿fuera en el jardín? b) ¿bajo/debajo de la mesa? c) ¿detrás del sofá? d) ¿dentro del microondas? e) ¿al fondo del armario?

23) A: Excuse me! Where's the Tourist Office?
B: It's behind the Town Hall, next to the bus station.
A: In front of the department store?
B: No, no, between the bank and the central/main pharmacy/chemist's.
A: Isn't it at the end of a street?
B: No, that's the train/railway station.
A: Oh yes, I understand. Thank you.

24) Reductions of up to 50%/half price sale on everything.

Page 161-162 (Quick Questions)

1) Voy/Vamos a reservar una habitación para dos personas. El año pasado pagué/pagamos treinta y cinco euros por un apartamento.

2) Este regalo es para tus padres.

3) In my opinion you are the nicest of all my English friends.

4) Fuimos de vacaciones para relajarnos/descansar pero papá alquiló un coche para cuatro días. Fuimos a Gibraltar por la carretera que pasa por Marbella. Salimos por la mañana. Llegamos por la noche. El tráfico/La circulación fue malísimo/a.

5) a) tú = singular informal, b) Vd./usted = singular formal
c) vosotros/as = plural informal, d) Vds./ustedes = plural formal

6) a) Lo vi en la tele. b) Los odio. c) Las quiero mucho.
d) La visité ayer. e) Nuestros amigos nos vieron en el supermercado.

7) a) ¿Los caramelos? ¡Los comimos todos el miércoles!
b) ¿Las chicas? Las vimos esta mañana.
c) ¿Eduardo y yo? Nos vieron en la discoteca.

8) a) Me gusta el vino español pero no me gustan las aceitunas españolas.
b) Nos gustan los calamares pero no nos gusta el pulpo.
c) Les gusta el chocolate pero no les gustan las galletas.
d) Le gustan los tomates pero no le gusta la lechuga.

9) a) ¡Escríbele una carta! b) ¡Mándale un regalo! c) ¡Envíales una postal!

10) A la derecha de mí está Emma, enfrente de ella está Lucy y a la derecha de ella está Daniel. Al otro lado de mí está Jason y enfrente de él está Tom.

11) a) conmigo, b) con ellos, c) con ella, d) contigo/con Vd.

12) a) Ven a Pablo todos los días. b) Estoy buscando a Teresa.
c) Quiero mucho a mis hermanas. d) Visitamos a mis tíos cada fin de semana. e) ¿Vas a encontrar a tus amigos en la discoteca? f) Quiero muchísimo a Elena. g) Buscan a nuestro profesor por todas partes.

13) a) Aquí está la persona que lo hizo.
b) Busco a mi hermanito que solamente tiene tres años.
c) Vamos a ver a nuestros tíos que viven en Nueva York.

14) a) Te doy las flores que costaron diez libras.
b) Vamos a vender los libros que están en la mesa.
c) Va a la playa que está a cien metros del hotel.

15) a) Dicen que va a llover.
b) Dicen que vamos a ganar el partido.
c) Creo/pienso que es verdad.

16) a) ¿Te lo presto? b) Nos la enviaron desde Málaga.

c) Te los mandamos la semana pasada. d) ¿Me las escribes?
e) Voy a prestártelo/ Te lo voy a prestar.

17) a) Se lo presto. b) Se la enviaron desde Málaga.
c) Se los mandamos ayer. d) ¿Se las escribiste?
e) Voy a prestárselo.

18) a) este perro, b) esta chica, c) esta canción, d) estas decisiones.

19) a) ¡Esta actriz es estupenda! b) Estos zapatos son demasiado caros.
c) Este libro es interesante. d) ¡Estas camisetas son baratas!

20) a) aquel hombre, b) aquella mujer, c) aquellos viajes, d) aquella calle.

21) A: What do you think of these trousers?
B: I prefer those in the (shop) window.
A: Don't you like this red T-shirt either?
B: Yes but that one in the window is white and it's better. Why don't you try them on with that blue hat?
A: But this one doesn't match those trousers!
B: Of course, but if you take that T-shirt, it *will* match. And if you wear these sunglasses, you won't see the difference in colours!

Page 169-170 (Quick Questions)

1) a) como b) comemos c) come d) comes e) coméis f) comen
g) (Vds.) comen h) (Vd.) come.

2) a) ii b) i c) vi d) iv e) v f) i g) ii
h) iii i) ii

3) a) Mi familia vive en una casa pequeña.
b) Los ascensores suben al décimo piso.
c) El tendero abre el supermercado a las siete.
d) (Tú) escribes una postal de Valencia.
e) (Yo) vivo en el norte de Inglaterra.
f) Subimos al primer piso.
g) Mis padres leen el periódico por la mañana.
h) (Vds.) escriben muchas cartas.

4) a) Escribes a menudo. b) Subo al quinto piso/la quinta planta a pie.
c) Abren el bar a las cinco de la tarde. d) ¿Vivís cerca de Manchester?
e) Vivimos en un apartamento.

5) a) Hablo español. b) ¿Habláis español?
c) Hablamos con nuestro/a profesor(a).
d) Tus padres hablan demasiado rápido.
e) ¿Habla (Vd.) inglés?

6) a) Vd. ayuda con mis deberes.
b) Nosotros miramos la ropa nueva en el escaparate.
c) El tren no llega siempre con retraso.
d) Paco y María Dolores estudian inglés en el instituto.
e) María Dolores e Isabel siempre escuchan con atención.

7) a) No aprendemos nada en el instituto porque no comprendemos nada.
b) Abren sus libros y escriben la respuesta perfecta.
c) ¿Cuando llegas a casa, descansas delante de la televisión?
d) Siempre escucho cuando mi profesor/a me habla.

8) a) Soy inglés/inglesa. b) Eres/Es Vd. un chico agradable.
c) ¡Elena es estupenda! d) Los niños son horribles.
e) Somos maravillosos/as. f) Sois/Son Vds. chicas inteligentes.
g) ¿Es Vd. el farmacéutico? h) Es médico.

9) a) (Nosotros) Estamos en casa. b) ¿Estás (tú) enferma?
c) Hoy (yo) estoy de buen humor.
d) Mi casa no está cerca del instituto.
e) ¿Dónde estáis (vosotros)?
f) ¡Vds. están sentados en nuestras plazas reservadas!

10) a) Julio es alto, moreno y guapo y está aquí.
b) Londres está en Inglaterra. Es la capital.
c) Tom es inglés pero está en España en este momento.
d) ¿Qué hora es? Son las diez cincuenta y dos y hoy es jueves.
e) ¿Dónde está el banco más cerca? Está en la plaza. Es el Banco Atlántico.

11) a) ¿Van Vds. de vacaciones a Inglaterra?
b) (Nosotros) Vamos al instituto juntos.
c) Las chicas van de tiendas los sábados. d) (Yo) voy al cine.
e) ¿Vais (vosotros/as) a la discoteca?

12) a) No quiero lavar los platos.
b) Mi padre no quiere comprar un lavaplatos.
c) ¿Se puede cambiar moneda extranjera aquí?
d) Podemos empezar mañana.
e) ¿Por qué no quieren estudiar la geografía?

13) a) The shops shut/close at 4 on Sundays.
b) My uncle begins work at 5 a.m. but my father starts at 8.45.
c) What do you think of María Dolores? She's coming to see us tomorrow.
d) My friends play on computers that cost a thousand pounds each.

Page 175-176 (Quick Questions)

1) a) Tom y James van a jugar para City. b) ¿Tú vas a bailar con María?
c) Yo voy a hacer mis deberes.
d) ¿Vds. van a ir de vacaciones a Inglaterra?
e) Paco va a salir con Nuria.

2) Voy a ir a España con mi familia. Vamos a alquilar un apartamento en la costa. Vamos a ir en avión y el vuelo va a durar dos horas. Vamos a estar allí por dos semanas y mi papá va a alquilar un coche porque vamos todos a visitar la catedral de Gaudí en Barcelona.

3) a) James y Tom dormirán en el autocar.
b) Eduardo y tú cogeréis el autobús.
c) Mi padre venderá el perro.
d) Tú y yo iremos a la discoteca.
e) Yo te telefonearé mañana por la mañana.

4) a) Vd. pondrá un suéter. b) Nosotros lo sabremos más tarde.
c) El tren no saldrá con retraso.
d) Paco y María Dolores vendrán a la fiesta.
e) María Dolores e Isabel querrán ir también.

5) a) mandado b) estudiado c) comido d) subido e) cerrado

6) a) ¿Has abierto todos tus regalos? b) ¿Qué ha hecho Vd. con mi toalla?
c) No me han escrito una carta. d) Mis padres han vuelto del trabajo.

7) a) Ya he ido a Mallorca. b) Ya he visto la Alhambra.
c) Ya he comido calamares. d) Ya he conocido a Tomás.

8) a) He visto Gibraltar. b) Ya hemos ido a Barcelona.
c) Te has puesto muy feo/a mientras que tu hermana se ha puesto muy guapa.

9) a) Han vuelto de sus vacaciones.
b) ¿Has dicho a María Dolores que ya has comprado los billetes?
c) Por favor/Perdón, señor. ¿Ha(n) encontrado Vd./Vds. mi pulsera?

10) a) Eric y Bobby jugaron al fútbol para United.
b) ¿Tú bailaste en la discoteca?
c) Yo pasé quince días en España.
d) ¿Tomó Vd. el tren?
e) Paco estudió medicina.
f) Elena y yo cenamos juntos/as.
g) Pedro y tú escuchasteis la radio.
h) Nuria e Isabel compraron sandalias nuevas.

11) a) Almorzamos. b) Estudió. c) Bailé. d) Cantó.
e) Vds. escucharon. f) Tú nadaste.
g) Nuria y tú comprasteis un bolso. h) Habló.

12) a) El camarero entendió/comprendió. b) Escribí a mi familia.
c) Isabel abrió la puerta. d) Subieron al quinto piso.
e) Comimos calamares fritos.

13) a) We were awful children but we went to a good school.
b) He was a doctor and he went to the United States, where he stayed for 12 years.
c) I spent 10 years in the north and at that time I was a hard-working boy but when I went to University I became lazy.
d) Didn't you go on holiday? No, I was ill so I didn't go. That summer was a disaster for me.
e) They went to see Natalia but she wasn't in/at home.

14) Fui a España con mi familia y alquilamos un apartamento en la costa. Fuimos en avión y el vuelo duró dos horas. Estuvimos allí durante dos semanas pero papá no alquiló un coche porque tuvo miedo del tráfico. Así que cogimos el tren. Pero perdió los billetes y tuvo que pagar otra vez. Estuvo de muy mal humor aquel día y fue un desastre. Dijo que no volvería nunca a España.

Page 182-183 (Quick Questions)

1) There was/were

2) a) Había un cine en el pueblo.
b) Aquellos zapatos eran demasiado caros.
c) Era muy duro estudiar.
d) Había mucha gente en la calle.

3) a) Mis abuelos vivían en Londres.

b) ¿Qué tiempo hacía?
c) Tú y yo telefoneábamos a nuestros padres todos los días.
d) Mi abuela me hablaba de su pasado.
e) Cuando yo era joven, ayudaba a mi madre.
f) ¿Salías tú con mi amiga?
g) A veces mi familia y yo íbamos al zoo donde mirábamos los monos que comían los cacahuetes que nosotros les lanzábamos.
h) Nuestros abuelos nos daban siempre regalos estupendos que nosotros abríamos muy rápidamente.

4) a) I would say so. b) We would all go out together.
c) They could/would be able to come in August.
d) You would have to bring your passport.
e) I would put on woollen clothing.

5) a) Mi hermano no lavaría los platos.
b) Mi padre no compraría un coche nuevo.
c) Yo cambiaría moneda extranjera en el banco.
d) Elena y yo empezaríamos otra vez mañana.
e) Yo no bebería el agua.

6) a) despertarse b) levantarse c) acostarse

7) a) Yo me siento mal.
b) Tú te despiertas temprano.
c) Tu hermana y tú os vais por la mañana.
d) Mi prima y mi hermana se llaman Teresa.
e) Mi familia y yo nos acostamos tarde.
f) Mi abuela siempre se viste de negro.

8) a) I am going to go to bed late.
b) My Spanish friend left/went (away) last Tuesday.
c) Every day we used to get up early.
d) Are you going to have a shower now?
e) My father woke up late this morning, he didn't have a shave but he went to work.

9) Me despierto a las …, me levanto … luego me lavo / ducho. Tomo el desayuno … y me voy al instituto … . Vuelvo a casa a las … . Ceno/cenamos … y me acuesto … .

10) a) You/One can park in the square.
b) English spoken here.
c) The bank opens at 9.30 and closes/shuts at midday.
d) No entry.
e) They say she's mad!
f) In Spain they/one eat(s) the evening meal at about 10.

11) a) Mi hermano no lavó los platos.
b) Mi padre no ha comprado un coche nuevo.
c) No cambié mis cheques de viaje en el banco.
d) No bebió mucho.
e) No van a ir a la piscina con nosotros.

12) He doesn't go clubbing any more because there aren't any buses after 10 pm. He doesn't go to the cinema because there's nothing interesting (on). He neither goes clubbing nor to the cinema so he doesn't see anybody.

13) No hay nada que hacer aquí. No hay nadie interesante. No veo nunca a mis amigos/as. Quisiera un bocadillo pero no hay ni pan ni mantequilla y no hay ningún bombón en la casa.

14) a) Elena quiere que yo pase la aspiradora.
b) Me alegro de que tú y yo podamos salir juntos.
c) Dudo que la discoteca esté abierta ahora.
d) Necesitamos una persona que sepa conducir un camión.
e) Cuando sea rica, compraré una pulsera de oro.
f) Vamos a España para que yo mejore mi español.
g) No creo que Nuria y tú tengáis problemas.
h) Espero que Vds. hablen mucho español.

15) A: I'm pleased that we are friends because when you have a lot of money I hope that you won't forget me.

B: Of course not! But I don't think that's possible and I doubt that it will happen, especially because before I can win, I need to buy a lottery ticket.

Page 187-188 (Quick Questions)

1) a) Put your hand up! (formal, singular)
b) Open the window! (informal, singular)
c) Listen! (formal, plural)
d) Come here! (informal, singular)
e) Do your homework! (informal, plural)
f) Lay the table! (informal, singular)

2) a) ¡Salid de aquí en seguida! b) ¡Venid con nosotros!
c) ¡Levantad la mano! d) ¡Terminad los deberes!
e) ¡Tened cuidado! f) ¡Esperad en la parada de autobús!

3) a) ¡Dejen las llaves en Recepción! b) ¡Cojan la segunda a la izquierda!
c) ¡Sigan todo recto! d) ¡Vayan con Dios!
e) ¡Hablen más despacio! f) ¡Aprenden los verbos!

4) a) Long live the King! b) Park the car in/on the square!
c) Pay when you leave! d) Give this parcel to your parents!

5) a) ¡No hable! b) ¡No coman en clase!
c) ¡No escriban en la mesa! d) ¡No arrojen papeles!
e) ¡No duerma aquí!

6) a) ¡No hables! b) ¡No comas en clase! c) ¡No vendas el gato!
d) ¡No escuches! e) ¡No nades en el río! f) ¡No duermas aquí!

7) a) ¡Levántate! b) ¡Vete! c) ¡Acuéstate!
d) ¡Ayúdame! e) ¡Ponte un suéter! f) ¡Llámale!
g) ¡Escríbele una carta! h) ¡Dime la verdad!
i) ¡Dame tu número de teléfono!

8) a) ¡Vete! b) ¡Llámame (por teléfono)!
c) ¡Dime cuándo! d) ¡Déjame tu número de teléfono!
e) ¡Envíame/Mándame un recado!

9) No (lo) sé pero mi madre (lo) sabe.

10) ¡(Lo) Sabemos todos eso!

11) That your friend knows how to ski but that (s)he can't at the moment because (s)he has a broken leg which (s)he did skiing!

12) Sé nadar pero en este momento no puedo porque tengo la gripe.

13) No, no la conozco. Mucho gusto/Encantado/a, Elena.

14) You: ¿Conoces Madrid?
Friend: I don't know Madrid but I know La Coruña very well. Do you know London?
You: Sí, lo conozco muy bien.

15) Can you go clubbing tonight?

16) ¿Podemos María Dolores y yo salir a la discoteca esta tarde?

17) No, you can't, because they've booked a table for the whole family at the restaurant to celebrate María Dolores' brother's birthday.

18) Can you help me with my English homework?

19) Puedo ayudarte si quieres.

20) Puedo/Podemos ir a Ibiza este verano pero conozco/conocemos muy bien Ibiza. Puedo/Podemos ir a Italia pero no sé/sabemos hablar italiano.

21) Translate the following sentences into English:
a) Sonia had arrived.
b) We had finished.
c) I had not yet eaten octopus.
d) My friends had already gone/left.
e) Had you called Elena on the phone?

22) Habíamos llegado muy tarde porque habíamos tenido un viaje terrible/horroroso. Había llovido todo el día y nos habíamos parado en una estación de servicio pero yo no había comido nada. Un viaje que dura normalmente dos horas había durado seis.

23) a) He is eating.
b) He is sleeping/asleep.
c) He is reading the newspaper.
d) He is serving in the bar.
e) He is playing football on the beach.

24) a) Estoy almorzando/comiendo.
b) Estoy hablando con Ricardo.
c) Estoy haciendo mis deberes de español.
d) Estoy fregando/lavando los platos.

25) a) We were looking for the apartment.
b) Elena was writing a letter when Ricardo arrived.
c) My friends were having a good time singing and dancing.

26) a) I have just had a wash.
b) Pedro and Isabel have just gone out/left.
c) We have just been for a walk.
d) María Dolores has just caught the return flight to Madrid.

27) a) Acabo de telefonear/llamar a Isabel (por teléfono).
b) Acaba de salir/irse.
c) Acaban de volver.
d) ¡Acabamos de terminar todos los ejercicios!

EXAM PAPER ANSWERS

Please note: The answers to the past exam questions have not been provided by or approved by the examining bodies (AQA, OCR and Edexcel Ltd.). As such, AQA, OCR and Edexcel Ltd do not accept any responsibility for the accuracy and method of the working in the answers given.
CGP has provided suggested solutions — other possible solutions may be equally correct.

Listening Exam

Section A:

1 a)	B	1 mark
b)	B	1 mark
c)	C	1 mark
d)	A	1 mark
2	D	1 mark
3 a)	Alicia N	1 mark
b)	Manuela P	1 mark
c)	Carlos P+N	1 mark
4 a)	12 de julio, 9.45, 42 75 50 (All the numbers must be right to get the mark.)	3 marks
b)	2 de mayo, 5.00, 57 80 80 (All the numbers must be right to get the mark.)	3 marks
c)	23 de octubre, 7.15, 38 96 71 (All the numbers must be right to get the mark.)	3 marks
5	Encarna - historia, **interesante**, **matemáticas**, muy complicadas	2 marks
	Raúl - **inglés**, la profesora es buena, ciencias, **aburridas**	2 marks
	Elena - **educación física**, le encanta el baloncesto, **geografía**, inútil	2 marks
	Rosa - informática, **la profesora es muy simpática**, **música**, **muy difícil**	3 marks
6	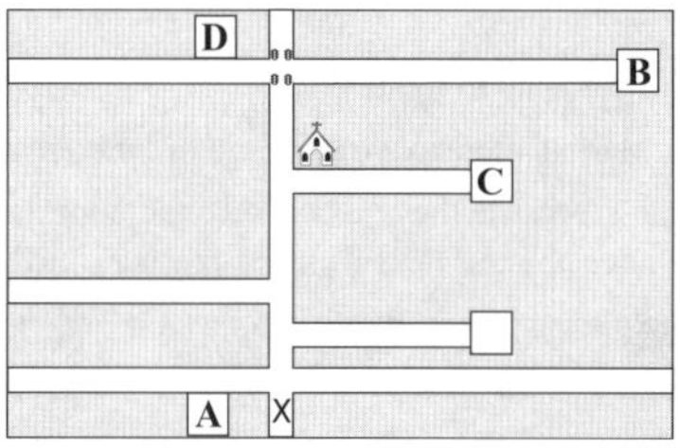	3 marks
7 a)	D	1 mark
b)	A	1 mark
c)	A	1 mark
d)	B	1 mark

Section B:

8 a) i)	Teenagers do not have a healthy diet these days.	1 mark
ii)	(Any of the following) They do not eat fruit or vegetables. They eat food that contains a lot of fat and salt. They love fast food.	1 mark
b)	No	1 mark
	(Any of the following) She doesn't like fast food. She likes her mother's home cooked food. She eats vegetables almost every day. She likes typical Spanish food. She has a healthy diet.	1 mark
9 a)	B	1 mark
b) i)	Cleaner	1 mark
ii)	The local government is introducing a 50 euro fine next year for people who drop litter.	1 mark

(Total marks available for the Listening Paper = 40 marks.)

Speaking Exam

Role Play 1:

	Task:	Marks (A maximum of 4 marks is available for each task.)
•	Your own choice of reason why not. E.g. *No puedo ir porque no tengo mucho dinero.*	4 marks if perfect, or one very minor error. 3 marks if there's up to 2 minor errors that don't change the meaning. 2 marks for more than two minor errors. 1 mark for a major error, but if the general idea is right, e.g. if you just say 'no' and don't give a reason. 0 marks if you don't manage to communicate the message.
•	Your own choice of yes or no, and a reason why or why not. E.g. *Sí, me encanta esquiar, porque me gusta estar en el aire libre, y me gusta la nieve.*	4 marks if perfect, or one very minor error. 3 marks if there's up to 2 minor errors that don't change the meaning (e.g. el nieve). 2 marks for more than 2 minor errors, or if you just gave a reason for liking skiing without saying that you liked it first. 1 mark for a major error, e.g. just 'sí' or 'no'. 0 marks if you don't manage to communicate the message.
•	Your own choice of **two** details of your holidays last year. E.g. *Fui con mi familia a Francia. Tomé sol y nadé en el mar.* *You should be using the past tense here.*	4 marks if perfect, or one very minor error. 3 marks if there's up to 2 minor errors that don't change the meaning. 2 marks for more than 2 minor errors. 1 mark if you don't give 2 details of your holiday, or if you use the wrong tense. 0 marks if you make a big error like only giving 1 detail of your holiday and you use the wrong tense.
•	Your own choice of **two** plans for September. E.g. *Estudiaré para el bachillerato, y también voy a buscar un trabajo a tiempo parcial.* *You won't lose marks if you don't manage the future tense here, but it looks good if you show you know it.*	4 marks if perfect, or one very minor error (using the infinitive or present tense is OK here and won't lose you marks). 3 marks if you make 2 minor errors. 2 marks if you make more than 2 minor errors. 1 mark if you only gave 1 detail, or if you used the past tense. 0 marks if you only gave 1 detail and you used the wrong tense too.

(16 marks)

Role Play 2:

	Task:	Marks (A maximum of 4 marks is available for each task.)
•	Your own choice of what you saw happen in the robbery. E.g. *Estaba en la calle en frente de la joyería, cuando el ladrón salió corriendo.*	4 marks if perfect, or one very minor error. 3 marks if there's up to 2 minor errors that don't change the meaning. 2 marks for more than two minor errors. 1 mark for a major error, but if the general idea is right. 0 marks if you don't manage to communicate the message.
•	Your own choice of description of the robber. E.g. *Es alto y delgado. Tiene el pelo moreno y a media melena. Llevaba un traje azul.*	4 marks if perfect, or one very minor error. 3 marks if there's up to 2 minor errors that don't change the meaning. 2 marks for more than two minor errors. 1 mark for a major error, but if the general idea is right, e.g. if you just say 'es alta'. 0 marks if you don't manage to communicate the message.
•	Your own choice of description of how he escaped. E.g. *El ladrón se escapó con las joyas en un coche negro.*	4 marks if perfect, or one very minor error. 3 marks if there's up to 2 minor errors that don't change the meaning. 2 marks for more than two minor errors. 1 mark for a major error, but if the general idea is right, e.g. if you used the wrong tense. 0 marks if you don't manage to communicate the message.
•	Your own choice of where you are staying. E.g. *En el hotel Buena Vista, en la Plaza Nueva.*	4 marks if perfect, or one very minor error. 3 marks if there's up to 2 minor errors that don't change the meaning. 2 marks for more than two minor errors. 1 mark for a major error, but if the general idea is right, e.g. if you just say 'en un hotel' and don't say what it's called. 0 marks if you don't manage to communicate the message.
•	Your own choice of what you plan to do tomorrow. E.g. *Mañana tengo que volver a Inglaterra — iré al aeropuerto a las nueve.*	4 marks if perfect, or one very minor error. 3 marks if there's up to 2 minor errors that don't change the meaning. 2 marks for more than two minor errors. 1 mark for a major error, but if the general idea is right, e.g. if you used the past tense. 0 marks if you don't manage to communicate the message.

(20 marks)

General Conversation:

The general conversation doesn't have a specific mark scheme because each person will say different things, so you can't just have one set of acceptable answers. Instead, the conversation is marked against a series of criteria, which will be something like the ones below (communication, fluency, (marked out of 4), use of language, accuracy and pronunciation (marked out of 6)).

Communication

Marks	4	3	2	1	0
Description	Almost all of the aspects of the topics are well-covered. You communicate ideas and opinions, giving full descriptions and accounts.	You've given a lot of information on most aspects of the topics, including descriptions, accounts and opinions.	You've given some information on most aspects of the topics. You expressed opinions and developed some topics.	You've given a little relevant information on some aspects of the topic, but your replies were quite short.	You haven't said anything relevant, or what you said didn't make any sense.

Fluency

Marks	4	3	2	1	0
Description	You kept the conversation flowing well and at a reasonable speed. You haven't always waited for a question from the teacher, and you've expanded some of the topics or the points made by the teacher.	You kept the conversation flowing fairly well, and you've talked about more than just the bare essentials of the topic.	You managed to keep the conversation going, and you didn't hesitate too much.	You were a bit hesitant, and your language didn't flow very well.	Your conversation was very hesitant and disjointed.

Use of language

Marks	6	5	4
Description	You've used a good range of vocabulary and tenses appropriately in complex and extended answers.	You've used a wide range of vocabulary and tenses appropriately in complex answers, some of which go some way beyond the original question from the teacher.	You've used some complex sentences with a wide range of vocabulary. Your replies refer to past, present and future events.

Marks	3	2	1	0
Description	Your replies are generally in simple sentences with limited vocabulary and sentence structure. You might use the occasional complex sentence.	Your replies rely on structures and vocabulary from the teacher's questions, and are quite limited. Some replies are in simple complete sentences.	You've just used simple vocabulary in lists, phrases or short sentences which sometimes communicate your message.	You've only used short answers which don't make much sense.

Pronunciation and accuracy

Marks	6	5	4
Description	You only made very minor errors in structure and pronunciation. You've got a good accent and intonation. You've got your message across accurately using a wide range of tenses.	Your structures and pronunciation were mostly accurate, with occasional communication problems. You used a variety of tenses accurately.	You've made some errors of structure or pronunciation which caused some communication problems. You did use some more complex sentences accurately. You used the right tenses, but they weren't always accurate.

Marks	3	2	1	0
Description	You made frequent errors in structures and pronunciation, but you still managed to get your message across. You used basic tenses accurately in simple sentences.	Your pronunciation was mostly recognisable, but you made frequent errors. You usually managed to get your message across.	You made frequent errors in pronunciation and structure, which made it hard to understand what you were saying.	It wasn't possible to understand what you were saying.

(20 marks)

(Total marks available for the Speaking Paper = 56 marks.)

Reading Exam

Q. no.		Answer:	Marks
1		A	1 mark
		C	1 mark
2		D	1 mark
3		Papá (P)	1 mark
		Nina (P & N)	1 mark
		Laura (P)	1 mark
4	a)	Engordaban (accept se aburrían y engordaban)	1 mark
	b)	(Los niños) (Los jóvenes) (Los pacientes) se mejoran más rápidamente (Do not accept se aburrían/veían demasiados programas de tele/engordaban)	1 mark
	c)	Estos (jóvenes/pacientes/niños) pueden seguir estudiando (desde su cama) (Do not accept pueden tener contacto con sus amigos por Internet)	1 mark
5		Carmen tomaba / **comida barata**	1 mark
		Carmen tomará / **comida picante**	1 mark
		Pedro toma / **bebidas sin gas**	1 mark
6	a)	pasaba	1 mark
	b)	robos	1 mark
	c)	más	1 mark
	d)	siente	1 mark
	e)	dejar	1 mark
7	a)	Fotógrafos/Fotografía/Photographo	1 mark
	b)	Los frenos fallaron.	1 mark
	c)	Para evitar ponerle nervioso/Un fotógrafo muerto era primo de un ciclista/Porque un fotógrafo era su primo/Porque los ciclistas, para evitar ponerles nerviosos/La carrera no había terminado (No marks for 'Ponerles nerviosos/No quiso evitar ponerles nerviosos /Evitar nerviosos').	1 mark
	d)	Camino al hotel/Tras la cuarta etapa/Cuando estaba en la carretera (No marks for 'En el hotel/al hotel/a la radio/más tarde').	1 mark
	e)	Era el líder/Porque ganó la carrera/Porque estaba el primer ciclista/Es la costumbre cuando ganas (No marks for 'Es la costumbre/Hay nuevo líder').	1 mark
	f)	Montañas/En alta sierra/Especializado en conseguir triunfos en alta sierra (No marks for 'Conseguir triunfos en alta sierra').	1 mark
	g)	Se cayó/Porque tras una caída/Tuvo una caída/Porque se quedó a sólo un segundo de ser líder tras una caída/tras una caída (No marks for 'Porque David Johnson era más rápido/ Ser líder tras una caída/Líder tras una caída').	1 mark
8	a)	Everything is going great but she's still unhappy. (You need to say both things here to get the mark.)	1 mark
	b)	Something important is missing / something is missing in her life. (Don't accept something is wrong with her life / she needs something important in her life.)	1 mark
	c)	Any one of: make others happy, look after less fortunate people, visit/help/befriend/accompany an ill/old person. (Do not accept: help others, take care of others.)	1 mark
9		In any order: D, E, G	3 marks
10	a)	People who love Seville.	1 mark
	b)	Outskirts of town / of Seville.	1 mark
	c)	The Palace lights are turned on.	1 mark
	d)	They will end up dancing.	1 mark
	e)	Famous as the <u>home</u> of bullfighting in Spain / the <u>most</u> famous bull-ring in Spain / the <u>oldest</u> bull-ring in Spain / the <u>most</u> traditional bull-ring in Spain. (Do not accept: famous (place/bull-ring) in Spain.)	1 mark

(Total marks available for the Reading Paper — 35)

Writing Exam

Different exam boards use different systems to assess their writing exams. The things they mark your work for are very similar though, and will be something like the mark scheme shown below. Like the speaking exam, it's very difficult to mark your own writing answers, because there isn't just one 'right' answer. However, you can get a rough idea by using a dictionary to see how accurate you have been, and ideally getting someone who's good at Spanish to mark your work using the mark scheme below.

Q1
(Total marks available for Q1 = 20 marks [8 marks for communication, and 6 marks each for use of language and accuracy].)

Communication

Marks	7-8	5-6	3-4	1-2	0
Description	You've included your opinions but also justified them. You've given a lot of relevant information, including narrating events and giving full descriptions.	You've given an opinion, and quite a lot of relevant information.	You've given some basic information, with occasional extra details like descriptions and simple opinions.	You've communicated simple facts and not much more.	You haven't managed to communicate any message at all.

Range/complexity of language

Marks	6	5	4
Description	You've used a wide range of vocabulary and structures. You're confident with longer, more complicated sentences, and you write fluently.	You've used a fairly wide range of vocabulary and structures to communicate descriptions and opinions. You use long sentences fairly successfully.	You've used a fairly good range of vocabulary and you have attempted longer sentences using linking words (pues, entonces etc.). You've managed to express your opinions and use more than one tense.

Mark	3	2	1	0
Description	You've used the correct vocabulary and structures, but there isn't much variety.	You've used the right basic vocabulary for the task. Your sentences are very simple, not very varied, and you don't really link them together.	You've only used simple vocabulary and structures, and your sentences are repetitive and use a lot of words that sound like English words (e.g. problema).	You've not really used much relevant vocabulary. Some of your words are recognisable, but your sentences don't make much sense.

Accuracy

Mark	6	5	4
Description	You've hardly made any errors. Your work is accurate even when you're using more difficult tenses or grammar structures.	You've only made minor errors, or a major error in a complicated sentence. You usually use verbs and tenses correctly.	There are quite a few minor errors and some major ones, but your work is still mostly accurate. Even when you make mistakes, the meaning is still obvious.

Mark	3	2	1	0
Description	There are a lot of minor errors and some major errors. You often make mistakes using verbs and tenses.	Most of your sentences have errors, and you rarely use verb forms accurately.	You've only managed to write very basic sentences correctly. Most of your sentences have major errors.	You haven't really managed to write anything correctly.

Q2

(Total marks available for Q2 = 30 marks [12 marks for communication, and 9 marks each for use of language and accuracy].)

Communication

Marks	10-12	7-9	4-6	1-3	0
Description	You've included your opinions but also justified them. You've given a lot of relevant information, including narrating events and giving full descriptions.	You've given an opinion, and quite a lot of relevant information.	You've given some basic information, with occasional extra details like descriptions and simple opinions.	You've communicated simple facts and not much more.	You haven't managed to communicate any message at all.

Range/complexity of language

Marks	8-9	6-7	4-5
Description	You've used a wide range of vocabulary and structures. You're confident with longer, more complicated sentences, and you write fluently.	You've used a fairly wide range of vocabulary and structures to communicate descriptions and opinions. You use long sentences fairly successfully.	You've used a fairly good range of vocabulary and you have attempted longer sentences using linking words (pues, entonces etc.)You've managed to express your opinions and use more than one tense.

Marks	3	2	1	0
Description	You've used the correct vocabulary and structures, but there isn't much variety.	You've used the right basic vocabulary for the task. Your sentences are very simple, not very varied, and you don't really link them together.	You've only used simple vocabulary and structures, and your sentences are repetitive and use a lot of words that sound like English words (e.g. café).	You've not really used much relevant vocabulary. Some of your words are recognisable, but your sentences don't make much sense.

Accuracy

Marks	8-9	6-7	4-5
Description	You've hardly made any errors. Your work is accurate even when you're using more difficult tenses or grammar structures.	You've only made minor errors, or a major error in a complicated sentence. You usually use verbs and tenses correctly.	There are quite a few minor errors and some major ones, but your work is still mostly accurate. Even when you make mistakes, the meaning is still obvious.

Marks	3	2	1	0
Description	There are a lot of minor errors and some major errors. You often make mistakes using verbs and tenses.	Most of your sentences have errors, and you rarely use verb forms accurately.	You've only managed to write very basic sentences correctly. Most of your sentences have major errors.	You haven't really managed to write anything correctly.

(Total marks available for the Writing Paper — 50)

Working Out Your Grade

- *Work out your average percentage for the whole exam.*
- *Look it up in this table to see what grade you got. If you're borderline, don't push yourself up a grade — the real examiners won't.*
- *These grades will only give you a rough guide — they're no guarantee that you'll get this grade in the real exam. It's really important that you do as much practice and revision as possible to help you get the grade you want.*

Average %	85+	74 – 84	61 – 73	47 – 60	37 – 46	29 – 36	22 – 28	15 – 21	under 15
Grade	**A***	**A**	**B**	**C**	**D**	**E**	**F**	**G**	**U**

Important:

- *This is a higher level paper, but it's still good practice if you're preparing for a foundation level exam. Don't be put off if you find some of the questions really difficult — they'll be more straightforward in the actual foundation exam.*

Track 1 Page 12

1)

a) Son las diez y cuarto.

b) Son las veinte horas cuarenta minutos.

c) Son las siete y media.

Track 2 Page 12

2) **Ejemplo** El cumpleaños de Berta es el quince de julio.

a) Julián cumple los años el dos de octubre.

b) El cumpleaños de Marisa es el dieciséis de septiembre.

c) Víctor va a organizar una fiesta para su cumpleaños, que es el día cinco de diciembre.

d) Voy a comprar un regalo para Sergio, pues su cumpleaños es el veinte de abril.

Track 3 Page 12

3) Soy Rosaura y vivo en un pueblo de la provincia de Huelva. Cuando termino el colegio, voy a clases de baile dos veces por semana; siempre hago mis deberes, y si hay tiempo, veo la tele antes de cenar. Los domingos voy a misa con mis padres y mi hermana. Me encanta el cine y voy a ver películas de estreno siempre que puedo; la semana pasada fui con mis amigas a ver 'El diario de Bridget Jones' y me reí mucho. Mi familia y yo vamos de vacaciones todos los años en el mes de agosto; tenemos un apartamento en la Costa de la Luz.

Track 4 Page 28

Ejemplo

F1 Juan, ¿es verdad que fuiste de vacaciones con tus tíos y tus primos?

M1 Sí, todos los años alquilamos un piso muy grande. ¡Vamos a la costa en dos coches!

F1 Y ¿qué hiciste?

M1 Fui a la playa muchos días porque me encanta.

F1 ¿Con quién? A tu hermana le gusta la playa, ¿no?

M1 Sí, le gusta, pero mi hermana estaba siempre con mi prima. Fui a la playa con mi hermano, Alejandro.

1)

F1 ¿Y jugaste al tenis?

M1 Sí, claro. Siempre juego al tenis cuando estoy de vacaciones. Cuando era pequeño jugaba con mi padre, pero ¡prefiero jugar con mi madre porque juego mejor que ella!

F1 ¡Así tú puedes ganar! ¿Y jugaste con tu madre entonces?

M1 Sí. Le encanta el tenis y a mí también.

2)

F1 ¿Fuiste de compras?

M1 Sí, pero sólo al supermercado. Tenemos que comprar mucha comida para dos familias, y siempre tengo que ayudar.

F1 ¿Con quién fuiste?

M1 Pues, el coche de mi padre es muy pequeño así que fui con mi tío.

3)

F1 ¿Y visitaste sitios de interés?

M1 Bueno, sí, un museo, pero la verdad es que no era muy interesante.

F1 ¿Con quién fuiste?

M1 Con mis primos, pero después de veinte minutos volvimos al piso porque era aburrido.

F1 ¡Ah, vale!

Track 5 Page 28

4)

F1 ¿Adónde irás de vacaciones el verano que viene, Raquel?

F2 Voy a ir a Francia en julio.

F1 Y, ¿cómo irás?

F2 Vamos a ir en avión de Madrid a París.

F1 ¿Y sabes qué harás allí?

F2 Vamos a visitar galerías de arte. Hay muchas en París.

Track 6 Page 28

5)

F1 Hotel Alhambra, ¡diga!

M1 Buenos días. Quisiera reservar una habitación doble.

F1 Muy bien. Todas las habitaciones dobles tienen ducha y balcón. ¿Para cuántas noches quiere la habitación?

M1 Quisiera quedarme cinco noches. ¿Cuánto es?

F1 Por noche son cuarenta euros, así que, en total son doscientos euros.

M1 Bueno, la tomo.

Track 7 Page 42

F1 He perdido mi bolso. Lo tenía ayer cuando estaba en la cafetería de la estación de trenes pero ahora no lo tengo.

M1 Ah sí, ¿cómo es el bolso?

F1 Es pequeño, negro y de cuero. Mi monedero estaba dentro.

M1 ¿Llevaba dinero?

F1 Sí, claro. Cincuenta euros.

M1 ¿Y algo más había?

F1 Vamos a ver … mi agenda, fotos de mi familia y las llaves de casa.

M1 Bueno, voy a ver si lo tenemos. ¿Cómo se llama usted y cuál es su número de teléfono?

F1 Me llamo Cristina Rodríguez y mi número de teléfono es el setenta y ocho, cuarenta y cinco, treinta y dos.

Track 8 Page 57

1)

F1 Ana, háblame de tu horario escolar.

F2 Vale, bueno, los lunes, miércoles y viernes hay seis clases por día. Por la mañana tenemos inglés a las ocho y media y las matemáticas a las nueve y veinte.
A las diez y diez tenemos un recreo que dura treinta minutos. Después del primer recreo tenemos historia y a las once y media tenemos informática. A las doce y veinte hay otro recreo de veinte minutos y después del segundo recreo tenemos música y a la una y media tenemos geografía. Las clases terminan a las dos y veinte.
Los martes y los jueves tenemos tres clases dobles que duran una hora y cuarenta minutos. Primero tenemos arte, y después del primer recreo hay ciencias. Después del segundo recreo hay educación física. Mis asignaturas preferidas son arte y educación física, así que me encantan los martes y los jueves en el instituto.

Track 9 Page 57

2)

M1 ¿En qué trabaja tu padre, Raquel?

F1 Hace unos años mi padre era dueño de una tienda en el centro de la ciudad, pero tenía que trabajar horas muy largas, incluso los fines de semana. Al final decidió estudiar otra carrera y ahora mi padre es ingeniero. Está mucho más contento ahora.

M1 ¿Cuántas horas trabaja por semana?

F1 Trabaja treinta y dos horas por semana y lo bueno es que no tiene que trabajar ni los sábados ni los domingos. Cuando era dueño de la tienda trabajaba sesenta horas por semana, como mínimo.

M1 ¿Y tu madre?

F1 Mi madre es enfermera pero detesta su trabajo porque es muy duro. El año que viene va a buscar otro trabajo a tiempo parcial. Le interesa hacer algo relacionado con los niños, como maestra de primaria.

M1 ¿Y tu hermana?

F1 Es secretaria. Sólo trabaja los martes, jueves y sábados pero no le gusta trabajar los sábados, preferiría trabajar los lunes, miércoles y viernes y estar libre los fines de semana. Gana treinta euros por día.

M1 ¿Y tú? ¿Tienes trabajo?

F1 Sí, trabajo en una peluquería los sábados pero no es lo que quiero hacer en el futuro. Es bastante aburrido y sólo gano cinco euros por hora. El año que viene voy a estudiar arte en la universidad porque me gustaría ser diseñadora de moda. ¡Es mi sueño!

Track 10 Page 72

1)

F1 ¿Qué haces en tus ratos libres, Sandra?

F2 Me encantan el tenis y el hockey. También, soy miembro de un club de bádminton. Pero no me gusta nada leer. ¿Y tú, Pilar?

F1 Lo que más me gusta es tocar el piano. Toco el piano todos los días en casa y también canto en un coro. Lo que no aguanto es practicar deportes como el baloncesto o el tenis de mesa.
¿Y tú, Carmen?

F3 A mí me gusta mucho estar al aire libre. Los fines de semana hago ciclismo con mi hermana o hago senderismo en el campo. Odio estar en casa con los videojuegos – en mi opinión es un pasatiempo muy aburrido.
¿Y tú, Roberto?

M1 Prefiero leer. Tengo muchos libros en casa y leo, por lo menos, dos novelas al mes. Lo que detesto es ver la tele. Para mí es mucho más interesante leer un libro que ver una película en la tele.

Track 11 Page 72

2)

F1 Hola Eva. ¿Qué quieres hacer mañana por la tarde?

F2 Bueno, no sé, podemos ir al cine o a la bolera. ¿Cuál prefieres tú, Luisa?

F1 Prefiero ir al cine pero, ¿por qué no vamos al teatro?

F2 La verdad es que no me gusta mucho ir al teatro, lo encuentro muy aburrido. ¿Te gustaría ir a la pista de hielo?

F1 Sí, me encantaría. ¿A qué hora nos encontramos?

F2 Pues, tengo una clase de aeróbic a las cuatro que dura una hora y después tengo que recoger a mi hermano de la piscina antes de las seis y media. ¿Te va bien las siete y media?
F1 Está bien. ¿Cuánto cuesta una sesión de patinaje sobre hielo?
F2 No lo sé exactamente. La última vez que fui costó dos euros cincuenta pero creo que ahora cuesta tres euros. Sí, estoy segura. Me lo dijo mi hermano.
F1 Vale. ¿Dónde nos vemos?
F2 Nos vemos al lado de la biblioteca. ¿Sabes dónde está?
F1 Pues, no, nunca voy a la biblioteca. ¿Por qué no nos vemos delante de Correos?
F2 Vale. Delante de Correos entonces. Hasta mañana.

Track 12 Page 72
3)
F1 ¿Quieres ir al cine Beatriz?
F2 Vale. ¿Qué ponen?
F1 Dame el periódico un momento… vamos a ver…. Ah, ponen 'El diario de Bridget Jones Dos' a las ocho y 'La Casa de Fantasmas' a las diez. ¿Cuál prefieres?
F2 La verdad es que no me gustan las comedias y sobre todo las comedias románticas. Vi la primera película de 'Bridget Jones' y pensé que la chica era muy tonta. El problema es que tampoco me gustan las películas de terror. La última vez que vi una película de terror no dormí durante muchas noches. ¿Cuál prefieres tú Lucía?
F1 Pues, odio las películas de terror porque me dan miedo y detesto las películas sangrientas. Las comedias me dan igual pero prefiero las películas de acción.
F2 Mira aquí, también ponen 'Misión Imposible Tres' a las diez y media. ¿Te interesa ver ésta?
F1 No mucho. Tom Cruise es muy feo en mi opinión y además es muy mal actor. Siempre hace los mismos papeles y me aburre bastante.
F2 ¿Qué hacemos entonces?
F1 Podemos ver un DVD. ¿Quieres ver 'Los Doce de Oceans'?
F2 Sí, tengo muchas ganas de verlo, ¡todos los actores son muy guapos! ¿Te interesa?
F1 ¡Sí, mucho! Me encantan las películas policiacas.

Track 13 Page 90
1)
Ejemplo
F1 Buenos días.
F2 Buenos días. ¿En qué puedo servirle?
F1 ¿Tiene tomates?
F2 Sí, son muy frescos. ¿Cuántos quiere?
F1 Póngame tres kilos…, pues no, ya tengo unos en casa, póngame dos.
F2 Muy bien. Dos kilos. ¿Algo más?
F1 No me acuerdo, voy a mirar la lista que tengo…a ver…ya he comprado queso, uvas, chorizo, pan y lechugas, ah sí, falta jamón. Pues deme ocho lonchas de jamón.
F2 Vale. Aquí tiene. Son dos euros setenta en total.
F1 Aquí tiene. Adiós.

A
F2 ¿En qué puedo servirle?
F1 Pues, voy a preparar una tortilla en casa. Ya tengo huevos y ajo pero no tengo patatas. ¿Me da un kilo de patatas y una barra de pan?
F2 Muy bien…un kilo de patatas y dos barras de pan, ¿verdad?
F1 No. Es una barra de pan.
F2 Ay, perdón. ¿Algo más?
F1 No. ¿Cuánto es?
F2 Un euro setenta.
F1 Aquí tiene.

B
F1 ¿Tiene uvas?
F2 No, no tenemos hoy pero tenemos cerezas muy dulces y naranjas muy ricas.
F1 Deme cuatro naranjas entonces.
F2 ¿Algo más?
F1 Sí, también quisiera dos botellas de agua.
F2 ¿Sin gas o con gas?
F1 Sin gas, a mi marido no le gustan las bebidas gaseosas.
F2 Aquí tiene. Pues, las naranjas cuestan un euro cuarenta y las botellas de agua cuestan un euro cada una así que son tres euros cuarenta en total.
F1 Gracias, adiós.

C
F2 Buenos días. ¿En qué puedo servirle?
F1 Necesito queso para los bocadillos de los niños.
F2 ¿Cuánto quiere?
F1 Quisiera cuatro lonchas.
F2 ¿Algo más?
F1 Sí, medio kilo de fresas.
F2 No tenemos fresas hoy.
F1 Pues, medio kilo de frambuesas.
F2 Lo siento pero tampoco tenemos frambuesas hoy. Había un problema con la entrega de fruta esta mañana, sólo tenemos cerezas.
F1 Vale. Pues, deme quinientos gramos entonces.
F2 ¿Eso es todo?
F1 Sí, ¿cuánto es?
F2 Son diez euros sesenta en total.
F1 ¡Diez euros!
F2 Ay, me he equivocado, quiero decir, dos euros sesenta.
F1 Vale. Aquí tiene.
F2 Gracias, adiós.

Track 14 Page 90
2)
F1 ¿Qué quieres, Juan?
M1 Me apetece la pasta con los champiñones pero no me gusta la salsa que lleva, así que voy a tomar un filete con patatas fritas.
F1 ¿Y de postre?
M1 Pues me encantan los postres y en este restaurante tienen todos mis favoritos – el arroz con leche, las natillas, – pero sobre todo me encanta el chocolate, entonces voy a escoger el pastel de chocolate.
F1 ¿Y para beber?
M1 Mmm…un zumo de manzana…pues no… tengo mucha sed…una cola para mí.
F1 Vale. ¿Y tú, Mariela?
F2 A mí me encantan las patatas fritas pero estoy a régimen y no puedo comer ni las patatas fritas ni las hamburguesas. Voy a tomar el bacalao con una ensalada.
F1 ¿Y de postre?
F2 La verdad es que tengo muchas ganas de comer algo dulce, como el pastel de chocolate, pero debería tomar fruta.
F1 ¿Y para beber?
F2 Un zumo de naranja aunque me gustaría beber un vaso de vino tinto.
F1 Zumo, muy bien. ¿Y tú, Raquel?
F3 Pues, como nunca como carne no puedo escoger ni el pollo ni el cerdo ni el filete. Quiero probar los calamares porque me han dicho que son muy ricos en este restaurante y de postre quiero un helado de fresa.
F1 ¿Y para beber?
F3 Una cerveza. ¿Qué vas a tomar tú, Belén?
F1 Pues, yo voy a tomar gambas a la plancha, aunque también me apetecen los calamares, de postre un yogur y para beber una cerveza, como tú.

Track 15 Page 107
1)
F1 ¿Cómo es tu dormitorio, Susana?
F2 Bueno, mi dormitorio es bastante pequeño y en mi opinión es bastante feo, pero es limpio. En mi dormitorio hay dos camas – porque comparto mi dormitorio con mi hermana – una mesa y dos sillas – donde hacemos los deberes – una alfombra de rayas, unos estantes en la pared y un armario. Antes había un ordenador en la mesa pero ahora está en el despacho de mi padre. No tenemos ni televisión ni equipo de música porque no hay sitio.

Track 16 Page 107
2)
Ejemplo
F1 ¿Qué le pasa?
M1 Me siento mal. Esta tarde comí muchos caramelos y ahora me duele mucho el estómago.
F1 Pues, tiene que beber agua, por lo menos dos vasos por hora, durante seis horas.
M1 Vale, doctor.

A
F2 ¿Qué le duele?
F3 ¡Todo! Estoy muy cansada y me duele todo el cuerpo.
F2 Pues, me parece que tiene gripe. Tiene que meterse en la cama durante dos días.

B

F1 ¿Qué le pasa?
F2 No me siento bien, doctora.
F1 ¿Qué le duele?
F2 Me duele la garganta y también tengo dolor de cabeza.
F1 Pues hay que tomar dos aspirinas cada tres horas. ¿Vale?

C

M1 ¿Qué le pasa?
F1 No sé, doctor. Pasé todo el día en la playa y ahora me siento mal. Estoy mareada y me duele mucho la cabeza.
M1 Es posible que tenga una insolación. Hay que quedarse en casa. Mejor no salir durante el día, ¿vale?

Track 17 Page 118

1)

M1 Hola, soy David. Quisiera dejar un mensaje para Roberto. Mira, Roberto, no tengo que trabajar en el restaurante mañana así que voy a salir con vosotros para celebrar el cumpleaños de José. ¿Vale?
F2 Buenos días señor Castillo, soy Carmen Cortázar. Tengo un problema. No encuentro mi raqueta de tenis. Lo siento mucho pero no puedo participar en el concurso de esta tarde.
F1 Hola Felipe, soy Penélope. Hay un retraso de una hora por la niebla, así que voy a llegar a las ocho y media, más o menos. Llámame cuando recibas este mensaje.
F3 Buenos días. Mi nombre es señora Piqueres y llamo para comprobar los detalles de mi reserva de una habitación doble con ducha el día once de agosto. Mi número de teléfono es cincuenta y dos, sesenta y uno, ochenta. Gracias.

Track 18 Page 118

2)

Ejemplo

F1 Hola. ¿Cuánto cuesta mandar una carta a Inglaterra?
F2 Un sello para Inglaterra cuesta sesenta céntimos.

A

M1 Buenos días. Quiero mandar tres paquetes a Alemania.
F1 A ver...pues, pesan casi un kilo cada uno, así que en total son dieciséis euros treinta y seis.

B

F1 ¿Tiene sellos?
F2 Sí, ¿cuántos quiere?
F1 Pues, tengo que mandar diez cartas a Italia. ¿Cuánto cuesta en total?
F2 Un sello para Italia cuesta cincuenta céntimos. En total son cinco euros.

C

F1 Hola. Quisiera mandar una tarjeta postal a mi abuela que vive en Australia. ¿Cuánto cuesta?
F2 Vale. Cuesta un euro noventa y dos mandar una tarjeta postal a Australia.

Track 19 Page 133

1)

F1 ¿Cómo fue tu experiencia laboral, Laura?
F2 Bueno, trabajé en un supermercado durante dos semanas y la verdad es que no me gustó nada porque el trabajo era muy aburrido y trabajaba horas muy largas – de las ocho de la mañana hasta las seis de la tarde – y llegaba a casa cansadísima. No quiero hacer este tipo de trabajo en el futuro porque no me interesa nada. ¿Y tú, Jorge?
M1 Pues, todo lo contrario. Trabajé en un taller de coches cerca de mi casa. El trabajo era bastante duro pero me encantaba trabajar con las manos y con gente simpática y entusiasta. Cuando termine mis estudios voy a hacer prácticas y en el futuro me gustaría ser mecánico porque es un trabajo muy variado. ¿Y tú, María?
F1 Pues yo trabajé en una peluquería en el centro de la ciudad. Conocí a mucha gente nueva pero el trabajo era un poco repetitivo. No tenía mucha responsabilidad, sólo me dejaban preparar tazas de té y café y barrer el suelo. Sin embargo es un trabajo que a mí me interesa mucho aunque no es un trabajo bien pagado.

Track 20 Page 133

2)

F1 ¿Qué opinas del medio ambiente, Ana?
F2 La verdad es que vivo en un pueblo pequeño muy cerca de un parque nacional y por eso no se notan mucho los problemas del medio ambiente. Pero antes vivía en el centro de la ciudad y allí había muchos problemas como la contaminación industrial y el humo de los coches. Mi amigo, José, vive en la costa y allí los turistas dejan basura en la playa y en las calles. José dice que a los turistas no les interesan ni la naturaleza ni los animales y que todo está muy sucio porque no utilizan las papeleras. En mi opinión la situación es bastante grave y hay que pensarlo bien. Tenemos que tomar medidas ahora mismo y salvar el planeta en interés de nuestros hijos.

Practice Exam

Track 21 Page 191

1)

F1 Carla, necesitamos unas cosas. ¿Puedes ir al centro esta mañana?
F2 Vale, Mamá. ¿Qué quieres?
F1 Pues, primero quiero pollo para hacer paella, y también necesito jamón. Tráeme seis lonchas de jamón.
F2 Vale, ¿qué más?
F1 A ver... ah sí, busca un regalo para tu prima Sara. Es su cumpleaños el lunes que viene y hay un vestido muy bonito en la tienda enfrente del supermercado. Es rosa con flores y es de algodón. Es de la marca Zig Zag.
F2 Sí, sí, lo vi la semana pasada cuando fui de compras con Marisol. ¡Es muy bonito!
F1 Pues el vestido rosa entonces, en la talla pequeña.
F2 Vale, ¿es todo?
F1 No, tu padre no se encuentra bien. Le duele la garganta y también la cabeza. Compra una botella grande de jarabe y una caja de aspirinas.
F2 Vale. ¡Hasta luego!

Track 22 Page 192

2)

M1 ¿Diga?
F1 Alvaro, soy Ana. ¿Qué tal?
M1 Bien, bien, ¿y tú?
F1 Bien. Mira, vamos a salir el sábado por la noche, Pilar, Miguel, David y yo. ¿Quieres salir con nosotros?
M1 Bueno, me gustaría pero no puedo.
F1 ¿Por qué no?
M1 Bueno, la verdad es que estudio todos los días para los exámenes y tengo muchas ganas de salir ... y no es cuestión de dinero porque en este momento tengo bastante. El problema es que tengo que trabajar en el restaurante de mis padres el sábado por la noche porque mi hermano está enfermo.
F1 ¡Qué pena! Pues, otra noche, entonces. ¡Hasta pronto!
M1 Adiós.

Track 23 Page 192

3)

F1 ¿Qué piensas de la comida, Emilia?
F2 Pues, si veo al camarero, le voy a decir que el pescado tiene muchas espinas y la salsa no tiene sabor. Es asqueroso. ¿Y tú? ¿Qué crees, Alicia?
F1 A mí tampoco me gusta la comida. La carne está quemada y las patatas fritas están frías. No sé qué ha pasado en este restaurante. Antes era muy bueno.
F3 ¡Qué dices!
F1 Pues, ¿a ti te gusta, Manuela?
F3 Sí, sí. A mí, sí. La paella está muy rica y me gusta mucho la decoración. ¡Queda muy bonita! Bien, dinos Carlos, ¿tú qué opinas?
M1 Pues, la comida es regular, pero hay una buena selección de vinos.

Track 24 Page 193

4)

Ejemplo

F1 Bueno María, ¿cuándo vamos de excursión a Salamanca?
F2 Vamos el cuatro de febrero.
F1 Y, ¿a qué hora nos encontramos?
F2 A las nueve y media de la mañana, ¿vale? En la Plaza Mayor.
F1 Muy bien. Si voy a llegar tarde, te llamaré. ¿Cuál es tu número de teléfono?
F2 Es el noventa y dos, veintiuno, treinta y tres.
F1 Vale, el noventa y dos, veintiuno, treinta y tres.
F2 Sí. Hasta el día cuatro entonces.

A

F1 Hola, Jorge.
M1 Hola, Susana. ¿Cuándo llegas?
F1 El doce de julio.
M1 ¡El doce! ¡Qué bien! ¿A qué hora?
F1 Llego a las diez menos cuarto de la mañana.

M1 Bueno, estaré en el aeropuerto. Te doy el número de mi móvil, es el cuarenta y dos, setenta y cinco, cincuenta. ¿Lo repito?
F1 Sí.
M1 Vale. Es el cuarenta y dos, setenta y cinco, cincuenta.
F1 Vale. Hasta luego.

B
F1 Ana, ¿quieres ir al cine conmigo el sábado que viene?
F2 El sábado que viene es el día dos de mayo, ¿verdad?
F1 Sí. Ponen 'Spiderman' a las cinco de la tarde. ¿Lo quieres ver?
F2 Pues, depende. Tengo que estudiar para los exámenes.
F1 Y yo también, ¡pero tenemos que relajarnos un poco!
F2 Tienes razón … y hace mucho tiempo que quiero ver 'Spiderman'. Vale, te veo a las cinco.
F1 Mi padre me va a llevar. Si quieres que te lleve, llámame. Es el cincuenta y siete, ochenta, ochenta.
F2 El cincuenta y siete, ochenta, ochenta. Muy bien.

C
F1 Raquel, ¿qué haces el miércoles de la semana próxima?
F2 ¿Qué fecha es?
F1 Es el veintitrés de octubre.
F2 No sé. No tengo planes todavía.
F1 ¿Quieres ir de compras? La última vez lo pasamos muy bien, ¿te acuerdas?
F2 Sí, ¡pero gasté mucho dinero! Vale. ¿Dónde nos encontramos?
F1 Enfrente de la estación de autobuses a las siete y cuarto. ¿Está bien?
F2 ¡Las siete y cuarto! Es muy temprano, ¿no? No tengo despertador.
F1 No hay problema. Te llamaré para despertarte. Dame tu número de teléfono.
F2 Es el treinta y ocho, noventa y seis, setenta y uno.
F1 Vale, el treinta y ocho, noventa y seis, setenta y uno. Hasta el miércoles entonces.

Track 25 Page 193
5)
F1 Bueno Encarna, ¿qué piensas de tus asignaturas en el colegio?
F2 Pues, mira, el año pasado no me gustaba la historia, pero ahora sí. Es interesante. Hay otras asignaturas que me interesan también, pero las matemáticas no. Son muy complicadas y no entiendo nada.

F1 Y tú Raúl, ¿qué opinas de tus asignaturas?
M1 La asignatura que más me gusta es el inglés. La profesora es muy buena. ¡Y en inglés se puede hablar en clase! Sin embargo, no me gustan nada las ciencias.
F1 ¿Por qué? ¿Piensas que son complicadas?
M1 No. Para mí son aburridas. Me duermo en clase.

F1 ¿Y tú Elena?
F3 En mi opinión la educación física es la asignatura más divertida porque me encanta el baloncesto.
F1 ¿Y qué más?
F3 Vamos a ver … las otras asignaturas pues, así así, pero no aguanto la geografía. Es inútil.
F1 ¿Inútil?
F3 ¡Si yo ya sé donde vivo!

F3 ¿Y tú, Rosa?
F1 Bueno, cuando era pequeña me gustaban mucho las matemáticas pero ahora mi asignatura favorita es la informática. La profesora es muy simpática.
F3 ¿Y la que menos te gusta?
F1 La música. De verdad, la detesto. Es muy difícil.

Track 26 Page 194
6)
Ejemplo
A
M1 ¡Perdone! ¿Para ir a la oficina de turismo?
F1 Ah sí. Mire, estamos aquí en su mapa. Tome la primera a la izquierda, Calle San Juan, y la oficina de turismo está a la izquierda.
M1 ¿A la izquierda?
F1 Sí, la verá en seguida.
M1 Gracias.
F1 De nada.

B
F1 Por favor, ¿conoce usted la ciudad?
F2 Sí, sí.
F1 ¿Me puede decir dónde está el castillo?
F2 Está un poco lejos … vamos a ver. Siga todo recto, pasando por delante de la catedral, gire a la derecha …
F1 ¿A la derecha?
F2 Sí, en el cruce de los semáforos, y luego el castillo está a cien metros todo recto.
F1 Muchas gracias.
F2 De nada.

C
F2 Señor, ¿hay un mercado por aquí? He ido a encontrarme con mis amigos allí, pero me he perdido.
M1 A ver… sí, está bastante cerca de aquí. Tome la segunda, no, la tercera, la tercera a la derecha y está al final de la calle.
F2 Vale. La tercera a la derecha, y al final de la calle. Muchas gracias.

D
M1 Señora, por favor, ¿la biblioteca está cerca de aquí?
F1 Sí, no está lejos, a unos quinientos metros más o menos. ¿Sabe dónde está el cruce de los semáforos?
M1 Sí, al final de esta calle.
F1 Eso es. Pues, siga todo recto hasta el cruce. Luego gire a la izquierda y la biblioteca está a la derecha.
M1 Vale, gracias.
F1 De nada.

Track 27 Page 195
7)
F1 Buenos días, señor.
M1 Buenos días. ¿A qué hora sale el próximo tren para Madrid?
F1 Sale a las diez y veinte.
M1 Vale, todavía tengo tiempo. ¿A qué hora llega?
F1 A las doce treinta.
M1 Bien, pues quisiera un billete de ida de segunda clase.
F1 ¿Cómo? ¿De ida y vuelta me ha dicho?
M1 No, no. Después me voy a Bilbao en avión. Quiero un billete sólo de ida.
F1 ¿Fumadores o no fumadores?
M1 Mejor no fumadores. ¿De qué andén sale?
F1 Del número siete.
M1 ¿Y hay que cambiar?
F1 No, es directo. Son nueve euros cuarenta en total.
M1 Aquí tiene. Ahora, me gustaría sentarme y leer el periódico mientras espero. ¿Hay sala de espera?
F1 Por supuesto. La tiene allí enfrente.
M1 Es verdad. Gracias.
F1 A usted. ¡Buen viaje!

Track 28 Page 196
8)
F1 ¿Qué piensas de la dieta de los jóvenes hoy en día, Víctor?
M1 Bueno, cuando yo era joven, no había tanta comida rápida, y comíamos bien. Ahora es terrible. Los jóvenes de hoy no comen nada de fruta ni verdura, sólo patatas fritas y pizza. Casi toda la comida que comen contiene mucha grasa y sal. A los jóvenes les encanta la comida rápida pero este tipo de comida engorda mucho. La mayoría de los jóvenes hoy en día no tienen una dieta sana.
F1 Vale, y tú María, ¿qué piensas?
F2 Lo siento, pero ¡los jóvenes no somos todos iguales! Yo tengo dieciséis años y no aguanto la comida rápida. Además es muy cara. Mi madre cocina muy bien y prefiero comer en casa. Como verduras casi todos los días y me encanta la comida típica española – el pescado, la tortilla, la paella, las ensaladas. Así que no estoy de acuerdo contigo Víctor. Yo tengo una dieta muy sana, y mis amigos también.

Track 29 Page 197
9)
F1 Me llamo Puri y vivo en un pueblo pequeño en el sur de España, cerca de la costa. La gente aquí es muy amable y como el pueblo no es muy grande, tengo todos mis amigos muy cerca. Mi pueblo no es muy bonito y el problema es que hay mucha basura en las calles. Hay suficientes papeleras pero la gente no las usa y la situación es bastante grave. El año que viene, el gobierno local va a introducir una multa de cincuenta euros si la gente deja basura en el suelo, y yo estoy totalmente de acuerdo. Creo que la situación va a mejorar porque la gente tendrá que utilizar las papeleras en el futuro si no quiere pagar la multa. ¡Eso espero!

Spanish — English Dictionary

A

la a f *a (letter)*
a prep *at, to*
abajo ad *down, downstairs, below*
el abanico m *fan*
abatido/a a *depressed*
la abeja f *bee*
abierto/a a *open*
el/la abogado/a mf *lawyer*
abonarse vr *to subscribe to*
el abono m *subscription, payment*
abrazar v *to hug*
el abrazo m *hug*
el abrebotellas m *bottle opener*
el abrelatas m *tin opener*
abrigar v *to shelter, keep warm*
el abrigo m *overcoat*
abril m *April*
abrir v *to open*
abrochar v *to fasten*
la abuela f *grandmother*
el abuelo m *grandfather*
aburrido/a a *bored, boring*
aburrirse vr *to be/get bored*
acabar v *to finish* acabar de *to have just…(done something)*
acampar v *to camp*
el acantilado m *cliff*
el aceite m *oil*
la aceituna f *olive*
acelerar v *to speed up*
aceptar v *to accept*
la acera f *pavement*
acerca de prep *about*
acercarse (a) vr *to get near (to)*
el acero m *steel*
acertar v *to guess, to be right*
acogedor(a) a *welcoming*
acoger v *to receive*
la acogida f *reception, welcome*
acompañar v *to accompany*
aconsejar v *to advise*
acordarse (de) vr *to remember*
acostarse vr *to go to bed*
la actitud f *attitude*
la actividad f *activity*
la actuación f *performance*
las actualidades fpl *news*
actualmente ad *nowadays*
actuar v *to act*
el acuerdo m *agreement*
adelantar v *to overtake, move forward*
adelante ad *forward*
además ad *in addition*
adentro ad *inside*
el adiós m & excl *goodbye*
adivinar v *to guess*
adjunto/a a *attached*
¿adónde? ad *where?*
adrede ad *on purpose*
la aduana f *Customs*
el/la aduanero/a mf *Customs officer*
advertir v *to warn*
el aerodeslizador m *hovercraft*
el aeropuerto m *airport*
afeitarse vr *to shave*
la afición f *hobby*
el/la aficionado/a mf *enthusiast, fan*
afuera ad *outside*
las afueras fpl *outskirts*
agarrar v *to grip*
la agencia de viajes f *travel agency*
agitar v *to wave, to shake*
agosto m *August*
agotar v *to wear out, extinguish*
agradable a *pleasant, helpful*
agradecer v *to thank*
agradecido/a a *grateful*
el agrado m *pleasure*
el agua f *water*
aguantar v *to put up with, stand*
aguardar v *to wait, to wait for*
agudo/a a *sharp, pointed*
la aguja f *needle*
el agujero m *hole*
ahí ad *there*
ahogarse vr *to drown/choke*
ahora ad *now*
ahorrar v *to save*
aislado/a a *isolated*
el ajedrez m *chess*
el ajo m *garlic*
al aparato *speaking (on phone)*
alargar v *to stretch*
el albañil m *bricklayer*
el albaricoque m *apricot*
el albergue m *hostel, shelter*
el alcalde m *mayor*
alcanzar v *to reach*
la aldea f *hamlet*
alegrarse vr *to be happy*
alegrarse de *to be pleased about*
alegre a *happy*
la alegría f *happiness, joy*
alejarse vr *to go/move away*
el alfiler m *pin*
la alfombra f *carpet*
algo pron *something, anything*
el algodón m *cotton*
alguien pron *somebody, anyone*
algún sitio ad *somewhere*
algunas veces ad *sometimes*
alguno/a a *some*
el aliento m *breath*
la alimentación f *food, nutrition*
el alimento m *food*
aliviar v *to relieve*
allá ad *there*
allí ad *there*
el almacén m *store, warehouse*
la almendra f *almond*
la almohada f *pillow*
almorzar v *to have lunch*
el almuerzo m *lunch*
alojarse v *to stay, to lodge*
el alpinismo m *mountain climbing*
el/la alpinista mf *mountain climber*
alquilado/a a *rented*
alquilar v *to rent, to hire*
el alquiler m *rent*
alrededor (de) ad *around, about*
alto/a a *high, tall*
la altura f *height*
el/la alumno/a mf *pupil*
el ama de casa f *housewife*
amable a *kind*
el amanecer m *dawn*
amar v *to love*
amargo/a a *bitter*
amarillo/a a *yellow*
el ambiente m *atmosphere*
ambos a/pron *both*
amenazar v *to threaten*
el/la amigo/a mf *friend*
la amistad f *friendship*
amistoso/a a *friendly*
el/la amo/a mf *owner, boss*
el amor m *love*
amplio/a a *large, spacious*
amueblado/a a *furnished*
añadir v *to add*
ancho/a a *wide*
anciano/a a *old*
el/la anciano/a mf *old man/woman*
andar v *to walk*
el andén m *platform*
el anfiteatro m *amphitheatre*
el anillo m *ring*
animado/a a *lively, animated*
animar v *to liven up, cheer up*
el año m *year*
anoche ad *last night*
el anochecer m *nightfall*
anteayer ad *day before yesterday*
antes (de) ad *before*
antiguo/a a *old, antique*
antipático/a a *unpleasant, horrible*
anunciar v *to announce*
el anuncio m *advert, announcement*
apagar v *to turn out, to put out, switch off*
el aparador m *sideboard*
el aparato m *appliance, telephone*
el aparcamiento m *car park*
aparcar v *to park*
aparecer v *to appear*
aparte a *separate,* ad *separately*
el apellido m *surname*
apenado/a a *sorry, sad*
apenas ad *hardly, scarcely*
la apertura f *opening*
apetecer v *to feel like, to crave*
apetitoso/a a *appetizing*
aplastar v *to crush, to squash*
aplicado/a a *conscientious*
el apodo m *nickname*
apoyar v *to lean, to support*
apreciar v *to like, to value*
aprender (a) v *to learn (to)*
apresurarse v *to hurry*
aprobar v *to pass (exam), to approve*
apropiado/a a *suitable*
aprovecharse (de) v *to take advantage (of)*
apto/a a *suitable, capable*
los apuntes mpl *notes*
aquel/aquella a *that*
aquél/aquélla pron *that, that one*
aquí ad *here*
aquí tiene *here it is*
el/la árbitro/a mf *referee, umpire*
el árbol m *tree*
el arbusto m *bush*
archivar v *to file*
arder v *to burn*
la arena f *sand*
el arma f *weapon*
el armario m *cupboard, wardrobe*
arrancar v *to pull out/start vehicle*
arreglar v *to arrange/settle/repair*
arreglarse vr *to get ready*
arrepentirse vr *to be sorry, regret*
arriba ad *above, upstairs, up*
arriesgar v *to risk*
arrojar v *to throw, to throw out*
el arroyo m *stream*
el arroz m *rice*
arruinar v *to ruin*
el arte dramático m *drama, theatre*
el artículo m *article*
asado/a a *roast*
asar v *to roast*
el ascensor m *lift*
el asco m *disgust*
asegurar v *to insure, secure*
los aseos mpl *toilets*
asesinar v *to murder*
el asesinato m *murder*
así ad *so, like this/that*
el asiento m *seat*
la asignatura f *subject (school)*
asistir v *to attend*
asomarse v *to look/lean out of*
asombrar v *to astonish*
asombroso/a a *amazing*
el aspecto m *aspect, appearance*
la aspiradora f *vacuum cleaner*
asqueroso/a a *disgusting*
el asunto m *matter, subject*
asustarse vr *to be frightened*
atacar v *to attack*
el ataque cardíaco m *heart attack*
atar v *to tie, to tie up*
el atasco m *obstruction, traffic jam*
atento/a a *attentive*
el aterrizaje m *landing (plane)*
aterrizar v *to land*
el ático m *attic*
el/la atleta mf *athlete*
el atletismo m *athletics*
atónito/a a *amazed*
el atraco m *holdup, robbery*
atraer v *to attract*
atrás ad *behind*
atrasar v *to be late, to be slow*
atravesar v *to go across*
atreverse vr *to dare*
atrevido/a a *daring, cheeky*
atropellar v *to run over*
el atún m *tuna fish*
el aula f *classroom, lecture room*
aumentar v *to increase*
el aumento m *increase*
aún ad *still, yet*
aunque conj *although*
el autobús m *bus*
el autocar m *coach*
la autopista f *motorway*
el/la autor/a mf *author*
la autoridad f *authority*
el autostop m *hitch-hiking*
el AVE m (alta velocidad española) *high speed train*
la avenida f *avenue*
la aventura f *adventure*
averiarse vr *to break down*
averiguar v *to find out*
el avión m *aeroplane*
avisar m *to inform, warn*
el aviso m *notice, warning*
la avispa f *wasp*
ay excl *ouch!, oh dear!*
ayer ad *yesterday*
la ayuda f *help*
ayudar v *to help*
el ayuntamiento m *town hall*
la azafata f *air hostess*
el azar m *chance, fate*
el azúcar m *sugar*
azul a *blue*

B

el bacalao m *cod*
el bachillerato m *secondary course/examination*
bachillerato elemental *lower certificate (GCSE)*
bachillerato superior *higher certificate (A Level)*
la bahía f *bay*
bailar v *to dance*
el baile m *dance*
bajar v *to take/go down*
bajar de *get off (a vehicle)*
bajo/a a *low, short*
bajo prep *low, below*
el balcón m *balcony*
el balón m *ball*
el baloncesto m *basketball*
el/la bañador/a mf *swimmer*
los bañadores mpl *bathing trunks*
bañar(se) v(r) *to bathe*
el/la bancario/a mf *bank employee*
la bandeja f *tray*
la bandera f *flag*
la bañera f *bathtub*
el baño m *bath, bathroom*
barato/a a *cheap*
la barba f *beard*
la barbacoa f *barbecue*
la barbaridad f *atrocity*
¡Qué barbaridad! *How awful!*
la barbilla f *chin*
la barca (de pesca) f *(fishing) boat*
el barco m *boat, ship*
la barra (de pan) f *loaf (of bread)*
la barra de labios f *lipstick*
barrer v *to sweep*
la barrera f *barrier*
el barrio m *district, neighbourhood*
bastante a/ad *enough, quite a lot*
¡Basta! *Enough!*
la basura f *rubbish*
el/la basurero/a mf *dustman/woman*
la bata f *dressing gown*
la batalla f *battle*
la batería f *battery, drums*
batido/a a *beaten*
el batido m *milk shake*
el bebé m *baby*
beber v *to drink*
la bebida f *drink*
belga a *Belgian*
Bélgica f *Belgium*
bello/a a *beautiful*
besar v *to kiss*
el beso m *kiss*
la biblioteca f *library*
la bicicleta f *bicycle* la bici *bike*
bien ad *well/good*
bien hecho *well done*
bienvenido/a a *welcome*
el biftec m *steak*
el bigote m *moustache*
el billete m *ticket* billete sencillo/de ida *single ticket*
billete de ida y vuelta/regreso *return ticket*
el billete m *bank note*
el billetero m *wallet*
el bistec m *steak*
blanco/a a *white*
el bloque m *block*
la boca f *mouth*
el bocadillo m *sandwich*
la boda f *wedding*
la bodega f *wine cellar/shop*
la bofetada f *slap*
la bola f *ball, scoop (of ice cream)*
la bolera f *bowling alley*
el boletín f *bulletin*
el bolígrafo/el boli m *ballpoint pen*
el bolo m *skittle* los bolos *skittles*
la bolsa f *bag*
el bolsillo m *pocket*
el bolso m *bag, handbag*
bolso de mano *handbag*
la bomba f *bomb, pump* lo pasé bomba *I had a wonderful time*
el bombero m *fireman*
la bombilla f *light bulb*
el bombón m *chocolate, sweet*
bonito/a a *pretty, nice*
el bonobús m *bus pass*
el boquerón m *fresh anchovy*
el borde m *edge*
a bordo m *on board*
borracho/a a *drunk*
el borrador m *(board) rubber*
borrar v *to rub out, delete*
la borrasca f *storm*
el bosque m *wood*
la bota f *boot*
el bote m *jar, pot*
bote de remo *rowing boat*
la botella f *bottle*
el botón m *button*
el brazo m *arm*
brevemente ad *briefly*
el bricolaje m *do-it-yourself*
brillar v *to shine*
la broma f *joke*
broncearse vr *to get a suntan, sunbathe*
la bruma f *mist*
brusco/a a *sharp, sudden, rude*
bucear v *to dive, go under water*
bueno/a a *good*
la bufanda f *scarf*
el búho m *owl*
el buque m *ship, boat*

ad: adverb **prep**: preposition **pron:** pronoun **interj**: interjection **conj**: conjunction **art**: article **excl**: exclamation

Spanish — English Dictionary

burlarse vr *to joke*
burlarse de *to make fun of*
el burro m *donkey*
buscar v *to look for, fetch*
la butaca f *armchair, seat (in cinema, theatre)*
el buzón m *post box*

C

el caballero m *gentleman, knight*
el caballo m *horse*
el cabello m *hair*
caber v *to fit*
la cabeza f *head*
la cabina f *booth*
el cable m *wire, cable*
el cabo m *cape, end*
la cabra f *goat*
la cacerola f *saucepan*
cada a *each, every*
la cadena f *chain*
caer v *to fall* caer enfermo *fall ill* caerse vr *to fall, fall over*
el café m *coffee, café*
la cafetera f *coffee pot/ machine*
la caja f *box, till* caja de ahorros *savings bank*
el/la cajero/a mf *cashier*
el cajero automático m *cash dispenser*
el cajón m *drawer*
los calamares mpl *squid*
el calcetín m *sock*
el caldo m *soup, broth*
calentar v *to heat*
la calidad f *quality*
caliente a *hot*
la calificación f *grade, mark, rating*
calificado/a a *qualified*
callado/a a *quiet, reserved*
callar(se) v(r) *to say nothing*
la calle f *street*
la callejuela f *side street*
el calor m *heat*
caluroso/a a *warm, hot*
calvo/a a *bald*
el calzado m *footwear*
calzar v *to wear (shoes etc.)*
los calzoncillos mpl *underpants*
la cama f *bed*
la cámara f *camera*
el/la camarero/a mf *waiter/ waitress*
el camarote m *cabin*
cambiar v *to change*
el cambio m *change, bureau de change*
caminar v *to walk*
la caminata f *long walk, hike*
el camino m *road, track, route*
el camión m *lorry*
la camioneta f *van*
la camisa f *shirt*
la camiseta f *T-shirt*
la campana f *bell*
la campaña f *campaign, countryside*
el/la campeón/a mf *champion*
el campeonato m *championship*
campesino/a a *rural*
el camping m *campsite*
el/la campista mf *camper*
el campo m *field, country*
la caña f *small glass of beer, stalk*
caña de pesca(r) *fishing rod*
el canal m *canal, channel*
la cancha f *court* cancha (de tenis etc.) *(tennis etc.) court, ground*
la canción f *song*
el cangrejo m *crab*
el canguro m *kangaroo* hacer de canguro *to baby-sit*
cansado/a a *tired*
cansador/a a *tiring*
el cansancio m *tiredness*
cansarse vr *to get tired*
el/la cantante mf *singer*
cantar v *to sing*
la cantidad f *quantity*
la capa f *cloak, layer*
capacitar(se) vr *to prepare yourself, qualify*
capaz a *capable*
la cara f *face*
el caracol m *snail*
caramba excl *good gracious*
el caramelo m *sweet, caramel*
la cárcel f *prison*
cargar v *to load*
carillo/a a *a bit expensive*
cariñoso/a a *affectionate*
el carnaval m *carnival*
la carne f *meat* carne de cerdo *pork* carne de vaca *beef*
el carnet m *card* carnet de conducir *driving licence*
la carnicería f *butcher's*
el/la carnicero/a mf *butcher*
caro/a a *expensive*
la carpeta f *folder, file*
el carpintero m *carpenter*
la carrera f *run, race, course, career*
la carretera f *road* la carretera nacional *"A" road*
el carro m *cart*
la carta f *letter, menu, card*
las cartas fpl *playing cards*
cartearse (con) vr *to correspond*
el cartel m *poster*
la cartelera f *billboard*
la cartera f *wallet, schoolbag*
el cartón m *cardboard*
la casa f *house*
casado/a a *married*
el casamiento m *marriage, wedding*
casarse vr *to get married*
el casco m *helmet*
casi ad *almost*
la casilla f *pigeonhole, hut*
el caso m *case*
castaño/a a *chestnut brown*
las castañuelas fpl *castanets*
castellano/a a *Spanish, Castilian*
el castellano m *Spanish (language)*
castigar v *to punish*
el castigo m *punishment*
el castillo m *castle*
el catarro m *cold, catarrh*
cavar v *to dig*
la caza f *hunting*
cazar v *to hunt*
la cebolla f *onion*
ceda el paso m *give way*
celebrar v *to celebrate*
célebre a *famous*
celoso/a a *jealous*
la cena f *dinner, evening meal*
cenar v *to have dinner*
el cenicero m *ashtray*
la central telefónica f *telephone exchange*
el centro m *centre*
cepillar v *to brush*
el cepillo m *brush*
cepillo de dientes *toothbrush*
cerca (de) ad *near (to)*
cercano/a a *close, nearby*
el cerdo m *pig*
el cereal m *cereal, grain*
la cereza f *cherry*
la cerilla f *wax match*
el cero m *zero*
cerrado/a a *closed*
con llave *locked*
la cerradura f *lock*
cerrar v *to shut*
el certificado m *certificate*
la cerveza f *beer*
la cervecería f *bar, brewery*
cesar (de) v *to stop*
el césped m *lawn*
la cesta f *basket*
el cesto m *basket*
el chaleco m *waistcoat, vest*
el champiñón m *mushroom*
el champú m *shampoo*
la chaqueta f *jacket*
la charcutería f *pork butcher's, cooked pork products*
charlar v *to chat*
el cheque m *cheque* cheque de viaje *traveller's cheque*
la chica f *girl*
el chicle m *chewing gum*
el chico m *boy*
chillar v *to shriek, scream*
la chimenea f *chimney, fireplace*
el chisme m *thingummy*
el chiste m *joke*
chocar v *to collide, crash, shock*
el chófer m *driver*
el choque m *crash*
el chorizo m *spicy hard pork sausage*
el chubasco m *heavy shower*
la chuleta f *chop, cutlet*
el churro m *flour fritter*
el ciclismo m *cycling*
el/la ciclista mf *cyclist*
ciego/a a *blind*
el cielo m *sky, heaven*
cien a *100*
la ciencia f *science*
cierto/a a *true, certain, sure*
la cifra f *figure, number*
el cigarrillo m *cigarette*
el cigarro m *cigarette, cigar*
la cima f *summit, peak*
el cine m *cinema*
la cintura f *waist*
el cinturón m *belt*
el circo m *circus*
la circulación f *traffic, circulation*
el círculo m *circle*
la ciruela f *plum*
el/la cirujano/a mf *surgeon*
la cita f *appointment, date*
citarse vr *to arrange to meet*
la ciudad f *city, large town*
el/la ciudadano/a mf *citizen*
claro/a a *clear, obvious, light (coloured)* ¡Claro! *Of course!*
la clase f *class, lesson*
clásico/a a *classical*
clasificar v *to classify*
el clavo m *nail*
el/la cliente mf *customer,client*
el clima m *climate*
climatizado/a a *air-conditioned*
la clínica f *clinic*
el club m *club*
cobarde a *cowardly*
el/la cobarde mf *coward*
el/la cobayo/a mf *guinea pig*
el/la cobrador/a mf *train/ bus conductor*
cobrar v *to charge, collect (cash)*
el cobro revertido m *reverse charge*
el coche m *car*
cocido/a a *boiled, cooked*
el cocido m *stew*
la cocina f *kitchen, cookery, cooker*
cocinar v *to cook*
el/la cocinero/a mf *cook*
codiciado/a a *sought after*
el código m *code*
el codo m *elbow*
coger v *to take, pick, hold, catch*
el cojín m *cushion*
cojo/a a *lame*
la col f *cabbage*
la cola f *queue, tail, glue*
el colchón m *mattress*
coleccionar v *to collect*
el/la colega mf *colleague*
el colegio m *school*
colgar v *to hang, hang up, put down (phone)*
la coliflor f *cauliflower*
la colina f *hill*
el collar m *necklace*
colocar v *to place, arrange*
el color m *colour*
el columpio m *swing*
la comedia f *comedy, play*
el comedor m *dining room*
comenzar v *to begin*
comer v *to eat*
los comestibles mpl *food, groceries*
cometer v *to commit*
la comida f *food, meal, lunch*
el comienzo m *start*
la comisaría f *police station*
el comité m *committee*
como ad *how, like, as, about*
¿Cómo? *How, Pardon?*
la cómoda f *chest of drawers*
la comodidad f *comfort*
cómodo/a a *comfortable*
el/la compañero/a mf *companion*
la compañía f *company*
compartir v *to share, divide*
complicado/a a *complicated*
componer v *to compose, make up*
el comportamiento m *behaviour*
comportarse vr *to behave*
la compra f *purchase*
comprar v *to buy*
las compras fpl *shopping*
comprender v *to understand*
el comprimido m *pill, tablet*
comprobar v *to check, confirm*
el compromiso m *commitment*
la computadora f *computer*
con prep *with*
el concierto m *concert*
concurrido/a a *busy, crowded*
el concurso m *competition*
conducir v *to drive, lead*
el/la conductor/a mf *driver, motorist*
el conejo m *rabbit*
el conejillo de Indias m *guinea pig*
la confianza f *confidence*
confiar v *to trust*
la confitería f *sweet shop, confectionery*
confortable a *comfortable*
el congelador m *freezer*
congelar v *to freeze*
conjunto/a a *joint, combined*
el conjunto m *group, outfit, team*
conmigo, contigo pron *with me, with you*
conocer v *to know, meet*
el conocimiento m *knowledge*
la consecuencia f *consequence*
conseguir v *to achieve, manage, get*
el consejo m *advice*
el conserje m *caretaker, janitor*
la consigna f *left-luggage office*
el constipado m *cold*
estar constipado/a *to have a cold*
el/la constructor/a mf *builder*
construir v *to build*
el consulado m *consulate*
la contaminación f *pollution*
contar v *to count, tell*
contenido/a a *controlled, restrained*
el contenido m *contents*
el contestador automático m *telephone answering machine*
contestar v *to reply, answer*
continuar v *to continue*
contra prep *against*
el/la contrabandista mf *smuggler*
el contrabando m *smuggled goods*
contrario/a a *opposing, opposite*
convencer *to convince*
la copa f *cup, trophy, wine glass*
copa mundial *World Cup*
el corazón m *heart*
la corbata f *tie*
el corcho m *cork*
el/la cordero/a mf *lamb*
el cordón m *cord, string, wire*
el coro m *choir, chorus*
corregir v *to correct*
el correo m *post, mail*
correo electrónico *e-mail*
correo aéreo *airmail*
Correos *post office*
correr v *to run*
el/la corresponsal mf *penfriend*
la corrida (de toros) f *bullfight*
el cortacésped m *lawnmower*
cortar v *to cut*
el corte de pelo m *haircut*
cortés a *polite*
la cortina f *curtain*
corto/a a *short*
la cosa f *thing*
coser v *to sew*
la costa f *coast*
costar v *to cost*
el coste m *cost*
costoso/a a *costly, expensive*
la costumbre f *custom*
la costura f *sewing*
cotidiano/a a *daily, everyday*
crear v *to create*
crecer v *to grow*
creer v *to think, believe*
crema a *cream, cream-coloured*
la crema f *cream*
crema bronceadora *suntan lotion*
la cremallera f *zip*
la criada f *maid*
criar v *to bring up (children), raise*
el crimen m *crime*
el/la crío/a mf *child*
el cristal m *glass, window pane*
criticar v *to criticize*
el cruce m *junction (road)*
el crucigrama m *crossword*
la cruz f *cross*
Cruz Roja *Red Cross*
cruzar v *to cross*
el cuaderno m *exercise book*
cuadrado/a a *square*
el cuadro m *square, picture, painting*
cual(es) pron pl *which, what*
cualquier/a a *any*
cuando ad *when*
¿Cuándo? *When?*
cuanto/a a *how much*
¿Cuánto/a? *How much?*
cuarto/a a *fourth*
el cuarto m *room, quarter*
cuarto de baño *bathroom*
cuarto de hora *quarter of an hour*
cubierto/a a *covered, overcast*
el cubierto m *cover, place setting*
el cubo m *bucket, cube*
cubo de basura *dustbin*
cubrir v *to cover*
la cucaracha f *cockroach*
la cuchara f *spoon*
la cucharada f *spoonful*
la cucharilla f *teaspoon*
el cuchillo m *knife*
el cuello m *neck*
la cuenta f *bill, sum, account*
el cuento m *short story*
la cuerda f *rope, string, cord*
el cuero m *leather*
el cuerpo m *body*
la cuesta f *slope, hill*
la cueva f *cave, wine cellar*
¡Cuidado! *Careful!*
cuidadoso/a a *careful*
cuidar v *to look after, take care of*
la culebra f *snake*
el culebrón m *soap opera*
la culpa f *blame*
culpable a *guilty*
cultivar v *to cultivate, grow*
la cumbre f *summit, top*
el cumpleaños m *birthday*
cumplido/a a *complete, full*
cumplir v *to carry out, complete*

*nouns — **m**: masculine **f**: feminine **pl**: plural **v**: verb **vr**: reflexive verb **a**: adjective*

Spanish — English Dictionary

el/la cuñado/a mf *bro/sister-in-law*
el cura m *priest*
la cura f *cure*
curar v *to cure*
la curiosidad f *curiosity*
el curso m *course*
la curva f *bend, curve*
cuyo/a a *whose, of whom*

D

dañar v *to harm, damage, spoil*
el daño m *harm, damage*
dañoso/a a *damaging*
dar v *to give*
darse cuenta *to realize*
los datos mpl *facts, data*
de prep *of, from*
deber v *to owe, must, should*
el deber m *duty*
los deberes mpl *homework, duties*
débil a *weak*
una decena f *ten*
decepcionado/a a *disappointed*
decidir v *to decide*
décimo/a a *tenth*
decir v *to say*
el dedo m *finger*
dedo del pie *toe*
dejar v *to leave, allow* dejar de (hacer) *stop (doing)*
dejar caer *drop*
el delantal m *apron*
delante (de) prep *in front (of)*
deletrear v *to spell*
delgado/a a *thin, slim*
el delito m *crime, offence*
demás a *other, others*
demasiado ad *too, too much*
la demora f *delay*
dentro (de) ad *inside*
denunciar v *to report, denounce*
el/la dependiente/a mf *shop assistant*
el deporte m *sport*
el/la deportista mf *sportsman/woman*
el depósito m *tank (petrol), warehouse, deposit*
deprisa ad *quickly*
la derecha f (dcha – abbrev.) *right* derecho/a a *straight*
el derecho m *right, law, duty*
los derechos mpl *rights*
desafortunado/a a *unfortunate*
desagradable a *unpleasant*
desaparecer v *to disappear*
desaparecido/a a *disappeared*
la desaparición f *disappearance*
el desastre m *disaster*
desastroso/a a *disastrous*
desayunar v *to have breakfast*
el desayuno m *breakfast*
descansar v *to rest*
el descanso m *rest, break*
descolgar v *to pick up (phone), to unhook*
desconfiar v *to distrust*
desconocido/a a *unknown*
el/la desconocido/a mf *stranger*
descortés a *impolite*
el descubrimiento m *discovery*
descubrir v *to discover, uncover*
el descuento m *discount*
descuidado/a a *careless, untidy*
desde prep *from*
desear v *to want*
desempleado/a a *unemployed*
el desempleo m *unemployment*
deshacer las maletas v *to unpack*
desierto/a a *bleak, deserted*
el desierto m *desert*
desmayarse vr *to faint*
desnudarse vr *to get undressed*
el desodorante m *deodorant*
el despacho m *office, study*
despacio ad *slowly*
despedirse vr *to say goodbye*
despegar v *to take off (plane), unstick*
despejado/a a *clear*
despejar v *to clear*
el despertador m *alarm clock*
despertarse vr *to wake up*
desplazar v *to move, transfer*
después (de) prep/ad *after, later on*
destruir v *to destroy*
el desván m *attic*
la desventaja f *disadvantage*
desviar v *to divert*
el desvío m *diversion*
el detalle m *detail, small gift*
detenerse vr *to stop*
detestar v *to detest, hate*
detrás (de) prep/ad *behind*
devolver v *to give back, return*
el día m *day*
la diapositiva f *slide (photographic)*
diario/a a *daily*
el diario m *daily newpaper*
dibujar v *to draw*
el dibujo m *drawing, art*
los dibujos animados mpl *cartoons*
el diciembre m *December*
el diente m *tooth*
difícil a *difficult*
¡diga! v *speak* ¡dígame! *speak to me (when answering the phone)*
dinámico/a a *dynamic*
el dinero m *money*
dinero de bolsillo *pocket money*
Dios m *God*
la dirección f *direction, address* dirección obligatoria *one-way*
directo/a a *straight, direct*
el/la director/a mf *director, head*
dirigirse vr *to speak to, head for, go towards*
el disco m *record, disc* disco compacto/CD *compact disc*
disculpar v *to forgive*
disculparse vr *to apologize*
el discurso m *speech*
discutir v *to argue*
el/la diseñador/a mf *designer*
diseñar v *to design*
el diseño m *design, sketch*
disfrutar v *to enjoy*
el disgusto m *quarrel, upset*
disminuir v *to diminish*
disponible a *available*
dispuesto/a a *arranged, ready*
la disputa f *argument*
distinguir v *to distinguish*
distinto/a (de) a *different (from)*
la/s distracción / distracciones f/fpl *entertainment*
distribuir v *to distribute*
divertido/a a *fun, funny, amusing*
divertirse vr *to enjoy yourself*
dividir v *to divide*
divorciado/a a *divorced*
el DNI m (documento nacional de identidad) *ID (identity) card*
doblar v *to turn, to fold*
doble a *double*
la docena f *dozen*
el documental m *documentary*
doler v *to hurt*
el dolor m *pain, ache*
el domicilio m *home, residence*
el domingo m *Sunday*
donde ad *where*
¿Dónde? *Where?*
dormido/a a *asleep*
dormir v *to sleep*
dormirse vr *to go to sleep*
el dormitorio m *bedroom*
la droga f *drug*
el/la drogadicto/a mf *drug addict*
la droguería f *chemist's without a pharmacy, drugstore*
la ducha f *shower*
ducharse vr *to have a shower*
dudar v *to doubt*
el/la dueño/a mf *owner, landlord*
dulce a/ad *sweet, soft, gentle*
durante prep *during*
durar v *to last*
duro/a a *hard*

E

echar v *to throw, throw away, put, pour, show*
echar al buzón *to post*
echar de menos *to miss*
echar sangre *to bleed*
echar una mirada/un vistazo *to glance*
la ecología f *ecology*
económico/a a *economic, cheap*
la edad f *age*
el edificio m *building*
EEUU abbrev (mpl) *USA*
el efecto m *effect*
eficaz a *effective, efficient*
egoísta a *selfish*
el ejemplo m *example*
el ejercicio m *exercise*
el ejército m *army*
el def. art. m *the*
el/la mío/a pron *mine*
la elección f *election*
la electricidad f *electricity*
eléctrico/a a *electric, electrical*
electrónico/a a *electronic*
el/la elefante/a mf *elephant*
elegir v *to choose*
elevado/a a *high, noble, important*
embarazada a *pregnant*
emborracharse vr *to get drunk*
el embotellamiento m *traffic jam*
emigrar v *to emigrate*
emocionante a *moving, exciting*
emparejar v *to pair, match*
el empate m *draw (match)*
empezar v *to begin*
el/la empleado/a mf *employee*
emplear v *to employ*
el empleo m *employment, work, job*
la empresa f *company, enterprise*
el/la empresario/a mf *businessman*
empujar v *to push*
en prep *in, on*
enamorado/a (de) a *in love (with)*
enamorarse (de) vr *to fall in love (with)*
encantado/a a *delighted*
encantar v *to bewitch*
me encanta *I love*
el/la encargado/a mf *manager*
encender v *to light, turn on, ignite*
encerrar v *to shut (up), enclose*
enchufar v *to plug in*
el enchufe m *plug, socket*
encima (de) prep/ad *on, above, over*
encogerse vr *to shrug*
encontrar v *to find*
encontrarse vr *to find, meet, be*
el encuentro m *meeting*
la encuesta f *survey*
el/la enemigo/a mf *enemy*
la energía f *energy*
el enero m *January*
enfadarse vr *to get angry*
la enfermedad f *illness*
el/la enfermero/a a *nurse*
enfermo/a a *ill*
enfrente (de) prep/ad *opposite, in front*
engañar v *to deceive, trick*
enganchar v *to hook (up)*
¡Enhorabuena! *Congratulations!*
enojar v *to anger*
enojarse vr *to get angry*
la ensalada f *salad*
el ensayo m *essay, test, trial*
la enseñanza f *education, teaching*
enseñar v *to teach, show*
ensuciar v *to dirty, get dirty*
entender v *understand*
entonces ad *then, after*
el entorno m *environs, surroundings*
la entrada f *entry, entrance, ticket*
entrar v *to enter*
entre prep *between, among*
la entrega f *delivery, handover*
entregar v *to deliver, hand over*
el entremés m *interlude*
los entremeses mpl *hors d'oeuvres*
entrenarse vr *to train*
entretanto ad *meanwhile*
la entrevista f *interview*
enviar v *to send*
envolver v *to wrap (up)*
la época f *age, period*
equipado/a a *equipped*
el equipaje m *luggage*
el equipo m *team, equipment*
la equis f *"X"*
la equitación f *horse riding*
equivocarse vr *to make a mistake*
la escala f *scale, stopover (on trip)*
escalar v *to climb*
la escalera f *stairs, ladder*
escapar(se) v *to escape, leak*
el escaparate m *shop window*
la escarcha f *frost*
la escena f *scene*
escoger v *to choose*
esconder v *to hide*
escribir v *to write*
escribir a máquina *to type*
el/la escritor/a mf *writer*
el escritorio m *desk, bureau*
escuchar v *to listen (to), hear*
la escuela f *school*
el/la escultor/a mf *sculptor*
la escultura f *sculpture*
la ese f *"S"*
ese/a a *that* ése/a pron *that one*
el esfuerzo m *effort*
la esgrima f *fencing, swordfighting*
eso pron *that*
el espacio m *space* espacio en blanco *blank space*
la espalda f *back*
espantar v *to scare*
espantoso/a a *frightening, scary*
el esparadrapo m *sticking plaster*
el espárrago m *asparagus*
la especialidad f *speciality*
la especie f *type, species*
el espectáculo m *show, performance*
el espejo m *mirror*
la esperanza f *hope*
esperar v *to hope, expect, wait for*
espeso/a a *thick, heavy*
las espinacas fpl *spinach*
el espíritu m *spirit, mind*
el/la esposo/a mf *husband, wife*
el esquí m *skiing*
esquiar v *to ski*
la esquina f *corner*
la estación f *station* estación del año *season of the year*
el estacionamiento m *car park*
estacionar v *to park*
el estadio m *stadium*
el estado m *state* (civil) *marital*
estadounidense a *US citizen*
estallar v *to explode, burst*
la estancia f *stay, ranch*
el estanco m *tobacco/cigarette shop*
estar v *to be*
la estatua f *statue*
este/a a *this*
éste/a pron *this one*
el este m *the East*
el estéreo m *stereo*
el estilo m *style*
esto pron *this*
el estómago m *stomach*
estrecho/a a *narrow*
la estrella f *star*
estremecer v *to shake, shudder*
estrenar v *to wear/use something for the first time*
el estrés m *stress*
estricto/a a *strict*
estropear v *to spoil/damage/break*
el estuche m *case (for glasses etc)*
el/la estudiante mf *student*
estudiar v *to study*
el estudio m *study*
los estudios mpl *studies*
estupendo/a a *wonderful*
estúpido/a a *stupid*
la etapa f *stage, phase*
la ética f *ethics*
evitar v *to avoid*
exagerar v *to exaggerate*
el examen m *examination*
exigente a *demanding*
exigir v *to demand*
el éxito m *success*
experimentado/a a *experienced*
la explicación f *explanation*
explicar v *to explain*
exponer v *to display, exhibit*
la exposición f *exhibition*
el expreso m *express train*
el extracto m *extract*
extranjero/a a *foreign*
el/la extranjero/a mf *foreigner*
extraño/a a *strange*

F

la fábrica f *factory*
fabricar v *to manufacture*
fácil a *easy*
la faena f *task, chore*
la falda f *skirt*
la falta f *lack*
faltar v *to lack, be missing, need*
la fama f *fame*
la familia f *family*
los familiares mpl *relations, relatives*
famoso/a a *famous*
el/la farmacéutico/a mf *chemist*
la farmacia f *chemist's*
el faro m *headlamp, lighthouse*
fastidiar v *to annoy*
el febrero m *February*
la fecha f *date*
la felicidad f *happiness*
felicidades/felicitaciones *congratulations*
felicitar v *to congratulate*
feliz a *happy*
feo/a a *ugly*
la feria f *fair, festival, market*
el ferrocarril m *railway*
la festividad f *festivity, holiday*
fiarse vr *to trust*
la ficha f *file, counter, token*
la fiebre f *fever, temperature*
la fiesta f *party, holiday, festival*
fijar v *to fix, focus*
la fila f *line, row*

***ad**: adverb* ***prep**: preposition* ***pron**: pronoun* ***interj**: interjection* ***conj**: conjunction* ***art**: article* ***excl**: exclamation*

Spanish — English Dictionary

el filete m *fillet*
el fin m *end*
fin de semana *weekend*
la finca f *farm*
la firma f *company, signature*
firmar v *to sign*
la física f *physics*
físico/a a *physical*
el/la físico/a mf *physicist*
flaco/a a *thin, skinny*
el flan m *crème caramel*
la flauta f *flute, recorder*
la flecha f *arrow*
flojo/a a *loose, weak*
la flor f *flower*
(silvestre) *wild flower*
el/la florero/a mf *florist*
el florero m *vase*
flotar v *to float*
el folleto m *brochure*
el fondo m *end, bottom, back*
el/la fontanero/a mf *plumber*
el/la forastero/a m *stranger, outsider*
la forma f *shape, way, method, form*
la formación f *training*
el formulario m *form*
forzar v *to force*
el fósforo m *match*
fracasar v *to make a mess of, fail*
la frambuesa f *raspberry*
franco/a a *frank, honest*
la frase f *phrase*
el fregadero m *sink*
fregar v *to wash*
freír v *to fry*
frenar v *to brake*
la frente f *forehead*
el frente m *front*
la fresa f *strawberry*
fresco/a a *fresh, cool*
el frigorífico m *refrigerator*
el frigo *fridge*
frío/a a *cold*
la fruta f *fruit*
la frutería f *fruit shop, greengrocer's*
el fuego m *fire*
fuegos artificiales mpl *fireworks*
la fuente f *fountain, dish, source*
fuera (de) prep/ad *outside (of)*
fuerte a *strong*
la fuerza f *strength, force*
el/la fumador/a mf *smoker*
fumadores mpl *smoking compartment*
fumar v *to smoke*
el/la funcionario/a mf *civil servant*
fundir v *to melt*
el futuro m *future*

G

las gafas fpl *(eye)glasses*
gafas de sol *sunglasses*
la galería (de arte) f *(art) gallery*
la galleta f *biscuit*
la gallina f *hen*
el gallo m *cockerel*
la gamba f *prawn*
el gamberro m *hooligan*
(la gana f) con ganas *with enthusiasm*
el/la ganador/a mf *winner*
ganar v *to earn, win*
ganarse la vida *to earn a living*
la ganga f *bargain*
el ganso m *goose*
el garaje m *garage*
el/la garajista f *garage owner/ attendant*
la garganta f *throat*
la gaseosa f *fizzy drink, soda*
la gasolina f *petrol* gasolina sin plomo *lead free petrol*
la gasolinera f *petrol station*
gastado/a a *worn, used*
gastar v *to spend (money), wear away*
el gasto m *expense, expenditure*
el/la gato/a mf *cat*
el gazpacho m *cold spicy soup*
el/la gemelo/a mf *twin*
generoso/a a *generous*
la gente f *people*
el/la gerente mf *manager*
el gimnasio m *gymnasium, gym*
la gimnasia f *gymnastics, P.E.*
la gimnástica f *gymnastics*
girar v *to turn, go round, spin*
la glorieta f *(large) roundabout*
el gobierno m *government*
el gol m *goal*
goloso/a a *sweet-toothed, greedy*
golpear v *to hit*
la goma f *glue, rubber*
goma (de borrar) f *eraser, rubber*
gordo/a a *fat*
la gota f *drop*
gozar v *to enjoy*
las gracias fpl *thanks*
gracias *thank you*
gracioso/a a *funny*
el grado m *degree, stage, grade*
el gramo m *gramme*
grande a *big, great*
los grandes almacenes *department store(s)*
el granizo m *hail*
la granja f *farm*
el/la granjero/a mf *farmer*
la grasa f *fat, grease*
gratis a/ad *free, for nothing*
grato/a a *pleasing*
gratuito/a a *free*
el grifo m *tap*
la gripe f *flu, influenza*
gris a *grey*
gritar v *to shout*
el grito m *shout*
grosero/a a *rude, vulgar*
grueso/a a *thick, stout, fat*
el grupo m *group*
el guante m *glove*
guapo/a a *beautiful, handsome*
guardar v *to guard, put away*
el guardarropa m *wardrobe, cloakroom*
la guardería f *nursery, play school*
el/la guardia mf *policeman/ woman, guard*
la guardia civil f *civil guard*
guay excl *great!, wonderful!*
la guerra f *war*
el/la guía mf *guide*
la guía (turística) f *guidebook*
guiar v *to guide*
el guisante m *pea*
la guitarra f *guitar*
gustar v *to like*
el gusto m *taste, pleasure*

H

la haba f *broad bean*
haber aux v *to have*
hábil a *skilful*
la habitación f *room, bedroom*
el habla f *speech, language*
hablar v *to talk, speak*
hacer v *to do, make*
hacerse vr *to become*
hacerse daño *to hurt yourself*
hacia prep *towards, about*
hallar v *to find*
hallarse vr *to be, find yourself*
el hambre f *hunger*
la hamburguesa f *hamburger*
la harina f *flour*
harto/a a *fed up, tired (of), full up*
hasta prep *until, up to*
hay *there is, there are*
he aquí *here are*
el hecho m *deed, fact*
el helado m *ice-cream*
helar v *to freeze*
la herida f *wound, injury*
herir v *to wound, hurt, injure*
herirse vr *to injure yourself*
el/la hermano/a mf *brother/ sister*
el/la hermanastra/o mf *stepbrother/sister*
hermoso/a a *beautiful*
la herramienta f *tool*
hervir v *to boil*
el hidrodeslizador m *hovercraft*
el hielo m *ice*
la hierba f *grass*
el hierro m *iron*
el hígado m *liver*
el higo m *fig*
el/la hijo/a mf *son/daughter*
hijo/a único/a mf *only child*
el hilo m *thread, yarn*
el/la hincha mf *fan*
hinchar v *to inflate*
el hipermercado m *hypermarket*
la historia f *story, history*
el hogar m *home, hearth*
la hoja f *leaf* hoja de solicitud *application form*
¡hola! excl *hello!*
el hombre m *man*
el hombro m *shoulder*
honesto/a a *honest*
honrado/a a *honourable, honest*
la hora f *hour*
hora de comer *lunch time*
hora punta *rush hour*
el horario m *timetable*
el horno m *oven*
horroroso/a a *dreadful, horrible*
la hortaliza f *vegetable*
hortalizas *garden produce*
hoy ad *today*
la huelga f *strike*
el huerto m *kitchen garden*
el hueso m *bone, stone (in fruit)*
el huésped m *guest*
el huevo m *egg*
la huida f *flight, escape*
huir v *to escape, flee*
húmedo/a a *damp*
el humo m *smoke*

I

la ida f *departure*
la identidad f *identity*
el idioma m *language*
la iglesia f *church*
ignorar v *to not know, ignore*
igual (a) a *equal (to)*
la imagen f *image*
impedir v *to prevent*
el impermeable m *raincoat*
imprescindible a *vital, essential*
impresionante a *impressive*
la impresora f *printer*
imprimir v *to print*
el impuesto m *tax, duty*
el incendio m *fire*
inclinar v *to lean, incline*
incluido/a a *included*
incluir v *to include*
incluso ad *even*
increíble a *incredible*
indicar v *to indicate, show*
el individuo m *individual*
la industria f *industry*
informar v *to inform*
informarse vr *to find out, get info*
la informática f *computing, IT*
el informe m *report*
el/la ingeniero/a mf *engineer*
Inglaterra f *England*
el inglés m *English (language)*
el/la inglés/esa mf *Englishman/woman*
el ingreso m *admission, entry,*
los ingresos *income*
injusto/a a *unjust, unfair*
inmediatamente ad *immediately*
inmenso/a a *immense*
inmóvil a *immobile, unmoving*
inquieto/a a *worried, unsettled*
la insignia f *badge, emblem*
la insolación f *sunstroke*
insoportable a *unbearable*
las instalaciones fpl *facilities*
instalar v *to install*
el instituto m *secondary school, college*
intentar v *to try*
intercambiar v *to exchange, swap*
el intercambio m *exchange*
interesar v *to interest*
interesarse vr *to be interested in*
el/la interno/a mf *boarder*
intervenir v *intervene, take part in*
introducir v *to insert, enter*
la inundación f *flood*
inútil a *useless*
el invierno m *winter*
la inyección f *injection*
ir v *to go* ir a + infinitive *to be going to (future tense)*
las Islas Baleares fpl *Balearic Isles*
las Islas Canarias fpl *Canary Islands*
irritar v *to irritate*
la isla f *island*
irse vr *to go away, leave*
el IVA m (impuesto sobre el valor añadido) *VAT*
la izquierda f *left*

J

el jabón m *soap*
jamás ad *never*
el jamón m *ham*
el jarabe m *syrup, cough syrup*
el jardín m *garden*
el jarro m *jug*
la jaula f *cage*
el/la jefe/a mf *boss, head, manager*
joven a *young*
el/la joven mf *young man/ woman*
la joya f *jewel* joyas *jewels, jewellery*
la joyería f *jewellery, jeweller's shop*
jubilarse vr *to retire*
la judía f *bean*
el/la judío/a mf *Jewish man/ woman*
el juego m *game, play*
el jueves m *Thursday*
el/la juez(a) mf *judge*
el/la jugador/a *player*
jugar v *to play*
el jugo m *juice*
el juguete m *toy*
el julio m *July*
el junio m *June*
junto/a a *together*
junto (a) prep/ad *near, next/ close(to)*
justo ad *just, exactly*
justo a *just, fair*
la juventud f *youth*
juzgar v *to judge*

K

el kilo m *kilo*
el kilómetro m *kilometre*

L

la art def *the (fem)*
el labio m *lip*
el lado m *side*
el ladrillo m *brick*
el ladrón m *thief*
el lago m *lake*
la lágrima f *tear*
lamentar v *to regret, be sorry*
la lámpara f *lamp*
la lana f *wool*
la langosta f *lobster, locust*
lanzar v *to throw, launch*
el lápiz m *pencil*
largo/a a *long*
la lástima f *pity,shame*
la lata f *tin, can*
el latín m *Latin*
latinoamericano/a *Latin American*
el lavabo m *washbasin, washroom*
el lavado m *washing*
la lavadora f *washing machine*
la lavandería f *laundry, launderette*
el lavaplatos m *dishwasher*
lavar v *to wash*
lavarse vr *to get washed*
el lavavajillas m *dishwasher*
la lección f *lesson*
la leche f *milk*
la lechería f *dairy*
la lechuga f *lettuce*
la lectura f *reading*
leer v *to read*
la legumbre f *pulse, vegetable*
lejano/a a *distant*
lejos (de) prep/ad *far, far away(from)*
la lengua f *language, tongue*
las lentes de contacto fpl / la lentilla f *contact lenses/lens*
lento/a a *slow*
el león m *lion*
la letra f *letter*
levantar v *to lift*
levantarse vr *to get up*
la ley f *law*
liberar v *to free, release*
la libra (esterlina) f *pound (sterling)*
libre f *free, available*
la librería f *bookshop, bookcase*
el libro m *book*
el/la licenciado/a mf *graduate*
la licenciatura f *degree*
la liga f *league*
ligero/a a *light, delicate, quick*
el limón m *lemon*
la limonada f *lemonade*
limpiar v *to clean*
la limpieza a seco f *dry cleaning*
limpio/a a *clean*
la línea f *line*
la linterna f *torch, lantern*
la liquidación f *sale*
liso/a a *smooth, straight*
la lista f *list*
listo/a a *ready, clever*
el litro m *litre*
la llamada f *call*
llamar v *to call, phone, knock*
llamarse vr *to be called*
la llave f *key*
el llavero m *key ring*
la llegada f *arrival*
llegar v *to arrive*
llegar a *come to*
llenar v *to fill, fill up*
lleno/a a *full*
llevar v *to wear, carry, take*
llevarse vr *to get on with*
llorar v *to cry*
llover v *to rain* llover a cántaros *to rain cats and dogs*
lloviznar v *to drizzle*
la lluvia f *rain*
lluvioso/a a *rainy*
lo art def
loco/a a *mad*
lograr v *to achieve, obtain*
la loncha f *slice*
Londres m *London*
la lonja f *slice*
la lotería f *lottery*
la lucha f *fight, battle, struggle*
luchar v *to fight, struggle*
luego ad *then, after*
luego con *therefore*
el lugar m *place*
el lujo m *luxury*
lujoso/a a *luxurious*
la luna f *moon*
el lunes m *Monday*
la luz f *light*

M

la madera f *wood, timber*
la madrastra f *stepmother*
la madre f *mother*
la madrugada f *early morning*
madrugar v *to get up early*

nouns — **m:** *masculine* **f:** *feminine* **pl:** *plural* **v:** *verb* **vr:** *reflexive verb* **a:** *adjective*

Spanish — English Dictionary

maduro/a a *mature, ripe*
el/la maestro/a mf *primary teacher, maestro*
el magnetofón/magnetofono m *tape recorder*
el magnetoscopio m *video recorder*
magnífico/a a *magnificent*
mal ad *badly, ill*
la maleta f *suitcase*
el maletero m *car boot*
malhumorado/a a *bad-tempered*
malo/a a *bad, wrong, ill, naughty*
la mamá f *mum, mummy*
la mancha f *stain*
manchar v *to stain*
mandar v *to send/order/be in charge*
manejar v *to use, handle*
la manera f *way, method*
la manifestación f *demonstration*
manifestar v *to show, demonstrate*
la mano f *hand*
la manta f *blanket*
el mantel m *tablecloth*
mantener v *to maintain/hold/keep*
mantenerse vr *to stay, remain*
la mantequilla f *butter*
la manzana f *apple, block of houses*
el manzano m *apple tree*
mañana ad *tomorrow*
la mañana f *morning*
el maquillaje m *make-up*
maquillarse v *to put on make-up*
la máquina f *machine*
el mar m *sea*
maravilloso/a a *marvellous*
la marca f *make, brand, mark*
marcar v *to dial, score, mark*
marcar una señal *put a sign*
la marcha f *march, progress, departure*
marcha atrás *reverse*
marcharse vr *to leave, go away*
la marea f *tide*
mareado/a a *dizzy, travel-sick*
marearse vr *to feel sick, dizzy*
el mareo m *dizziness, sickness*
el marido m *husband*
el/la marinero/a mf *sailor*
los mariscos mpl *seafood*
marrón a *brown*
el martes m *Tuesday*
el marzo m *March*
más ad *more*
más allá *further away*
más o menos *more or less*
el matador m *bull-fighter*
matar v *to kill*
la matrícula f *registration, enrolment, car registration number*
el matrimonio m *marriage*
el mayo m *May*
el/la mayor mf *oldest, eldest*
la mayoría f *the majority*
me pron *me, to me*
me da igual *I don't mind*
me gusta mucho *I like it/him/her a lot*
el/la mecánico/a mf *mechanic*
el mechero m *cigarette lighter*
la media pensión f *half board*
mediano/a a *medium, average*
las medias fpl *tights, stockings*
el medicamento m *medicine*
el/la médico/a mf *doctor*
la medida f *measure, measurement*
medio/a a *half*
el medio m *middle, centre,way*
medio ambiente *environment*
el mediodía m *midday*
medir v *to measure*
la mejilla f *cheek*
el mejillón m *mussel*
mejor a *better*
el/la mejor mf *best*
mejorar v *to improve*
mejorarse vr *to get better*
el melocotón m *peach*
el melón m *melon*
mencionar v *to mention*
menor a *younger, smaller*
el/la menor mf *youngest, smallest*
menos ad *less*
al menos *at least* menos cuarto *quarter to*
el mensaje m *message*
mensaje electrónico *email*
mentir v *to lie*
la mentira f *lie*
mentiroso/a a *untruthful, lying*
el menú m *menu*
el mercado m *market*
merecer v *to deserve*
la merienda f *teatime snack, picnic*
la mermelada f *jam*
el mes m *month*
la mesa f *table*
meter v *to put in, insert*
el método m *method*
el metro m *metre, underground*
mezclar v *to mix*
mezquino/a a *mean, miserly*
el microondas m *microwave*
el miedo m *fear*
la miel f *honey*
el/la miembro/a mf *member*
mientras conj *while, meanwhile*
mientras que *whereas*
el miércoles m *Wednesday*
militar a *military*
la milla f *mile*
el millón m *million*
el/la minero/a mf *miner*
mínimo/a a *minimum, minute*
el/la ministro/a mf *minister*
minusválido/a a *disabled*
mirar v *to look at, look, watch*
la misa f *mass*
mismo/a a *same, very, self*
misterioso/a a *mysterious*
la mitad f *half*
mixto/a a *mixed*
la mochila f *backpack, rucksack*
la moda f *fashion*
el modelo m *model*
el modo m *way, method, type*
mojado/a a *damp, wet, soaked*
mojarse vr *to get wet*
molestar v *to trouble, disturb*
molestarse vr *to get upset, trouble yourself*
la molestia f *bother, trouble*
la moneda f *coin*
el monedero m *purse*
el/la monitor/a *instructor, coach*
el mono m *monkey*
mono/a a *pretty*
el monopatín m *skateboard*
montar v *to ride, put together*
el monte m *mountain, hill*
el montón m *pile, large amount*
el monumento m *monument*
la moqueta f *fitted carpet*
morado/a a *purple*
morder v *to bite*
moreno/a a *dark-haired, brunette, tanned*
morir v *to die*
la mosca f *fly*
la mostaza f *mustard*
el mostrador m *counter*
mostrar v *to show*
la moto(cicleta) f *motorbike*
mover v *to move*
móvil a *mobile*
el móvil m *mobile phone*
el/la mozo/a mf *waiter/'tress, porter*
el/la muchacho/a mf *boy/girl*
la muchedumbre f *crowd*
mucho/a a *a lot, many*
la mudanza f *house move*
mudar v *to change*
mudarse de casa *move house*
el mueble m *piece of furniture*
la muela f *tooth, back tooth*
la muerte f *death*
muerto/a a *dead*
la mujer f *woman, wife*
la multa f *fine*
el mundo m *the world*
la muñeca f *doll, wrist*
el muro m *wall*
el museo m *museum*
muy ad *very*

N

nacer v *to be born*
nacido/a a *born*
el nacimiento m *birth*
la nación f *nation*
la nacionalidad f *nationality*
las Naciones Unidas fpl *UN*
nada pron *nothing*
nada ad *not at all*
de nada *don't mention it*
nadar v *to swim*
nadie pron *nobody*
el naipe m *playing card*
la naranja f *orange*
la nariz f *nose*
la nata f *cream*
la natación f *swimming*
la naturaleza f *nature*
la Navidad f *Christmas*
la neblina f *mist*
necesario/a a *necessary*
negar(se) vr *to deny (refuse)*
el negocio m *business, shop*
negro/a a *black*
el neumático m *tyre*
nevar v *to snow*
la nevera f *refrigerator*
ni conj *neither, nor*
¡ni hablar! *no way!*
la niebla f *fog*
el/la nieto/a mf *grandson/daughter*
la nieve f *snow*
el nilón m *nylon*
la niñez f *childhood*
ninguno/a a *none, no*
el/la niño/a mf *boy, girl*
el nivel m *level*
no ad *no, not* no cuelgue *don't hang up, please hold*
no hay de qué *don't mention it*
no importa *it doesn't matter*
no me importa *I don't mind*
la noche f *night*
la Nochebuena f *Christmas Eve*
la Nochevieja f *New Year's Eve*
el nombre m *name* nombre de pila *first name, Christian name*
el nor(d)este m *north-east*
el noroeste m *north-west*
el norte m *north*
la nota f *note, mark, grade*
notar v *to notice*
la noticia f *piece of news*
la novela f *novel*
noveno/a a *ninth*
el noviembre m *November*
el/la novio/a mf *fiancé(e), boy/girlfriend*
la nube f *cloud*
nublado a *cloudy, overcast(sky)*
nuboso a *cloudy*
la nuera f *daughter-in-law*
nuevo/a a *new*
la nuez f *walnut*
el número m *number* (zapatos) *shoe size*
nunca ad *never*

O

la o f *o (the letter)*
o/u conj *or* o/o *either/or*
obedecer v *to obey*
el objeto m *object, aim*
la obra f *work, deed* obra de teatro *play, theatrical production*
el/la obrero/a mf *workman/woman*
la ocurrencia f *idea*
ocho a *eight*
el ocio m *leisure*
octavo/a a *eighth*
el octubre m *October*
ocupado/a a *occupied, engaged*
ocuparse de vr *to look after*
ocurrir v *to happen, occur*
odiar v *to hate*
el oeste m *west*
la oferta f *offer*
la oficina f *office*
ofrecer v *to offer*
el oído m *ear (inner)*
¡Oiga! (v) excl *Listen! Excuse me!*
oír v *to hear, listen to*
¡Ojalá! excl *I wish! I hope so!*
el ojo m *eye* ¡Ojo! *Look out!*
la ola f *wave*
¡Olé! excl *Hooray!*
oler v *to smell*
el olor m *smell*
olvidar v / olvidarse de vr *to forget*
la ONU f (Organización de las Naciones Unidas) *UN*
opinar v *to think, give your opinion*
la oportunidad f *opportunity*
la orden f *order (command)*
ordenar v *to arrange, order*
la oreja f *ear (outer)*
el orgullo m *pride*
orgulloso/a a *proud*
el origen m *origin*
la orilla f *bank, edge*
el oro m *gold*
la orquesta f *orchestra*
os pron *you, to you*
la oscuridad f *dark, darkness*
oscuro/a a *dark*
el oso m *bear*
la ostra f *oyster*
el otoño m *Autumn*
otro/a a *other, another*
la oveja f *sheep*

P

el/la paciente mf *patient*
pacífico/a a *peaceful*
el padrastro m *stepfather*
el padre m *father*
la paella f *paella (rice dish)*
la paga f *pay, wages, pocket money*
pagar v *to pay*
la página f *page*
el pago m *payment*
el país m *country*
el paisaje m *landscape*
el pájaro m *bird*
la palabra f *word*
el palacio m *palace*
pálido/a a *pale*
el pan m *bread*
la panadería f *bakery, baker's*
el/la panadero/a mf *baker*
el panecillo m *(bread) roll*
la pantalla f *screen*
el pantalón m / los pantalones mpl *trousers* pantalón corto/pantalones cortos *shorts*
el panti/panty m / los pantys *tights*
el pañuelo m *handkerchief, headscarf*
el papá m *daddy*
el Papa m *Pope*
el papel m *paper*
la papelera f *wastepaper basket/bin*
la papelería f *stationer's, stationery*
el/la papelero/a mf *stationer*
el paquete m *packet, parcel*
el par m *pair, couple*
para prep *for, in order to, so that*
el parabrisas m *windscreen*
la parada f *stop*
parada de autobuses *bus stop*
parado/a a *stopped, still, unemployed*
el parador m *(state-run) hotel*
el paraguas m *umbrella*
parar v *to stop*
pararse vr *to stop, come to a stop*
parecer v *to seem, appear, look like*
me parece *it seems to me*
parecerse a vr *to look like*
parecido/a a *similar*
la pared f *wall*
la pareja f *couple, partner*
el/la pariente/a mf *relative, relation*
el paro m *unemployment, stoppage*
el parque m *park*
la parrilla f *grill*
la parte f *part*
el partido m *match/game, party (political)*
pasado/a a *past, last*
pasado mañana *the day after tomorrow*
el pasado m *the past*
el/la pasajero/a mf *passenger*
pasar v *to pass, spend (time), happen*
pasar (la) lista *to take the register*
pasar (por) *to go past, through*
pasar la aspiradora *to vacuum*
pasarlo bien *to have a good time*
el pasatiempo m *hobby, pastime*
pasear v *to take a walk*
pasearse vr *to go for a walk/stroll*
el paseo m *walk, stroll*
el pasillo m *corridor*
el paso m *step, way* paso a nivel *level crossing* paso de peatones *pedestrian crossing* paso prohibido *no entry* paso subterráneo *subway*
la pasta de dientes f *toothpaste*
el pastel m *cake, pie*
la pastelería f *baker's, cake shop*
la pastilla f *tablet, pill*
la pata f *leg (animal/furniture)*
la patada f *kick*
la patata f *potato*
patatas (fritas) *chips, crisps*
el paté m *paté*
el patín m *skate*
patín de ruedas *roller skate*
el patinaje m *skating*
patinar v *to skate*
el pato m *duck*
el/la patrón/ona mf *employer, owner, landlord/lady*
la pausa f *pause, break*
el pavo m *turkey*
el/la payaso/a mf *clown*
la paz f *peace*
el peaje m *toll*
el peatón m *pedestrian*
el pecho m *chest*
el pedazo m *piece*
el pedido m *order, request*
pedir v *to order, ask for*
pedir prestado *to borrow*
pegar v *to stick, hit*
pegar fuego *to set fire to*
el peinado m *hairdo*
peinarse vr *to comb your hair*
el peine m *comb*
pelar v *to peel*
la pelea f *quarrel, fight*
pelear v *to quarrel, fight*
la película f *film*
el peligro m *danger*
peligroso/a a *dangerous*
pelirrojo/a a *red-haired*
el pelo m *hair*
la pelota f *ball*

ad: *adverb* **prep**: *preposition* **pron**: *pronoun* **interj**: *interjection* **conj**: *conjunction* **art**: *article* **excl**: *exclamation*

Spanish — English Dictionary

la peluquería f *hairdresser's*
la pena f *sorrow, shame*
el pendiente m *earring*
la pendiente f *slope*
pensar v *to think*
la pensión f *guest house*
peor a *worse*
el/la peor mf *worst*
pequeño/a a *small, little*
la pera f *pear*
percibir v *to perceive, notice*
perder v *to lose*
la pérdida f *loss*
perdón excl *sorry!, pardon me*
perdonar v *to forgive*
perezoso/a a *lazy*
la perfumería f *perfume shop*
el periódico m *newspaper*
el/la periodista mf *journalist*
el periquito m *parakeet*
permanecer v *to stay, remain*
el permiso m *permission, licence*
permitido/a a *permitted, allowed*
permitir v *to allow*
pero conj *but*
el/la perro/a mf *dog*
la persiana f *(Venetian) blind*
el personaje m *celebrity, character*
el personal m *staff, personnel*
pertenecer v *to belong*
la pesadilla f *nightmare*
pesado/a a *heavy, difficult, boring*
pesar v *to weigh*
la pesca f *fishing*
la pescadería f *fishmonger's*
el pescado m *fish (dead, for cooking/ eating)*
el/la pescador/a mf *fisherman*
pescar v *to fish*
el peso m *weight*
el petróleo m *oil, petroleum*
el pez m *fish* pez de colores/ pez dorado *goldfish*
la picadura f *prick, sting, bite*
picante a *hot, spicy*
picar v *to sting, bite, prick*
picar un billete *to clip a ticket*
el pico m *beak, peak* son las dos y pico *it's just after two*
el pie m *foot*
la piedra f *stone, rock*
la piel f *skin*
la pierna f *leg*
la pieza f *piece*
la pila f *sink, battery*
la píldora f *pill*
la pimienta f *pepper (spice)*
el pimiento m *pepper (vegetable)*
la piña f *pineapple*
pinchar v *to get a puncture*
el pinchazo m *puncture*
pintado/a a *painted*
el pintalabios m *lipstick*
pintar v *to paint*
el/la pintor/a mf *painter*
pintoresco/a a *picturesque*
la pintura f *painting, paint*
la pipa f *pipe, pip, seed*
los Pirineos mpl *the Pyrenees*
pisar v *to walk on, tread on*
la piscina f *swimming pool*
el piso m *flat, floor*
la pista f *court, track, piste*
pista de hielo *ice rink*
pista de patinar *skating rink*
la pizarra f *blackboard*
el placer m *pleasure*
la plancha f *iron, grill*
planchar v *to iron*
plano/a a *flat*
el plano m *plan, map*
planta baja *ground floor*
la plata f *silver*
el plátano m *banana*
el platillo m *saucer*
el plato m *plate, dish, course*
plato combinado *one course set meal*
plato del día *dish of the day*
la playa f *beach*
la plaza f *square*
plaza de toros *bullring*
plaza mayor *main square*
el plomo m *lead*
la pluma f *feather, pen*
la población f *population*
pobre a *poor*
la pobreza f *poverty*
poco/a a *little, few*
poco ad *little* poco hecho *rare, slightly cooked*
poco m un poco *a little*
poder v *to be able, can*
la policía f *the police, policewoman*
el policía m *policeman*
el polideportivo m *sports centre*
el/la político/a mf *politician*
el pollo m *chicken*
el polvo m *dust*
la pomada f *ointment, cream*
el pomelo m *grapefruit*
poner v *to put*
poner la mesa *lay the table*
ponerse vr *to become*
ponerse a *to begin to*
ponerse la ropa *to put clothes on*
por prep *for, through, by, along*
por ciento *percent*
el porcentaje m *percentage*
porque conj *because*
¿Por qué? interrogo *Why?*
el portamonedas m *purse*
portátil a *portable*
el/la portero/a *caretaker, concierge*
la portezuela f *small door (train)*
el porvenir m *future*
la posibilidad f *possibility*
la postal f *postcard*
el postre m *sweet, dessert*
potable a *drinkable, drinking*
practicar v *to practise*
práctico/a a *practical*
las prácticas fpl *apprenticeship*
el prado m *meadow, pasture*
el precio m *price*
preciso/a a *necessary, precise*
predilecto/a a *favourite*
preferido/a a *favourite*
preferir v *to prefer*
la pregunta f *question*
preguntar v *to ask*
preguntarse vr *to wonder*
el premio m *prize*
la prensa f *the press, newspapers*
la preocupación f *worry*
preocupar v *to worry, trouble*
preocuparse vr *to worry*
prescindir de v *to do without*
la presentación (oral) f *presentation*
presentar v *to present, introduce*
presentarse vr (para un empleo) *to turn up (for a job)*
la presión f *pressure*
prestar v *to lend*
la primavera f *spring*
primero/a a *first*
el/la primo/a mf *cousin*
la princesa f *princess*
el príncipe m *prince*
el principio m *beginning*
la prioridad f *priority*
la prisa f *hurry*
privado/a a *private*
el probador m *changing room*
probar v *to try, test, prove, taste*
probarse vr *to try on*
el problema m *problem*
procedente (de) a *coming from*
el procesador de textos m *word processor*
producir v *to produce,*
producirse vr *to take place*
el/la profesor/a mf *teacher*
la profundidad f *depth*
profundo/a a *deep, profound*
el programa m *programme*
el progreso m *progress*
prohibir v *to prohibit, ban*
prometer v *to promise*
el pronóstico m *forecast*
pronto ad *soon, early, quickly*
el/la propietario/a mf *owner*
la propina f *tip*
propio/a a *own*
proponer v *to propose, suggest*
proporcionar v *to supply*
el propósito m *purpose*
proteger v *to protect*
la proximidad f *proximity, closeness*
próximo/a a *next*
el proyecto m *project*
la prueba f *proof, test*
publicar v *to publish*
la publicidad f *publicity, advertising*
el público m *public, audience*
el pueblo m *village, people*
el puente m *bridge*
el/la puerco/a mf *pig/sow*
el puerro m *leek*
la puerta f *door, gate*
el puerto m *port*
pues conj *well, then*
el puesto m *post, position, job*
puesto que conj *since*
el pulpo m *octopus*
la pulsera f *bracelet*
el puño m *fist*
el punto m *dot, point, spot, place*
el pupitre m *desk*
puro/a a *pure*

Q

que pron/conj *that, who, which*
¡Qué! ad *how!* ¿Qué? interrog. *What?, Which?*
quebrar v *to break*
quedar v *to remain, stay, suit (clothing)*
quedarse vr *to arrange, stay*
los quehaceres mpl *tasks*
la queja f *complaint*
quejarse vr *to complain*
la quemadura f *burn*
quemar v *to burn*
querer v *to want, love*
querer decir *to mean*
querido/a a *dear*
el queso m *cheese*
quien pron *who, whom*
la química f *chemistry*
el/la químico/a mf *chemist a chemical*
la quincena f *fortnight, two weeks*
quinto/a a *fifth*
el quiosco m *kiosk, news stand*
quisiera v *I/he/she/you would like*
quitar v *to remove, take away*
quitar el polvo *to dust*
quitarse vr *to take off (clothes)*
quizá(s) ad *perhaps*

R

el ramo m *bunch*
el rango m *rank*
la ranura f *groove, slot*
rápidamente ad *quickly*
rápido/a a *fast*
el rápido m *express train*
raramente ad *rarely*
raro/a a *strange*
el rascacielos m *skyscraper*
rasgar v *to tear, rip*
la rata f *rat*
el ratero m *pickpocket*
el rato m *while, amount of time*
el ratón m *mouse*
el rayo m *ray, flash of lightning*
la razón f *reason*
real a *royal*
realizar v *to carry out, achieve*
la rebaja f *reduction, sale*
las rebajas fpl *sales*
la rebanada f *slice*
la rebeca f *cardigan*
el recado m *message, errand*
la receta f *recipe*
recibir v *to receive*
el recibo m *receipt*
recientemente ad *recently*
recoger v *to pick up, collect*
la recogida f *collection*
la recompensa f *reward*
reconocer v *to recognize*
recordar v *to remember*
el recreo m *break, playtime*
recto/a a *straight, honest*
el recuerdo m *souvenir, memory*
recuerdos *regards*
el recurso m *resource*
la red f *net, network*
redondo/a a *round*
el reembolso m *reimbursement*
reflexionar v *to reflect, think about*
el refresco m *soft drink*
regalar v *to give (as a present)*
el regalo m *present, gift*
regar v *to water, irrigate*
la regla f *regulation, ruler*
regresar v *to return*
la reina f *queen*
el Reino Unido m *United Kingdom*
reír(se) v *to laugh*
relajar v *to relax, loosen*
relajarse vr *to relax*
el relámpago m *flash of lightning*
el relato m *story, account*
rellenar v *to fill up, stuff, fill in (form)*
el reloj m *watch, clock* reloj de pulsera *wristwatch*
la relojería f *watchmaker's shop*
remar v *to row*
el remedio m *remedy, alternative*
el remite m *return address*
el/la remitente mf *sender*
rendido/a a *exhausted*
reñir(se) v *to quarrel*
reparar v *to repair*
repartir v *to share, divide*
repasar v *to revise*
el reportaje m *report, article*
resbalar v *to slip, skid*
rescatar v *to save, rescue*
el rescate m *rescue*
resfriado/a a *having a cold*
respetar v *to respect*
el respeto m *respect*
respirar v *to breathe*
responder v *to respond, reply*
la respuesta f *reply, answer*
el resultado m *result*
el resumen m *summary, résumé*
retener v *to keep, hold*
el retraso m *delay*
el retrovisor m *rear-view mirror*
la reunión f *meeting*
reunirse vr *to meet, reunite*
el revés m *back*
al revés *backwards*
el revisor m *ticket collector, inspector*
la revista f *magazine*
revoltoso/a a *naughty, unruly*
revolver v *to stir*
el rey m *king*
rezar v *to pray*
rico/a a *rich, wealthy, delicious*
el riesgo m *risk*
riguroso/a a *severe, harsh, tough*
el rincón m *corner*
el río m *river*
la riqueza f *wealth, richness*
la risa f *laugh*
el ritmo m *rhythm*
rizado/a a *curly*
robar v *to rob, steal*
el robo m *theft, robbery*
la roca f *rock*
rodear v *to surround, enclose*
la rodilla f *knee*
rogar v *to ask, beg*
rojo/a a *red*
romper/se v/vr *to break*
roncar v *to snore*
ronco/a a *hoarse, husky*
la ronda f *round*
la ropa f *clothes*
ropa interior *underwear*
la rosa f *rose*
rosado/a a *pink*
el rostro m *face*
roto/a a *broken*
el rotulador m *felt tip pen*
rubio/a a *blonde, fair-haired*
la rueda f *wheel*
el ruido m *noise*
ruidoso/a a *noisy*
la ruta f *route*

S

el sábado m *Saturday*
la sábana f *sheet*
saber v *to know*
sabio/a a *wise, learned*
el sabor m *flavour, taste*
saborear v *to taste*
el sacacorchos m *corkscrew*
el sacapuntas m *pencil sharpener*
sacar v *to take out, get*
el saco m *bag, sack*
sacudir v *to shake*
la sal f *salt*
la sala f *room, living room*
salado/a a *salty, charming*
el salario m *salary, wage*
la salchicha f *sausage*
la salida f *departure, exit*
salir (de) v *to go out (of/ from), leave, depart*
el salón m *lounge, living room*
la salsa f *sauce*
saltar v *to jump, jump out*
la salud f *health* ¡Salud! *Cheers!*
saludar v *to greet*
el saludo m *greeting* saludos *greetings, best wishes*
salvaje a *wild*
salvar v *to save*
el salvavidas m *lifebelt, life jacket*
salvo/a a *safe*
salvo prep *except for*
la sandía f *water melon*
la sangre f *blood*
la sangría f *sangria (drink)*
sano/a a *healthy*
santo/a a *holy*
el/la santo/a mf *saint*
la sartén f *frying pan*
el/la sastre/a mf *tailor*
satisfecho/a a *satisfied*
se pron *to him/her/you/ them, him/her/your/oneself/ themselves*
se trata de *it's about*
el secador de pelo m *hairdrier*
la secadora f *tumble drier*
secar v *to dry*
seco/a a *dry*
el/la secretario/a mf *secretary*
la sed f *thirst*
la seda f *silk*
seguir v *to follow, continue*
según prep *according to*
segundo/a a *second*
la seguridad f *security, safety*
seguro/a a *safe, certain, sure*
el sello m *stamp*
la selva f *jungle, rainforest*
el semáforo m *traffic lights*
la semana f *week*
semanal a *weekly*
la señal f *signal, sign, mark*
las señas fpl *address*
sencillo/a a *simple, single*

*nouns — **m**: masculine* *f: feminine* *pl: plural* *v: verb* *vr: reflexive verb* *a: adjective*

Spanish — English Dictionary

el senderismo m *hiking*
el sendero m *path*
el/la señor/a mf *man/woman, mr/mrs, sir/madam*
la señorita f *miss, young lady*
sensible a *sensitive*
sentarse v *to sit down*
el sentido m *meaning, feeling, sense*
el sentimiento m *feeling, sorrow*
sentir v *to feel*
lo siento *I'm sorry*
separar v *to separate*
el se(p)tiembre m *September*
séptimo/a a *seventh*
ser v *to be*
ser de (+ material) *to be made of*
ser de (+ place) *to come from*
la serie f *series, serial*
serio/a a *serious*
el servicio m *service, toilet*
los servicios *the toilets*
la servilleta f *serviette*
servir v *to serve*
el se(p)tiembre m *September*
el seto m *fence*
el sexo m *sex*
si conj *if*
sí ad *yes*
sí pron *himself, herself, itself*
la sidra f *cider*
siempre ad *always*
la sierra f *mountain range*
la siesta f *short sleep (after lunch)*
el siglo m *century*
significar v *to mean*
el signo m *sign*
siguiente a *next, following*
silbar v *to whistle*
la silla f *chair*
el sillón m *easy chair, armchair*
la silueta f *silhouette*
la simpatía f *warmth, friendliness*
simpático/a a *nice, friendly*
sin prep *without*
sin plomo *lead free*
el síntoma m *symptom*
el/la sirviente mf *servant*
el sitio m *place, space, room*
situado/a a *situated*
sobrar v *to be left over, remain*
el sobre m *envelope*
sobre prep *on, about, around (time)*
sobre todo *above all*
el/la sobrino/a m *nephew/ niece*
la sociedad f *society*
el/la socio/a mf *member*
socorrer v *to help*
el/la socorrista mf *lifeguard*
el socorro m *help, aid*
el sol m *sun*
solamente/sólo ad *only, just*
el/la soldado mf *soldier*
soleado a *sunny*
solicitar v *to apply for*
sólido/a a *solid*
solo/a a *alone*
el solomillo m *sirloin steak*
soltero/a a *single, unmarried*
la sombra f *shadow, shade*
el sombrero m *hat*
soñar (con) v *to dream (about)*
sonar v *to ring, sound*
el sonido m *sound*
sonreír(se) vr *to smile*
la sonrisa f *smile*
la sopa f *soup*
soplar v *to blow, blow out/ away*
sordo/a a *deaf*
sorprender v *to surprise*
la sorpresa f *surprise*
el sorteo m *draw, raffle*
la sortija f *ring*
la sospecha f *suspicion*
el sostén m *support, bra*
sostener v *to support, hold*
Sr abbrev (Señor) *Mr.*
Sra/s abbrev (Señora) *Mrs.*
Sres abbrev (Señores) *Messrs*
Srta abbrev (Señorita) *Miss, Ms.*
suave a *smooth, soft, gentle*
la subida f *rise, increase, ascent*
subir v *to go up, rise*
subir a *get into (a vehicle)*
súbito/a a *sudden*
suceder v *to happen*
sucio/a a *dirty*
la sucursal f *branch (office)*
sudar v *to sweat*
el/la suegro/a mf *father/mother-in-law*
el sueldo m *salary, wage, pay*
el suelo m *floor*
suelto/a a *loose*
el sueño m *dream, sleep*
tener sueño *to be sleepy, tired*
la suerte f *luck, chance*
el suéter m *sweater*
sufrir v *to suffer*
sugerir v *to suggest*
sujetar v *to hold, fix*
la suma f *addition, total, sum*
la super f *four-star petrol*
superar v *to surpass, overcome*
el supermercado m *supermarket*
suplementario/a a *supplementary*
suponer v *to imagine, suppose*
el sur m *south*
surfear el Internet v *to surf the net*
el sureste m *southeast*
el suroeste m *southwest*
el surtido m *selection, range*
sustituir v *to substitute*
el susto m *shock*

T

la tabacalera f *tobacconist's, stationer's*
el tabaco m *tobacco*
la taberna f *bar, tavern*
la tabla f *plank, board*
tal a *such* tal vez *perhaps*
el Talgo m *inter-city express train*
la talla f *size (clothes)*
el taller m *workshop*
el talonario de cheques *chequebook*
el tamaño m *size*
también ad *also*
el Támesis m *Thames*
tampoco ad *neither*
tan ad *so, such*
tanto/a a *so much*
tantos/as a *so many*
la tapa f *lid, top, snack* tapas *snacks*
la taquilla f *box office, ticket office*
tarde ad *late*
la tarde f *afternoon, evening*
la tarea f *task* las tareas *homework*
la tarifa f *rate, price*
la tarjeta f *card*
la tarjeta postal f *postcard*
el tarro m *jar, pot*
la tarta f *cake, tart* tarta casera *homemade cake/tart*
la tasa f *rate*
el/la taxista mf *taxi driver*
la taza f *cup*
el tazón m *bowl, mug*
te pron *you, to you*
el té m *tea*
el teatro m *theatre*
el tebeo m *comic*
el techo m *ceiling*
el teclado m *keyboard*
técnico/a a *technical*
el/la técnico/a mf *technician*
el tejado m *roof*
los tejanos mpl *jeans*
la tela f *cloth, material*
telefonear v *to phone*
el teléfono m *telephone*
teléfono móvil *mobile phone*
la telenovela f *soap opera*
el televisor m *television set*
el tema m *theme, subject*
temblar v *to tremble*
la tempestad f *storm*
templado/a a *mild, temperate*
la temporada f *season, time period*
temporal a *temporary*
temprano ad *early*
el/la tendero/a mf *shopkeeper*
tenderse v *to lie down*
el tenedor m *fork*
tener v *to have*
el TER m *inter-city express train*
tercero/a a *third*
terco/a a *stubborn*
terminar v *to finish*
la ternera f *veal*
la terraza f *terrace*
el terremoto m *earthquake*
el terreno m *ground, land*
el/la testigo/a mf *witness*
la tetera f *teapot*
tibio/a a *cool, tepid*
el tiempo m *time, weather*
la tienda f *shop, tent*
tienda de campaña *tent*
la tierra f *earth*
tieso/a a *stiff*
el tigre m *tiger*
las tijeras fpl *scissors*
el timbre m *bell (electric), stamp (official)*
tímido/a a *shy, timid*
tinto a *red (wine)*
el tío m *uncle*
típico/a a *typical*
el tipo m *type, kind*
tirar v *to throw, throw away, pull*
tirarse vr *to throw oneself*
el título m *title, qualification*
la tiza f *chalk*
la toalla f *towel*
el tobillo m *ankle*
el tocadiscos m *record player*
el tocador m *dressing table*
tocar v *to play (instrument) / touch*
tocarle a uno *to be someone's turn* (te toca a ti *it's your turn)*
todavía ad *yet, still*
todo/a/os/as a *all, every*
tomar v *to take, have*
tomar el sol *to sunbathe*
el tomate m *tomato*
el tono m *tone*
la tontería f *silliness, nonsense*
tonto/a a *silly, stupid*
el tópico m *topic*
torcer v *to turn, twist*
la tormenta f *storm*
el torneo m *tournament, competition*
el tornillo m *screw*
el toro m *bull*
torpe a *slow, dim, clumsy*
la torre f *tower*
la tortilla f *omelette*
la tortuga f *tortoise*
la tos f *cough*
toser v *to cough*
la tostada f *slice of toast*
trabajador/a a *hardworking*
el/la trabajador/a mf *worker*
trabajar v *to work*
el trabajo m *work, job*
traducir v *to translate*
el/la traductor/a mf *translator*
traer v *to bring*
el tráfico m *traffic*
tragar v *to swallow*
la tragedia f *tragedy*
el traje m *suit* (de baño) *swimsuit*
tranquilo/a a *calm, quiet*
transbordar v *to transfer, change*
el transbordo m *change*
hacer transbordo *to change (trains etc)*
el/la transeúnte mf *passer-by*
el tranvía m *tram, local train*
el trapo m *rag, cleaning cloth*
el tratamiento de textos m *word processing*
tratar v *to try, treat, deal with*
la travesía f *crossing, voyage*
travieso/a a *naughty*
el trayecto m *journey, route*
el tren m *train*
el triángulo m *triangle*
el trimestre m *term*
triste a *sad*
la trompeta f *trumpet*
tronar v *to thunder*
el trozo m *piece, bit*
la trucha f *trout*
el trueno m *thunder*
tu a *your*
tú pron *you (familiar)*
el tubo m *tube, pipe*
tumbarse vr *to lie down*
el túnel m *tunnel*
el turismo m *tourism*
el/la turista mf *tourist*
tutear v *to use the informal "tú" when talking to someone*

U

ubicado/a a *located, situated*
la UE f (Unión Europea) *EU*
últimamente ad *recently*
último/a a *last, latest, final*
único/a a *only, unique*
la unidad f *unit, unity*
unido/a a *united, close*
el uniforme m *uniform*
la universidad f *university*
un/a art indef *a, one*
uno/a pron *one*
unos/as pron *some*
la uña f *fingernail*
la urgencia f *urgency, emergency* urgencias *emergency services*
usar v *to use*
usted(es) pron *you s/pl (formal)*
útil a *useful*
utilizar v *to use*
la uva f *grape*

V

la vaca f *cow*
las vacaciones fpl *holidays*
vaciar v *to empty*
vacío/a a *empty*
el vagón m *coach, carriage, wagon*
la vainilla f *vanilla*
la vajilla f *dishes, crockery*
vale excl *ok, fine*
valer v *to be worth, cost*
válido/a a *valid*
valiente a *brave*
el valle m *valley*
el valor m *value*
el vapor m *steam*
los vaqueros mpl *jeans*
variar v *to vary, change*
varios/as a *several, various*
el vaso m *glass (drinking)*
la vecindad f *neighbourhood, area*
el/la vecino/a mf *neighbour*
el/la vegetariano/a mf *vegetarian*
el vehículo m *vehicle*
la vela f *candle, sailing*
la velocidad f *speed*
vencer v *to overcome, defeat*
la venda f *bandage*
el/la vendedor/a mf *vendor, seller*
vender v *to sell*
venir v *to come*
la venta f *sale*
la ventaja f *advantage*
la ventana f *window*
la ventanilla f *(vehicle/bank) window, box office*
ver v *to see, watch*
veranear v *to spend summer hols*
el verano m *summer*
la verbena f *fair, festival*
la verdad f *truth*
es verdad *it's true*
verdaderamente ad *truly, really*
verdadero/a a *true*
verde a *green*
la verdulería f *greengrocer's shop*
la(s) verdura(s) fpl *vegetables*
la vergüenza f *shame, embarrassment*
la versión f *version*
verter v *to pour, spill*
el vestíbulo m *hall, foyer*
vestido/a a *dressed*
el vestido m *dress*
vestirse vr *to get dressed*
el vestuario m *clothes, wardrobe, dressing room*
el/la veterinario/a mf *vet, veterinary*
la vez f *time, occasion*
la vía f *way, lane (motorway), track*
viajar v *to travel*
el viaje m *journey*
el/la viajero/a mf *traveller*
la víctima f *victim*
la vida f *life*
el videojuego m *video game*
el vidrio m *glass (material)*
viejo/a a *old*
el/la viejo/a mf *old man/woman*
el viento m *wind*
el vientre m *stomach, belly*
el viernes m *Friday* Viernes Santo *Good Friday*
vigilar v *to supervise, guard*
la viña f *vine, vineyard*
el vinagre m *vinegar*
el vino m *wine*
la visibilidad f *visibility*
la visita f *visit*
el/la visitante mf *visitor*
visitar v *to visit*
la víspera f *day before*
la vista f *view, sight*
el/la viudo/a mf *widower/widow*
la vivienda f *home, dwelling*
vivir v *to live*
vivo/a a *alive, lively*
el vocabulario m *vocabulary*
volante a *flying*
el volante m *steering wheel*
volar v *to fly*
volcar v *to knock over, tip out*
el voleibol m *volleyball*
volver v *to return, turn*
volver a + inf *to do again*
volver de *to have just*
volverse vr *to turn round, back*
vomitar v *to vomit, be sick*
vosotros pron pl *you (pl informal)*
la voz f *voice*
el vuelo m *flight*
la vuelta f *return* la vuelta al colegio *return to school* dar una vuelta *go for a spin/stroll*

W

el wáter m *toilet*
el windsurf m *windsurfing*

Y

y conj *and*
y media *half past, and a half*
ya ad *already, yet, now*
el yerno m *son-in-law*
el yogur m *yoghurt*

Z

la zanahoria f *carrot*
la zapatería f *shoeshop*
el/la zapatero/a mf *shoemaker*
la zapatilla f *slipper*
la zapatilla de deporte f *trainer*
el zapato m *shoe*
la zona f *zone, area* zona peatonal *pedestrian precinct*
el zoo m *zoo*
el/la zorro/a mf *fox/vixen*
el zumo m *juice*

ad: adverb **prep**: preposition **pron**: pronoun **interj**: interjection **conj**: conjunction **art**: article **excl**: exclamation

Index

Index